Language, Discourse, Society

General Editors: **Stephen Heath, Colin MacCabe** and **Denise Riley**

Selected published titles:

Norman Bryson
VISION AND PAINTING
The Logic of the Gaze

Elizabeth Cowie
REPRESENTING THE WOMAN
Cinema and Psychoanalysis

Theresa de Lauretis
TECHNOLOGIES OF GENDER
Essays on Theory, Film and Fiction

Mary Ann Doane
THE DESIRE TO DESIRE
The Woman's Film of the 1940s

Jane Gallop
FEMINISM AND PSYCHOANALYSIS
The Daughter's Seduction

Peter Gidal
UNDERSTANDING BECKETT
A Study of Monologue and Gesture in the Works of Samuel Beckett

Piers Gray, edited by Colin MacCabe and Victoria Rothschild
STALIN ON LINGUISTICS AND OTHER ESSAYS

Alan Hunt
GOVERNANCE OF THE CONSUMING PASSIONS
A History of Sumptuary Law

Ian Hunter
CULTURE AND GOVERNMENT
The Emergence of Literary Education

Jean-Jacques Lecercle
DELEUZE AND LANGUAGE

Patrizia Lombardo
CITIES, WORDS AND IMAGES

Colin MacCabe
JAMES JOYCE AND THE REVOLUTION OF THE WORD
Second edition

Jeffrey Minson
GENEALOGIES OF MORALS
Nietzsche, Foucault, Donzelot and the Eccentricity of Ethics

Laura Mulvey
VISUAL AND OTHER PLEASURES

Christopher Norris
RESOURCES OF REALISM
Prospects for 'Post-Analytic' Philosophy

Denise Riley
'AM I THAT NAME?'
Feminism and the Category of 'Women' in History

Jacqueline Rose
PETER PAN, OR THE IMPOSSIBILITY OF CHILDREN'S FICTION

Moustapha Safouan
SPEECH OR DEATH?
Language as Social Order: a Psychoanalytic Study

Moustapha Safouan
JACQUES LACAN AND THE QUESTION OF PSYCHOANALYTIC TRAINING
(*Translated and introduced by Jacqueline Rose*)

Stanley Shostak
THE DEATH OF LIFE
The Legacy of Molecular Biology

Lyndsey Stonebridge
THE DESTRUCTIVE ELEMENT
British Psychoanalysis and Modernism

Raymond Tallis
NOT SAUSSURE
A Critique of Post-Saussurean Literary Theory

David Trotter
THE MAKING OF THE READER
Language and Subjectivity in Modern American, English and Irish Poetry

Geoffrey Ward
STATUTES OF LIBERTY
The New York School of Poets

Language, Discourse, Society
Series Standing Order ISBN 0–333–71482–2
(*outside North America only*)

You can receive future titles in this series as they are published by placing a standing order. Please contact your bookseller or, in case of difficulty, write to us at the address below with your name and address, the title of the series and the ISBN quoted above.

Customer Services Department, Macmillan Distribution Ltd, Houndmills, Basingstoke, Hampshire RG21 6XS, England

---

Cities, Words and Images

From Poe to Scorsese

Patrizia Lombardo
Professor of French and Comparative Literature
University of Geneva

First published 2003 by
PALGRAVE MACMILLAN
Houndmills, Basingstoke, Hampshire RG21 6XS and
175 Fifth Avenue, New York, N. Y. 10010
Companies and representatives throughout the world

PALGRAVE MACMILLAN is the global academic imprint of the Palgrave
Macmillan division of St. Martin's Press, LLC and of Palgrave Macmillan Ltd.
Macmillan® is a registered trademark in the United States, United Kingdom
and other countries. Palgrave is a registered trademark in the European
Union and other countries.

ISBN 0–333–69628–X

This book is printed on paper suitable for recycling and made from fully
managed and sustained forest sources.

A catalogue record for this book is available from the British Library.

Library of Congress Cataloging-in-Publication Data
Lombardo, Patrizia.
   Cities, words and images : from Poe to Scorsese / Patrizia Lombardo.
     p. cm. — (Language, discourse, society)
   Includes bibliographical references and index.
   ISBN 0–333–69628–X
    1. Cities and towns in art. 2. Arts, Modern—19th century. 3. Arts,
Modern—20th century. I. Title. II. Series.

NX650.C66 L66 2002
700'.4321732'09034—dc21

                                 2002072323

10 9 8 7 6 5 4 3 2 1
12 11 10 09 08 07 06 05 04 03

Printed and bound in Great Britain by
Antony Rowe Ltd, Chippenham and Eastbourne

Contents

Preface

In spite of the current academic fixation on the idea that all is rhetoric, it seems impossible to deny that cities are concrete realities. A city is a living body, which can be harmed and maimed. Words and images have long been used to describe the presence of cities, their physical and mental impact on human life. In this book, I am interested in words and images – or in literature, criticism, and the visual arts – in so far as they are concerned with urban reality, aware that such a reality creates a way of life and new conditions for modern art. This book would like to emphasize the cultural role of the city.

The city is a recurrent and essential theme in literature, painting, architecture, photography, and film. Cities have been scrutinized from a great variety of perspectives. A substantial bibliography presents diverse visions of a number of cities in different historical periods, as well as of the urban phenomenon in general as a mode of living. A classic book on this theme is *The City in History: Its Origins, its Transformations, and its Prospects*, by Lewis Mumford, which explores the architecture of a number of cities from the classical age to the twentieth century. In *Cities, Words and Images*, the historical period I investigate corresponds to the two centuries of modern life and modern art, 'from Poe to Scorsese', as suggested by the subtitle. I endorse the modernist vision of the nineteenth century as the epoch when the urban phenomenon became overwhelming and affected the way in which people lived and thought. From the German school of urban sociology at the beginning of the twentieth century (Max Weber, Georg Simmel), to Walter Benjamin and Raymond Williams, many critics and thinkers have felt that literature and the arts – or words and images – changed thoroughly when human beings had to face the rise of massive industrial production and urbanization. The metropolitan experience hinges on the continuous exchange process that, as suggested by Max Weber, has characterized the city and its market since the Middle Ages, and, as hinted by Simmel, has increased since the advent of the nineteenth-century city, with the rapid circulation of money and goods. This experience is fundamental for the understanding of modern art, whatever the media, of the culture of modernity, regardless of national frontiers. The metropolitan phenomenon is at the basis of today's world.

Edgar Allan Poe and Charles Baudelaire are inevitable references. They are not simply two writers who described cities – so many writers have done so. They represent, in opposition to their contemporaries, the awareness that the urban or, more precisely, the metropolitan land-scape is the place where modern sensitivity and modern art begin. The emergence of the metropolis in the nineteenth century was an awesome phenomenon: Paris and London profoundly impressed those who observed their tantalizing growth. But the rise of metropolises belongs also to the geography of the mind, since it entails a new way of perceiving, feeling, thinking, and acting. This book reflects on the link between the changes in human perception created by urbaniza-tion, and the way in which these changes were expressed in the arts. In order to cope with the complexity of urban reality, city dwellers had to develop their faculty of abstraction. As understood by Poe and Baudelaire, modern art had to include a high level of abstraction. Poe and Baudelaire are the key figures of modernity for the most celebrated twentieth-century critics, such as Walter Benjamin, whose visions of the metropolitan experience have become standard references in the global market-place of ideas.

Within Western culture, the opposition of the natural and the urban has long inspired critical choices in aesthetics and politics. This book first focuses on ardent reactions to the metropolitan explosion in the nineteenth century. The visions of Poe and Baudelaire are contrasted with those of some of their contemporaries, and I give great import-ance to their attempt to create literary forms consistent with the pace of modern life. Poe insisted on questions of composition and tech-nique and thought that short forms such as the poem or the short story best responded to the speed of contemporary life. Baudelaire's aesthetic conceptions integrate the relationship between the metro-politan reality and an art capable of representing modern life, both its concrete manifestations and its powerful abstract component. His com-ments on Delacroix and Constantin Guys are as crucial for modern aesthetics as his themes and style, in the verses of *Les Fleurs du Mal* and in the prose poems of *Le Spleen de Paris*.

More recent, often incompatible attitudes towards the city are then probed, in Europe and the United States, from rejection to idolatry. The artistic movements in Vienna at the end of the nineteenth century and at the beginning of the twentieth were an immediate response to the growth of the Hapsburg capital; and they became the object of further theoretical investigation in the late twentieth century. The urban theme makes it necessary to consider the visions of several architects and theoreticians of architecture: two central chapters in this book treat this topic. The Italian architect Aldo Rossi conceived, from the early 1960s, of a close relationship between the city and architecture itself; in his reading of the Viennese architect Adolf Loos, the Italian philosopher Massimo Cacciari provided in the 1970s the ground for the discussion of different ideologies on the urban phenomenon.

Finally, my inquiry concentrates on a third medium: the cinema. The works of certain film-makers, such as David Lynch and Martin Scorsese, and particular critical issues in contemporary film theory raised by André Bazin, Raymond Williams and Fredric Jameson, bring into focus the role of images in our world. Films have represented various cities for more than a century. Nevertheless, not unlike literature, film can do much more than merely capture the visual aspect of urban landscapes. First of all, because cinema in general is itself the realization of what has been called 'the aesthetic of disappearance', which characterizes the conditions of perception in modern life. Second, because film techniques, for example in Scorsese's masterpieces, render the rhythm of metropolitan life.

As I have already suggested, I am interested in the metropolitan theme in its connection with the problem of representing and expressing modern life both in terms of content and form. Without the spark of that connection, the urban landscape in literature or the arts is mere décor, and the thematic approach remains a mere list of descriptive examples. My perspective aims at being dynamic: this requires a continuous interplay between theoretical concern and analytical concentration on specific cases. Textual scrutiny, intellectual history, and aesthetic study do not involve, in my opinion, antagonistic methods, just as disciplines are not isolated realms. The same urban theme or motif links writers, architects, historians, critics and film-makers, as it links the nineteenth century and the contemporary world, European experiences and American ones. As I propose in one chapter, cultural phenomena do not tally with the model of evolution but with that of contagion.

Cultural phenomena spread like viruses, breaching temporal and geographical boundaries. Cities are at the centre of cultural life. It seems to me that Poe's vision of the man of the crowd as the allegory of the metropolis, as well as the insights of Baudelaire's aesthetics, should be drawn on if many contentions about modern art and modern life are to be cogent. For that reason, I interpret David Lynch's or Martin Scorsese's choices in filmmaking in the light of Baudelaire's ideas. This book studies the real Paris of Baudelaire, the fantasized London and Paris in

Poe's short stories, Hofmannsthal's or Musil's Vienna, New York as seen by Aldo Rossi and Martin Scorsese, and Trieste, Venice, Parma, etc., as conceived by architects, writers, film-makers. All these images of cities shift like a kaleidoscope that spins again and again, arranging the same pieces in unique configurations. The visions of the artists I consider are joined with the interpretations of contemporary critics, historians and philosophers, for instance Massimo Cacciari, Manfredo Tafuri, Carl Schorske, Raymond Williams, Fredric Jameson.

I always try to recreate debates within the atmosphere in which they took place. In my reading of Cacciari, while reconstructing an intellectual context now almost three decades old, I retrace the rather complex background that makes up the general set of references for a European scholar of my generation, who lived and taught in Europe and in the United States. This book responds to the realization that the metropolitan theme has been a constant preoccupation in my research, throughout time, a range of institutions, major influences, the real and virtual debates with people and books, and changes in my intellectual life. *Cities, Words and Images* is the result of the images and culture of the cities that have been at the centre of my thinking and my personal experience – from years studying in Venice and Paris, to years teaching in the USA, in Princeton, Los Angeles, and Pittsburgh, and later in Geneva.

Following a distinctive characteristic of modern aesthetics, I have never been inclined to separate the arts and the disciplines. Cities, images and words constitute a network of relationships that jeopardize disciplinary divisions within the human sciences, and enhance a critical vision suspicious of post-structuralist dogmas. Although I do not attempt to construct a linear history of the urban theme, but rather concentrate on clusters of intellectual debate, I resist the ahistorical trend typical of postmodernism and the contemporary mistrust of reason; I keep away from ideological interpretive grids characteristic of the theory of the last 30 years (logocentrism, hegemonic versus subaltern, female versus male, high culture versus low culture, etc.). If my perspective is obviously influenced by contemporary critical issues, nevertheless it remains distinct both from the traditional methods of literary history and the latest fads of cultural studies. I could also say that, following the logic of my metropolitan theme, I take a clear stand in favour of the modern as opposed to the postmodern. Or I could repeat what Roland Barthes used to say in the last years of his life: 'I am not afraid of being outmoded.' On the contrary, I deplore the proliferation of clichés in academic research in literature and culture: there is now a pressing need to refurbish some of the main mottoes of the seventies that my generation believed in, as in a sacred but subversive word, and which are now so rooted in critical productions that they have become mere academic tools. To renew might mean to go back, within another frame of mind, to what seemed surpassed in the outburst of the late sixties and seventies. For example, I hold – without any idealist or biographical purpose, simply for practical and aesthetic reasons – to the controversial notions of authorship, work of art, and representation. Literary criticism would probably be less dull and repetitive if it gave up its most popular topics and reconsidered the role of aesthetic evaluation – a work is good or bad, successful or not successful, for example, in expressing some reality. I actually try in this book to identify some moments and ideas that are at the dividing line between a rational analysis and an ideological reduction. I am also convinced, like many others today, that a proper textual analysis cannot be sustained without an effort to recreate the context or the contexts in which the specific example gets and takes its meanings.

My method is comparative, since I believe that, in criticism, contentions are made up of examples and counter-examples, of similarities and differences, of close readings and attempts at generalization. Therefore, I often present contrasts between two texts or authors, and I refer, especially in the case of Baudelaire, to the same texts or even quotations more than once in the course of this book. To focus on the metropolitan theme also indicates that, in my opinion, literary criticism deals essentially with topics and issues rather than with purely theoretical puzzles. The thematic approach should finally allow us to see that, in spite of the difference of media and notwithstanding the myth that all is rhetoric, cinema carries on today many of the important ends of literature, in particular of the novel in the nineteenth century: to represent the external and the internal world, to express emotions and ideas.

If the subject of this book is the metropolitan motif in literature, architecture and film, its form is the most typical of modern and contemporary criticism: the essay, a collection of essays. Several modern critics have reflected on the form of the essay, from Simmel to Benjamin, Musil and Barthes. The essay, as Sartre defined it, is a hybrid genre, which blends journalistic and academic traits. It responds to the modern need for relatively short pieces, which are adapted to today's rhythm of life and to the numerous situations and opportunities in which writing may occur. The essay derives from the struggle to render the nervous beat of an argumentation that has to be brief, effective and persuasive. Contemporary experience cannot but reinforce the *raison d'être* of this form. We are bombarded by empty words and images; in the age of internet and the remote control, we are used to jumping from one image to another: repetitions and differences spasmodically converge and diverge. The true form of the essay resists such scattering of perception. If it is shaped by the tensions of the contemporary world, it nevertheless aims at an ancient value: of being composed, finished and polished like a crafted object. Suspended between journalism and erudition, research in the libraries and the impulse to speak to the contemporary world, blurring past and present, the essay is the form that encompasses an intellectual search and a stylistic necessity where form and content are one.

In the emblematic 'Man of the Crowd', Poe's protagonist moves around the metropolis in a circuitous and repetitive way. Often, and particularly in the first essay on Poe and in the last on Scorsese, I try to construct my argument in accordance with that circuitous return to the same point. It is, in my own stylistic terms, my homage to the city, whose cultural values I want to endorse, all the more so after what recently happened to New York. As Anthony Vidler wrote on 23 September 2001 in *The New York Times*:

> real community, as evident over the last week, is bred in cities more strongly than suburbs. The street as a site of interaction, encounter and the support of strangers for each other; the square as a place of gathering and vigil; the corner store a communicator of information and interchange. These spaces, without romanticism or nostalgia, still define an urban culture, one that resists all efforts to 'secure' it out of existence.

Acknowledgements

Versions of some of the chapters of this book originally appeared, usually in very different form, in periodicals and edited books, and some were first presented as lectures. Chapter 3 is reprinted from *Home and its Dislocations in Nineteenth-Century France*, edited by Suzanne Nash; by permission of State University of New York Press © 1993. Chapter 4 was published as 'Lieu de retour ou lieu de fuite? De Slataper à Bazlen', *Critique*, 435–6 (1983). Chapter 5, as 'Piazza d'Italia: l'architecture d'Aldo Rossi', *Critique*, 447–8 (1984). Chapter 6 was the introduction to Massimo Cacciari, *Architecture and Nihilism: On the Philosophy of Modern Architecture* ('Theoretical Perspectives in Architectural History and Criticism', Mark Rakatansky, editor), translated by Stephen Sartarelli (New Haven and London: Yale University Press, 1993), copyright © 1993 by Yale University Press. Chapter 7 appeared in Colin MacCabe and Duncan Petrie, eds, *New Scholarship from BFI Research* (London: British Film Institute, 1996). I am grateful to the respective publishers for permission to reprint.

I am profoundly grateful to Colin MacCabe, who first suggested that I write this book: his friendly encouragement was as precious to me as our team-teaching at the University of Pittsburgh. Many thanks to Thomas Martin for helping with the translation of the texts that had been initially written in French, and to Joanna Jellinek for her thorough rereading of the texts written in English. I am greatly indebted to Antoine Compagnon and Kevin Mulligan, who read and criticized my manuscript with generosity and acuity.

1
Edgar Allan Poe: The Domain of Artifice

This interpretation of Poe is based on some of his most important critical principles and emphasizes his appeal for artifice and for imagination.[1] His essays, poems and short stories are strikingly coherent with his aesthetic beliefs and judgements. Sometimes his tales, so often connected with fear and terror, are fictions constructed on a deep rejection of his contemporaries, and their ethical and aesthetic myths. Although Poe did not often mention Ralph Waldo Emerson, he relentlessly attacked his ideas and American Transcendentalism in general. His praise of artifice was meant to jeopardize the ideal of nature so overwhelming all through the nineteenth century, and in the United States in particular. I will identify key oppositions confirming the main opposition between nature and artifice, such as a type of symbolism which understands nature as a sign of God, as opposed to a type of symbolism which is completely formal. In order to highlight the struggle that Poe fought against the Transcendentalists, I lay great stress on two very different ways of treating the term 'eye'. While for the Transcendentalists the eye is a powerful symbol of the spirit, for Poe it is either a concrete object – a part of the body which can be separated from the whole – or an isolated word – oral and written.

Perhaps it is the destiny of literature and art, as much as that of the urban setting: to trigger off an array of examples, connections, similarities and contrasts. Meanings have to be found in this network of relationships. My reading of Poe starts with a similarity with Bataille: the veiled eye of Poe's 'The Tell-Tale Heart' and the eye in Bataille's 'Histoire de l'oeil'. My reading of this imaginative link leads into an analysis of several essays, poems and tales by Poe, developing the motifs implied in them, suggesting and confirming a strong formal intention in his work. Poe was, in the first half of the nineteenth century, aware of the need for a certain type of order in writing: he called it 'the poetic principle', the mastery of the flux of images and words by the work of composition (one of his famous essays is called 'The Philosophy of Composition'). Rejecting any romantic myth of prophetic inspiration, Poe was convinced that the author of a literary text could be something other than an almost divine creator, could in effect be a technician using pen, paper and words, a rational human being using logic and thought in the process of writing and composing. Even the new was, in Poe's opinion, the result of composition: it was the reconstitution of old elements according to a different order. He liked to mention other writers:

> Some Frenchman – possibly Montaigne – says: 'People talk about thinking, but for my part I never think, except when I sit down to write.' ... It is certain that the mere act of inditing, tends, in a great degree, to logicalization of thought. Whenever, on account of its vagueness, I am dissatisfied with a conception of the brain, I resort forthwith to the pen, for the purpose of obtaining, through its aid, the necessary form, consequence and precision.[2]

The pen is the sole means we have to create the necessary order and precision in thinking.

The image of the veiled eye which appears in 'The Tell-Tale Heart' may recall the eye that appeared much later, in the twentieth century, in Bataille's short story. The eye motif and a crime are present in both stories. But a more striking justification for the association has to do with the way in which a story is 'technically' composed with words. The work of composing and its logic often form the basis of the strangest short narratives. At the end of the 'Story of the Eye', Bataille sets out to account for the composition of his story, and for the twists and turns of his imagination.[3] He had already thought out in some detail the scene in the church, and Simone's sexual behaviour, when a host of images crowded into his mind: images from his own lived experience fused with other mental images, which were joined by the bookish memory of Hemingway and his account of a corrida. Then came two other sequences of very violent images. The first sequence turned upon a surgical, organic vision of the testicles of a bull, and of their resemblance to the eye, while the second involved a childhood memory of his blind father and of the white cornea of his eyes. All these images apparently formed the basis of a mental fixation. The images in the 'Story of the Eye' thus derive at one and the same time from books, from real life, from scientific observation and from a psychic interiorization. This heterogeneity in turn gives rise to an association of the eye with other elements, such as the egg that recurs continually throughout the text. An alliterative link between the *oe* in *oeil* and the *oe* in *oeuf* establishes an anagrammatic association. The image is then confused with the sound: the white of the cornea and the white of the egg, the roundness of the eyeball and the roundness of the bull's testicles.

Roland Barthes thinks that the 'Story of the Eye' is not the story of something or of someone, but rather the story of an object, the eye.[4] It is a sequence of migrations of this object and a linguistic game that simply reverses the terms of ordinary language and the figures in every-day use. The narrative is disquieting because it is the eyes, not the eggs, that are broken. The conventional correspondences are disrupted, and it is no longer a matter of *casser un oeuf* ('breaking an egg') and *crever un oeil* ('blinding an eye'), but of *casser un oeil* ('breaking an eye') and *crever un oeuf* ('blinding an egg').

What could be more violent or more scandalous than to treat the eye as a banal object, to be trampled, forgotten, broken, reduced to detritus, annihilated in the violence of death and blood? For the eye is the quintessential romantic and idealist symbol, representing know-ledge and the perfection of nature. It is the privileged locus of the myth of expressivity, and signifies the transparency of the soul and of the subject, the metaphor of truth – so dear to Goethe and his follower Emerson. Above all else, the eye must not be veiled, although that is precisely what happens in the case of the old man in Poe's 'The Tell-Tale Heart'.

In the texts of Bataille and of Poe, the eye loses both its scientific and its metaphysical dignity, its value as moral symbol and as an instrument of precision. It loses its ideal transparency and its clinical cleanliness, becoming instead an obscene thing and the object of an absurd act and of a veritable fixation.

The eye as object

Poe rehearsed many possible readings of the eye as object. Thus, Annabel Lee has eyes that shine like stars:

> And the stars never rise, but I feel the bright *eyes*
> Of the beautiful ANNABEL LEE.[5]

In the poem 'To Helen', the poet sees celestial eyes:

> All – all expired save thee – save less than thou:
> Save only the divine light in thine *eyes* –
> Save but the soul in thine uplifted *eyes*.
> I saw but *them – they* were the world to me.
> I saw but *them* – saw only *them* for hours –
> Saw only *them* until the moon went down.[6]

And the narrator of 'Eleonora' while telling the sad story of the death of his beloved cousin Eleonora recalls that 'the bright eyes of Eleonora grew brighter at my words'.[7] Above all there are the eyes of Ligeia in 'Ligeia'. The setting and mood of this tale are romantic, even to excess: like characters in a Gothic novel, the narrator and his beloved, Ligeia, live in an isolated castle, worshipping solitude, literature and metaphysics. The large black eyes of Ligeia are suffused with an expression which transcends any physical attribute, touching the very soul. The narrator tries to describe Ligeia's eyes, their extraordinary effect: 'The "strangeness," however, which I found in the eyes was of a nature distinct from the formation, or the color, or the brilliancy of the features, and must, after all, be referred to the *expression.*'[8]

The expression of the eyes of Ligeia is so compelling that the narrator loses himself in the eyes of his beloved, resolved to discover the secret hidden in their expression. 'I found, in the commonest objects of the universe, a circle of analogies to that expression.' Words and phrases in this avowal derive from transcendentalist thought, which both Ligeia and the narrator are familiar ('Her presence, her readings alone rendered vividly luminous the many mysteries of the transcendentalism in which we were immersed'). Thus, 'circle', 'analogy' and 'expression' are terms that seem to be taken directly from R. W. Emerson's theory of symbols; perhaps from 'Circles', an essay devoted entirely to eyes and their transcendental power. However, using this same terminology, Poe in fact undermines Emersonian doctrine.

Once Poe's narrator realizes that Ligeia's eyes are extraordinary, he reverses the equivalencies posited by the Transcendentalists. For Emerson, neither the universe nor any objects in it could ever compare with the expression of eyes. On the contrary, it was the eye which gave meaning to the beauty of the universe – a reference to the perfection of the Spirit. (Emerson read Hegel belatedly, and was astonished to find how similar their conceptions were). The key Emersonian formula is 'each and all', which is the title of one of his poems[9]: 'each' – the detail, microcosm, little object or singular thing – could be a representation of 'all', of the whole. The microcosm only has meaning as part of the macrocosm. Thus, Emerson would speak of the shells that captivated him, and that he loved to gather by the seashore. When he returned home, however, and looked at the shells, separated from their whole, from the sea, the sun and the sand – in short, from the organic system of which they were a part – they lost their beauty and were no more than dull little grey objects. Each thing has its meaning in the whole to which it belongs.

Ligeia's eyes are a part, or a physical detail, but they mean everything in themselves. Poe's narrator seeks to bend the whole – all the objects in the universe – in order to regain something of this detail that he loves so much. He completely reverses the transcendentalist relation between microcosm and macrocosm. The separate object has much more meaning then the wholeness of nature. Moreover, vision was for idealist thinkers the least sensual of the senses. Indeed, it was held to be a spiritual sense allowing a glimpse of God, or of the divine forms. S. T. Coleridge, who had exerted a profound influence upon all the American transcendentalists and upon Poe, reckoned that 'nothing is wanted but the eye, which is the light of this House, the light which is the eye of this soul. The seeing light, this enlightening eye, is Reflection.'[10] Emerson would sometimes elaborate still further upon this religious symbolism, derived from Saint Matthew, who had called the eye the light of the body. In his famous essay 'Nature', the New England transcendentalist relived the Saint's ecstatic experience of the universality of Spirit:

> Standing on the bare ground, – my head bathed by the blithe air and uplifted into infinite space, – all mean egotism vanishes. I become a transparent *eyeball*. I am nothing; I see all; the currents of the Universal Being circulate through me; I am part or parcel of God.[11]

The eye, in Emerson's opinion, has a natural magic, and is capable of becoming transparent and of apprehending nature as representation of Spirit. This chain of idealist symbols is infinite. Emerson, concerned to define precisely what an idealist is, insists that, rather than denying 'the sensuous facts', the idealist indeed yields to the evidence, but at the same time knows how to see beyond: 'He does not deny the presence of this table, this chair, and the wall of this room, but he looks at these things as the reverse side of the tapestry, as the *other end*, each being a sequel or completion of a spiritual fact which nearly concerns him.'[12] The sensuous fact is supposed to be merely the other side of a spiritual fact.

Emerson uses the image of the tapestry and, given that the eye is a symbol, the tapestry becomes one also: they both lead to nature and the Spirit. Poe, having reversed the idealist's 'each' and 'all' in his quest for objects in the universe that might resemble the expression in Ligeia's eyes, disrupts the Emersonian image of the tapestry still more. He takes the image literally, for metaphor in his texts merges into words and casts off their symbolism (in 'The Facts in the Case of M. Valdemar', Valdemar can say quite literally 'I am dead', because he was mesmerized at the very moment he dies, in *articulo mortis*). In 'Ligeia', the protagonist of the story, confined to his decadently furnished apartment, after Ligeia's death, is hemmed in and haunted by the tapestry, on the other side of which there is indeed something, namely mechanical objects that produce a wind and cause the fabric to move with a hideous and disturbing animation: 'The phantasmagoric effect [of the tapestry] was vastly heightened by the artificial introduction of a strong continual current of wind behind the draperies – giving an hideous and uneasy animation to the whole.'[13] The spirit behind things has become a technical device pure and simple and nothing more.

One cannot forget that, despite all the tenets of Romantic naturalism and symbolism, Ligeia's eyes resemble (the Greek for resemble is *symballein*) something that is not of the order of nature, but of reading or of books. What the narrator feels upon seeing the extraordinary eyes of his wife is a sensation markedly similar to the impression left 'by certain sounds from stringed instruments, and not infrequently by passages from books'.[14]

Not only does Ligeia have eyes that may be compared to passages taken from books, but she is herself a woman who lives, and has lived, among books. The narrator says at the beginning of the story: 'I have spoken of the learning of Ligeia: it was immense',[15] as was that of Morella, another woman in Poe's tales, whose life was taken up with serious study and intense discussion of 'the wild Pantheism of Fichte; the modified Παλιγγενεσια of Pythagoreans; and, above all, the doctrines of *Identity* as urged by Schelling'.[16]

The women in Poe's stories have often been likened to ghosts or vampires, and critics have interpreted them in biographical terms, as if they suggested that Poe was impotent or haunted by women who were life and death at one and the same time.[17] But in fact these women are often the materialization of a reading, of a book, or of a fragment of a text. Ligeia, for example, dies because of the lack of will shown by human beings when faced with death, yet she mysteriously returns after death by an act of will when the narrator's second wife is on her deathbed. Ligeia did not wish to die, nor to be dead. She is pale and delicate, slender as the leaf of a book; the characteristics of German erudition are embodied in her. Like a philologist in the Romantic tradition, 'in the classical tongues [she was] deeply proficient', and, the narrator continues, 'as far as my own acquaintance extended in regard to the modern dialects of Europe, I have never known her at fault'.[18] Thus does her husband, who is the narrator, describe her, and for him her whole being, her fascination, charm and beauty are summed up in a passage taken from a book by Joseph Glanvill. Ligeia *is* this quotation, which stands as an epigraph at the beginning of the tale, and which is repeated when the narrator says that her eyes have the same effect on him as the reading of certain passages. The passage quoted, one of a thousand which might equally well have been chosen, runs as follows:

And the will therein lieth, which dieth not. Who knoweth the mysteries of the will, with its vigor? For God is but a great will pervading all things by nature of its intentness. Man doth not yield himself to the angels, nor unto death utterly, save only through the weakness of his feeble will.[19]

This passage forms Ligeia's own story, until, by her extreme act of will, she comes back, or appears in person, in front of her husband at the end of the tale.

Likewise, the story of Morella, a woman who dies giving birth to a child whom the narrator will call by the mother's name, is merely the enactment of a passage from Schelling on identity. The identity of the two Morella is such that the narrator is not surprised to discover, when burying his daughter, that her mother's tomb is empty. He laughs a long and bitter laugh. For he had never been truly seized by love for this deeply learned woman, despite the genuine affection he felt for her, and he had never shared her passion for mysticism and for German literature. If he allows himself be drawn into the study of the accursed pages, entering the labyrinth of Morella's reading, it is not without a sense of terror, and a shadow falling across his soul. Morella, for her part, touches him with her cold hand, which seemed like the hand of a dead woman, gathering up a few strange words 'from the ashes of a dead philosophy'.[20] The hand is chill as death, and dead too is the philosophy upon which Morella fed. The narrator is anything but fascinated by all that Morella loves, whether it is theological morality, or the theories of Fichte and of Schelling. Elsewhere, in an aphorism from his 'Marginalia', Poe says that nine times out of ten it is a pure waste of time to expect to extract any meaning from a German maxim. Here, in 'Morella', German philosophy, the doctrines of identification and of the totality of the self, and the faith in the eternally homogeneous (the initial epigraph, on unity, is taken from Plato's *Symposium:* 'Itself, by itself solely, ONE everlasting, and single'), are judged to be dead.

Like 'Ligeia', 'Morella' is also the story of the relationship with books, but Morella materializes books that are not loved, and that are concerned with a philosophy the narrator cannot accept. Although Poe had written a prose poem on unity, entitled *Eureka*, this tale is a critique of idealism and of its mystical aspect:

> Morella's erudition was profound.... . I soon, however, found that, perhaps on account of her Pressburg education, she placed before me a number of those mystical writings which are usually considered the mere dross of the early German literature. These, for what reason I could not imagine, were her favourite and constant study – and that, in process of time they became my own, should be attributed to the simple but effectual influence of habit and example.
>
> In all this, if I err not, my reason had little to do. My convictions, or I forget myself, were in no manner acted upon the ideal, nor was any tincture of the mysticism which I read, to be discovered, unless I am greatly mistaken, either in my deeds or in my thoughts.[21]

'Morella' is to some extent the negative image of 'Ligeia'. For the two tales do in fact form part of what one may term the cycle of women, along with 'Berenice' and 'Eleonora'. But the latter two women are vital, full of energy, agile, graceful and youthful, while Morella and Ligeia are erudite, one educated at Pressburg, the other from an old German family. Both are immersed in their books, steeped in their culture. But Ligeia is like a beautiful and beloved quotation, and loved in much the same fashion; and she writes a poem, 'The Conqueror Worm', which also features among Poe's own poems; like a beautiful quotation, and one that has made an impression on us, she does not die, she comes back. As the figure for the will to live, she can finally win death, in accordance with the passage from Glanvill that inspired the same feelings as her eyes had done. Conversely, Morella, who is not wholly loved, returns a second time as the baleful outcome of her own reading; once dead, she lives again in her own daughter, named after her, in order to die yet again, so that she may efface herself in the absolutely identical, in the terrible identity of death. Should we not hear in the name of both mother and daughter the initial letters of the sombre Latin word *mors*?

Poe's tales are peopled with books, readings and libraries, but the book as object differs completely from the book as symbol of the Transcendentalists. The Bible, the book of the truth according to them, and to Emerson in particular, effaces all the other books, since it is the one book capable of saying everything, and renders all the others pointless. The Good Book would thus be unique, and would annihilate the thousands upon thousands of quotations from various texts that gave so much pleasure to the narrator of 'Ligeia'. Emerson, on the other hand, praised Plato in terms of a paradox that would be quite inconceivable for Poe's characters: 'Among secular books, Plato only is entitled to Omar's fanatical compliment to the Koran, when he said: "Burn the libraries; for their value is in this book."'[22] Anti-Transcendentalists cannot conceive of the one and only Book, but seek out the plurality of objects, and thus of books in their infinite quantity, or fragmented into the innumerable passages that could be reconstituted here and there, according to a hidden order. If, in his tales, Poe invariably, or almost invariably, feels obliged to refer to a book, or to a sentence that he has read, it is because he realizes that nothing exists in the first degree, that life is already in books, that, in some ways, there is no difference between literature and life and that we live in a forest of references. Before Borges, Poe constructed his stories around erudite or fictitiously erudite references.[23]

There is an uncountable number of books. Since the world is not nature, the world is a library, an infinite collection of sheets of paper accumulated over time. Hermann Melville laid down an equally violent challenge to the transcendentalist love of nature. In a chapter of *Moby Dick* called 'Cetology', he classifies the family of whales. Yet it is not exactly a zoological sketch, for these mammals are catalogued after the fashion of books in libraries, as quarto, octavo, folio, etc.:

First: According to the magnitude I divide the Whales into three primary BOOKS (subdivisible into CHAPTERS), and these shall comprehend them all, both small and large. 1. The FOLIO WHALE, 2. The OCTAVO WHALE, 3. The DUODECIMO WHALE. As the type of the FOLIO I present The Sperm Whale, of the OCTAVO, The Grampus, of the DUODECIMO, The Porpoise.[24]

What could be more anti-transcendentalist? Melville completely over-turns Emerson's concept of nature, seeing the organic in non-natural terms, in that order of written objects known as books.

Objects are artificial, constructed, produced by a technique, and are something other than nature. Where Emerson loved the countryside and the open air, Poe, and his narrators, love objects, rooms furnished in curious ways, as in 'The Philosophy of Furniture', and cities, like London, as in 'The Man of the Crowd', or Paris, as in 'The Murders in the Rue Morgue'. The anti-transcendentalist programme was to denaturalize nature, to treat symbols as objects or as mathematical symbols, and to love artifice. Nature is not perfect. Mr Ellison, the wealthy heir in 'The Domain of Arnheim, or the Landscape Garden', is quite prepared to play down the role of nature:

> In the most enchanting of natural landscapes, there will always be found a defect or an excess – many excesses and defects ... In short, no position can be attained on the wide surface of the *natural* earth, from which an artistical eye, looking steadily, will not find matter of offence in what is termed the 'composition' of the landscape.[25]

Artistic vision and analytic observation lay bare the shortcomings of the natural landscape. Poe's character delivers on nature a judgement that reverses Emerson's pronouncement regarding shells: for Mr Ellison it is in the detail that nature can defy 'the highest skill of the artist'.[26] How could one ever hope to imitate the colours or the proportions of flowers? Yet human skill is far more effective than nature when it comes to combining and assembling: the same mathematical laws and the same variations and contrasts in style may be employed in the art of designing a garden as are used in the construction of a building. The totality of nature that so delighted Emerson failed to satisfy Poe, for whom the whole had to be the effect of a calculated combination. Besides, for Poe, original beauty is not the greatest beauty. Where Emerson regretted the loss of natural synthesis when he looked at shells separated from the sea, the fortunate owner of the domain of Arnheim asserted his anti-transcendentalist principle: 'The original beauty is never so great as that which may be introduced.'[27] Mr Ellison treats nature as one might treat objects, or the parts of a machine.

Ligeia's eyes are a whole world in themselves, and yet they undergo a dangerous, hallucinatory metamorphosis, which completely transforms them into objects. These big black eyes, that bear comparison with no others, will appear long after the death of Lady Ligeia, at the wake for the second dead wife, Lady Rowena, when the narrator is gripped by a profound doubt. An 'inexpressible madness' makes him think that she whom he sees rising up again from her deathbed is not

Lady Rowena, but Ligeia. The eyes are the proof, for they are not pale blue, as those of the English woman are, but black:

> And now slowly opened *the eyes* of the figure which stood before me. 'Here then, at least,' I shrieked aloud, 'can I never – can I never be mistaken – there are the full, and the black, and the wild eyes – of my lost love – of the Lady – of the LADY LIGEIA.[28]

In her psychoanalytical study, Marie Bonaparte, Freud's student, took the view that the four tales concerned with women were a cycle that hinged upon the theme of the living-dead mother, and she noted the importance of Ligeia's eyes, interpreting their appearance as a veritable obsession, with the big black eyes being those of Elisabeth Arnold, Poe's mother. 'It is with this exalted fervour,' she wrote, 'that Edgar Poe spoke, without knowing it, of the maternal eyes, which had remained forever living in his unconscious memory.'[29] Marie Bonaparte further emphasizes that Poe himself had recalled that the tale of Ligeia had been conceived 'after a dream in which some eyes, simply some strange and fascinating eyes, had appeared to him'.[30] The eyes are themselves perceived as isolated, separated from everything else, as if they were pure objects. They thus disturb the habitual paths of meaning, because they offer themselves literally, eluding romantic metaphor and moral symbolism. Poe, like Bataille, sees eyes as objects. One could do what one wished with those little round objects. One could look at them through a microscope, as Bataille does, to discover if they resemble something else. One could also remove them from a head, a temptation that can assail even the mildest of men, such as the narrator of 'The Black Cat'. The poor wretch had drunk too much one night, came home late, was scratched by the cat and, possessed by a furious rage against the animal, drew 'from his waistcoat-pocket a *penknife*', a tiny little object, and 'opened it, grasped the poor beast by the throat, and deliberately cut one of its eyes from the socket!'[31] He removed one of the eyes, just as one might remove the stone of an apricot: 'I blush, I burn, I shudder, while I *pen* the damnable atrocity.'[32] In English, of course, you merely have to delete an *s* to pass from *eyes* to *eye*. Language thus lends its authority to the deed: why not do with 'a penknife' what one can do with 'a pen', in the most innocent of grammatical exercises, and add or take away the plural?

As objects, the eyes can become unbearable, and betoken disgust, monstrosity or obscenity. This is because 'eye' or 'eyes', taken for the totality of the body and its spiritual existence, then cease to be treated as a direct expression of love and of the soul, and come to be regarded as a metaphor for the gaze that can see all – that is, the eye of God. Without the metaphor of knowledge, Oedipus would stand condemned; without the natural symmetry of the body, you would have a monster like Polyphemus. For the blind have a symbolic dignity. Thus, Oedipus could only see when he could no longer see in the physical sense; Homer and Milton, with their blinded eyes, are the quintessential poets. But the one-eyed man prompts the violence of the sacred; he provokes laughter (Bataille) or horror (Poe). The single eye, the literal eye or the eye-as-object, detached from the body and from medical observation, is anti-natural, escapes the organically natural, the naturally accepted metaphors. Taking a metaphor literally means perverting meanings, passing from a symbol burdened with signification to the material violence of the word; it means treating a word as a thing or as another kind of symbol, no longer moral but mathematical, and one which does not refer to some higher transcendental entity. Words for poets are like colours for painters or notes for musicians: the matter upon which or with which the artists manufacture their work. The poetic word is not a message, and is not didactic; it has a life of its own, combines with other words, and is then open to suggestions and associations. Suggestion is the opposite of a clear-cut message, and is akin to a subterranean current of thoughts, invisible and indefinite, as Poe likes to point out in his 'Philosophy of Composition'. It is the nakedness of a word, like that of an object, that alone can engender a cascading sequence of images. In his essay, Poe speaks of the bare word that shocks the eye and the ear of the artist and therefore gives rise to suggestion. 'Nevermore', the adverb which continually comes back in the poem 'The Raven', has to be said, uttered, heard, repeated, expected in the refrain, and it carries 'the most delicious because the most intolerable of sorrow'.[33] As Mallarmé observed, one merely has to speak of a flower and 'out of the oblivion to which my voice consigns no outline, there rises up musically, as something other than the flower's known chalices, the idea itself, and sweet, the fragrance of all posies'.[34]

Suppose we take the word eye – sole, isolated – and let it become voice or sound. We then have to listen to it, to hear it and to rehearse all its virtualities. Suppose we complete the isolation of the word, as Mallarmé suggests, suspending the swing between 'meaning and sound', and we can feel 'the surprise of never having heard such a banal fragment, at the same time as we feel that the reminiscence of the said object is bathed in a new atmosphere'.[35]

Eye-I

Where as Ligeia's eyes and the eye of the cat in 'The Black Cat' are treated as single objects, the eye of the old man in 'The Tell-Tale Heart' is both a specific object and a word-as-object, 'eye'. As I have suggested at the beginning, the composition of texts is a theme of great importance in Poe's criticism. Baudelaire translated 'The Philosophy of Composition' under the title 'La Génèse d'un poème'. The term 'composition' has two advantages over 'genesis'. It does not refer to anything natural or organic and it belongs wholly within a technical or artisan terminology. In this essay, Poe countered the Transcendentalist exaltation of content with an insistence upon form. He deemed a formalist approach essential to the composition of a poem. It matters little whether Poe wrote his poem 'The Raven' before he formulated his theory or vice versa, for what counts is that he behaved as a poet confronting the bareness of the isolated word: the word is a precise matter for the poet and it is a source of suggestion, an infinite vagueness.

Poe identified two types of the vague: one negative the other positive. Negative vagueness is confusion in the brain, the lack of clarity in thought, which demands the work of the pen in order to think, as in the passage from 'Marginalia' quoting Montaigne above. Positive vagueness is the element of 'indefinitiveness' that produces a 'spiritual effect'. Praising Tennyson, Poe wrote in 1844: 'There are passages in his works which rivet a conviction I had long entertained, that the indefinite is an element of the true ποιησις... . I *know* that indefinitiveness is an element of the true music – I mean of the true musical expression.'[36]

Poe was particularly entranced by diction and by the letters of the alphabet. He contemplated the effects of sounds and written letters with 'the attentive faculty' that characterized many of his protagonists, both the dreamy types such as Egaeus, for example, and the ratiocinative types such as Dupin. He was fascinated with various alphabets, alliterations, anagrams, rebuses, secret codes, and the peculiar mixture of sound and meaning that is in itself a word or sometimes a single letter. As Poe explained in 'The Philosophy of Composition', his poem 'The Raven' was composed as a kind of music owing its rhythm to the refrain 'Nevermore', its sound conjuring a flux of melancholy dreams – what in the article on Tennyson he called the 'luxury of dreams' or the 'atmosphere of the mystic'.[37] The sequence of rhymes, and letters were to him akin to musical notes, with a life of their own, and with the power of suggestion. These principles are at the root of his poetics. Poe would allow himself to be captivated by the sound of letters to the extent of confusing the written letter with the sound; he chose names full of liquid and nasal sounds such as 'Morella', 'Ligeia' or 'Annabel Lee'. He was as acquainted with the music of vowels as the symbolist poets of the second half of the century, and he knew how to listen to anagrams and alliterations. This is the case with the protagonist of 'Berenice', Egaeus, who, shut up in his library, surrounded by his precious books, would endlessly repeat a word until all its meaning was quite lost, and only the fascination with the pure sound remained. And then there is the suggestive effect of that name: 'Berenice! – I call upon her name – Berenice! – and from the gray ruins of memory a thousand tumultuous recollections are startled at the sound!'[38]

In Poe's oeuvre, then, the highly rich, vague and elusive, and the extremely precise, are two complementary sides of the same temptation. He speaks both of 'ratiocinative tales' and of 'suggestive tales', and for him rigorous mathematic is one aspect of poetry, as implied in the essay 'The Rationale of Verse', the other aspect being suggestion. Traditionally, critics have acknowledged this dual aspect of poetry in Poe, but have turned it into an opposition between the rational and the irrational. It is a matter, however, of two tendencies deriving from a single movement: a concern with the possibilities of sounds and letters. The relationship between logic and suggestion is of the same order as that between theory and practice. Literature and poetry do not arise from the kind of spontaneous impulse, that would be characteristic of 'a simple soul', according to the belief of many of Poe's American contemporaries, for example the poet James Russel Lowell, who was 'infected with the poetical conventionalities of the day'.[39] To argue in such terms is to fall into a 'common error', failing to acknowledge the importance of theoretical principles in the work of a writer. Theory means a thorough consideration of the effect upon the reader. It implies rhetorical awareness, since all the parts of rhetoric are important to Poe, as is evident in his critical works: *inventio*, *dispositio*, *elocutio* and *actio*, or the subject, the composition of the different parts, the words and figures chosen, and finally the diction.

Logic and suggestion both possess the same exacting quality, for analysis is essential to each, with the writer needing to consider the smallest details and be adept at cutting up or laying bare the elements of speech. Division, and work on the separate parts is followed by recombination, as in a laboratory experiment. Poe himself employs terms drawn from chemistry in his discussion of the imagination, a faculty crucial both to suggestion and to logic:

> The *pure Imagination* chooses, from *either Beauty or Deformity*, only the most combinable things hitherto uncombined; the compound,

as a general rule, partaking, in character, of beauty, or sublimity, in the ratio of the respective beauty or sublimity of the things combined – which are themselves still to be considered as atomic – that is to say, as previous combinations. But, as often analogously happens in physical chemistry, so not unfrequently does it occur in this chemistry of the intellect, that the admixture of two elements results in a something that has nothing of the qualities of one of them, or even nothing of the qualities of either.[40]

A concern with details, or the most minuscule parts of things, may eventually become a reverie, even a fixation. This was the case with Egaeus in 'Berenice', who, in his fascination with the monotonous repetition of a word, was capable of studying for days a small drawing on the cover of a book. He explains his 'morbid irritability of those properties of the mind in metaphysical science termed the *attentive*':

> To muse for long unwearied hours, with my attention riveted to some frivolous device on the margin or in the typography of a book; to become absorbed, for the better part of a summer's day, in a quaint shadow falling aslant upon the tapestry or upon the floor; to lose myself, for an entire day, in watching the steady flame of a lamp, or the embers in a fire; to dream away whole days over the perfume of a flower; to repeat, monotonously, some common word, until the sound, by dint of frequent repetition, ceased to convey any idea whatever to the mind.[41]

This intense contemplative activity leads Egaeus to become obsessed with Berenice's teeth:

> The teeth! – the teeth! – they were here, and there, and everywhere, and visibly and palpably before me; long, narrow, and excessively white, with the pale lips writhing about them ... Then came the full fury of my *monomania*, and I struggled in vain against its strange and irresistible influence. In the multiplied objects of the external world I had no thoughts but for the teeth.[42]

It may be that the object of the fixation, the word subject to detailed analysis, is eye. Thus, in Bataille's 'Story of the Eye' there is a fixation with *oeil-oeuf* (eye-egg), while in Poe's 'The Tell-Tale Heart' there is a fixation with 'eye-I'. 'Eye' and 'I' are homophones in English, and Poe, in order to disrupt romantic metaphors, puts a terrible, maddening leucoma upon the eye, 'a pale blue eye, with a film over it'[43]. The narrator, who lives with the old man, becomes obsessed with the white eye of the old man.

The Transcendentalists, and Emerson in particular, had often been the target of Poe's polemics, and 'The Tell-Tale Heart' seems to be a veiled comment on Emerson, who had expressly written 'Circles' in order to vaunt the moral value of the eye as a symbol. Poe's judgement is clear: 'When I consider the true talent – the real force of Mr. Emerson, I am lost in amazement at finding in him little more than a respectful imitation of Carlyle.'[44] The conclusion to this passage, which involves a comparison between Emerson and Aruntius, the historian of the Punic Wars and imitator of Sallust, is still more cutting in tone: 'If there is any difference between Aruntius and Emerson, this difference is clearly in favor of the former, who was in some measure excusable, on the ground that he was as great a fool as the latter *is not.*' Poe, who was well acquainted with Emerson's *Essays*, rejected both their ideology and their style.

If for the Transcendentalists, followers of Fichte, the eye represented the fullness of the self, the plenitude of spiritual vision and of idealist Reason, of the world and the soul, eye could never be understood as a pure sound, or as a naked word, and could never be cut free from the chains of Spirit. For, transcendentalist Reason was not the mathematical logic of 'The Rationale of Verse'. Conversely, the reason of which Poe speaks corresponds to the formal and metrical technique employed in the composition of poems. For the Transcendentalists, Reason is more or less equivalent to the Hegelian Spirit. Poe only mentions Hegel twice: once in order to qualify as 'jargon' the language of the philosopher,[45] and a second time in order to criticize the 'shamefully over-estimated' poet Rufus Dawes,[46] who was terribly keen on German philosophy and its obscurity. 'The Tell-Tale Heart', the short story of the eye, should be read as a profound critique of the blindness of idealist reason, and begins with an allusion to madness. The transcendental symbol of the eye has become the object of an absurd crime, of an intricate mental operation that questions the boundary between reason and madness:

> True! – nervous – very, very dreadfully nervous I had been and am; but why *will* you say that I am mad? ... How, then, am I mad? Hearken! and observe how healthily – how calmly I can tell you the whole story.[47]

The crime had no precise object, and yet the narrator soon realizes that he wished to kill the old man because of his veiled eye, which resembled that of a vulture. It was the eye that haunted him. 'Object there was none', but it was on account of the object-eye that the narrator committed his crime, for he had nothing against the old man. It was necessary to be rid of this eye, perhaps because the object was not very clear, for the eye was veiled. The first person, the I, has consciousness, and consciousness – Emerson would claim – is transparent to itself and apprehends itself as such. But in 'The Tell-Tale Heart' subject and object coincide and there is little room for consciousness: everything depends on 'I'/'eye', a word, a sound, a little piece that can be composed and recomposed. The narrator has then to 'rid [him]self of the eye forever'. This may appear the act of a madman, yet the crime is executed with such care and intelligence that it seems to represent the purest logic.

So it is that the tale translated by Baudelaire under the title 'Le Coeur révélateur' begins with an allusion to both logic and madness. However, *révélateur* is not an accurate rendering of the term 'tell-tale', which contains a verb and a noun, and functions as an adjective. 'Eye' and 'I' share the same sound, so that the shift from the written to the oral word opens up a gulf of suggestions. For the poet who was mesmerized by 'Nevermore', suggestions come both from sound and meanings. 'Tell-tale' produces a burst of alliterations around the letters *t* and *l*, modulated across a scale of vowels that runs from the sound *e* to the sound *a*, while the lexicon likewise causes the grammar to shelter verb, noun and adjective in the heart of words: '*Tell-tale* hear*t* (title)' – 'True'! (the first word of the text). Within the acrobatic movement of alliteration, the tale thus begins with a judgement qualifying the statement as true.

A logical absurdity (killing someone because of his veiled eye, and not for his money), is also a moral absurdity (you must not kill), but here the dividing line between positive and negative is uncertain. So much for Kantian morality in Poe's view (Poe knew Kant through Coleridge): his scorn for the great masters of morality among his contemporaries is evident in his reduction of questions of moral duty of to a linguistic game. Human consciousness in Poe's stories is either the world of crime and fear or what he called 'the attentive faculty of the mind' – the capacity of concentrating intellectually and emotionally on a detail.

The narrator of 'The Tell-Tale Heart' continues his account of events up to the crime and the final revelation to the police. Why should you think me mad if I have committed my crime by means of actions so precisely performed that they seem to embody the most perfect logic? This is the argument of the narrator who, being a sort of pathological Cartesian, knows that if one can reason, one cannot be mad. 'You fancy me mad. Madmen know nothing.' He carefully applies all the rules of reason: his self is the subject of his knowledge: 'Object there was none. Passion there was none... . For his gold I had no desire.' Subsequently, the evidence appears, and he attains certainty: 'I think it was his eye! yes, it was this!'[48]

The initial utterance ('True!') is immediately merged with the emphatic adverbs 'very, very dreadfully', and the twice-repeated adjective 'nervous' lends an air of excess to the word *I* when it first appears, reinforced by the inversion of the whole sentence, which runs: 'nervous – very, very dreadfully nervous I had been and am'. *I*, the subject, shows up, while speaking. But who is this subject? And who is he speaking to?

In 'Morella', Poe undermines Fichte's doctrine of the absolute subject. Here Poe constructs a dark and sardonic parody of the subject, who hallucinates around a detail, the veiled eye, and a sound in language, *I*. Poe often complained about the lack of a satirical tradition within American poetry; he wrote many humorous tales – namely *The Tales of the Grotesque and Arabesque* – and he burned, in the presence of his friends, his very first work, a comic tale entitled 'Gaffy'.[49] The pathological quality of Poe's characters has therefore a double aspect: on the one hand it investigates the labyrinth of mental terror, and on the other it is the satirical, exaggerated representation of a theory taken to such extreme consequences that it inevitably fails. Thus, the narrator of 'The Tell-Tale Heart' is both the parody of a Cartesian and a haunted mind. This second aspect explains Poe's strong appeal to the modern appetite for the tragic and the negative, but too often his satirical or even sardonic mood is neglected.

Poe knows that a well-thought-out composition makes a strong emotional impact on the reader, and that some stereotypes are effective; he maintains that 'The Raven' is constructed on the combined effects of the musical refrain of 'Nevermore' and the image of a beautiful dead woman. Why should a tale not work in the same way as a poem? It can play simultaneously on the powerful idea of murder and on the effect of words with the same sound and different meanings. So the elements of the alchemy can simply be 'eye'-'I' and a crime: then it is up to the writer to combine all this in the most extraordinary way.

The writer, or the poet, is an alchemist, a technician of the pen, working with letters, words, sentences and images – just as a mathematician works with numerals. For there are only twenty-six letters, and all these little symbols are combined to form words, which in their turn make up sentences – just as numerals combine to form complex numerals and equations. There are also laws of composition, language allowing a constant interplay between rules and freedom. I can choose my words but I must subject them to some rules, and bind them together according to syntax.

Words are akin to numeral symbols; they are not moral symbols. They are abstract, not spiritual, correspondences of Nature and God. A non-natural conception of language, such as Poe had, entails an investigation of anagrams, since these are a real linguistic game and show the 'chemistry' of letters and phonemes. Poe in fact built up a whole story around an anagram, 'A Tale of the Ragged Mountains'. The tale featured a Mr Bedloe, who had an extraordinary adventure. One day, while taking his customary walk in the mountains, a sequence of curious events befell him. He found himself in the Indies, with the battle of Benarez raging around him. This battle had taken place some years before, and had cost the life of a dear friend of Dr Templeton, the doctor who was then treating Bedloe with mesmerism techniques. The name of the friend in question was Oldeb, an anagram of Bedloe. The latter found himself transported back to the battle of Benarez just when the doctor was writing the unfolding of the event. Bedloe is as fragile and evanescent as a word written in ink, and responsive to the tricks of an anagram. The new word, produced through an operation performed upon letters, is at once the same and an other word; it can interweave an old story with the one under way.

To write a word or a sentence implies a sort of surgical operation, taking the words and laying them on the operating table that is the white page. There the writer operates, works, arranges the letters in different ways, combining them in various patterns. Poe took just such a pleasure in filling the pages of his article 'A Few Words on Secret Writing' with letters and schemes of the alphabet and of a crypto-alphabet.[50]

A word, a single word, or a proper name was for Mr Bedloe what a sentence, or the quotation of a sentence, had been for Ligeia. Poe thus manipulates books and letters: a fragment, a passage, a citation, a phoneme here, a phoneme there. He cuts, breaks into pieces, puts together, *cites* in the etymological sense of the term, which implies a movement (*cire* = to come). Suppose there is a passage from a book: the writer can set it in motion, can cite it, in a certain order and context (Poe was much taken with quotations, 'misapplication of quotations' and their 'capital effect when well done'[51]). Suppose there is a single word: it can be cut it up into letters, aptly, so as to compose another word or another name. There will no doubt be remainders, for example, passages that have not been quoted, letters that have not been recombined, such as the *e* in the anagram BEDLOe-OLDEB. In fact, after the death of Mr Bedloe, a conversation takes place around that little *e* between the narrator and the editor of the newspaper announcing the death of Mr Bedloe, whose name had been misspelled.

If the editor suggests that 'it is a mere typographical error', the narrator knows the mystery:

> 'Then,' said I mutteringly, as I turned upon my heel, 'then indeed has it come to pass that one truth is stranger than any fiction – for Bedlo, without the *e*, what is it but Oldeb conversed! And this man tells me it is a typographical error.'[52]

In these ways, Edgar Allan Poe could combine his passion for books, libraries and reading with his obsession for cryptography and hiero-glyphs. He wrote an essay, 'Cryptography' on the subject of ciphered codes. The well-known tale 'The Gold Bug' deciphers a message on parchment left by Captain Kidd. Artifice is at the root of reading and writing. This is the law of the domain of Arnheim: original beauty is never as great as the beauty that can be produced through the elaboration of artifice. The natural landscape has to be reworked, almost rewritten, by human skill; only thus can it be original and artistic. If Arnheim is a perfect place, it is because it is the product of arrangements. Indeed, its canal, trees, foliage, gorges, ravines and architectural elements are really quotations. The 'closely scrutinized', separated, well-analysed details are first disman-tled and then reassembled, like a code in cipher; they form a new set on the basis of preconceived data. Gardening is subjected to the same princi-ple as the anagram. The letters of the alphabet, like the elements of nature, belong to the realm of artifice and of intellectual construction. The artificial is not founded upon a transcendent nature, and it implies a complete network of necessary laws in order for it to be a system.

But the most extreme case of the presence of the alphabet is elab-orated in Poe's novel *Arthur Gordon Pym*. Hills, grottoes and the figures of what is termed the natural world become here letters of the alpha-bet, or indeed of three different alphabets, Ethiopian, Arabic and Egyptian, as the long, concluding note to the novel explains. Just as Melville's whales had become books and chapters, the physical forms of the region where Gordon Pym disembarks have become huge letters in several different languages. The most unexpected hieroglyphs conceal all the mystery of nature within the convention of language. The whole adventure is totally determined by two roots: the root for the Arabic verb 'to be white' and the Egyptian word meaning 'the region of the south'. Nature thus takes on the form of letters, the meaning of roots and words; it complies with the alphabet. The first root gives 'all the inflections of shadow and darkness', the second one 'all the inflections of brilliancy and whiteness'.[53] And, as the Egyptian word presaged, white was the colour in which Gordon Pym's adventure was to be forever engulfed: 'We were nearly overwhelmed by the white ashy shower which settled upon us and upon the canoe.'[54] This immense whiteness is also always in contrast with the darkness. What Poe himself called 'the power of words' is realized in that the roots of two verbs steer the destinies of Gordon Pym and of his friend. Dark and white, or black and white, like ink on the page: 'The darkness had materially increased, relieved only by the glare of water thrown back from the white curtain before us.'[55] Finally, in the mysterious conclusion to the novel, a huge human figure is conjured up, in 'the wide and desolate Antarctic Ocean',[56] 'and the hue of the skin of the figure was of the perfect whiteness of snow'.[57] (This reminds the reader of that other case of a famous unnatural whiteness: Melville's Moby Dick.)

This terrifying whiteness is also the main feature of Berenice's teeth, upon which Egaeus, the narrator, constructs his terrible hallucination: 'the white and ghastly *spectrum* of the teeth'.[58] Poe's character is deeply immersed in the volumes of the family library: there he can cultivate his obsessions, being haunted by the quotation from Tertullian on the resurrection of Christ and by the quotation from the poet Ebn Zaiat on the sepulchre of the beloved, the quotation that stands as epigraph to the tale: 'Dicebant mihi sodales, si sepulchrum amicae visitarem, curas meas aliquar tulum fore levatas.'[59] ('My friends told me that if I had visited my friend's grave, my sorrow would for a while be relieved.') These words are so powerful that they dictate the narrator's acts. Thus, after the death of the young woman, he visits her tomb, extracts her teeth, and mixes them up with surgical instruments. Egaeus blurs the organic boundary between life and death, and disfigures the still-living body of his beloved cousin, just as he breaks into pieces the box in which he has hidden the extracted teeth:

> in my tremor, it slipped from my hands, and fell heavily, and burst into pieces; and from it, with a rattling sound, there rolled out some instruments of dental surgery, intermingled with thirty-two small, white, and ivory-looking substances that were scattered to and fro about the floor.[60]

In opposition to the group of American idealists, Melville and Poe asserted the strength of culture – in the form of books and language – over nature. The white whale and the white land of Gordon Pym manifest themselves as a terrifying mockery of Emerson's idea of nature, and his conception of language. For him, indeed, language was a natural tool: 'Nature is the vehicle of thought and in a simple, double, and three-fold degree.'[61] This is the starting-point for idealist symbolism, and for the chain of symbols and representations that refer to spirit. Idealist symbols are meant to be the sign of some transcendent reality. Gradation and sequence are necessary, and everything stems from a simple origin. Hence Emerson sees the moral realm as being derived from nature: 'every word which is used to express a moral or intellectual fact, if traced to its root, is found to be borrowed from some material appearance.'[62] In his essay 'Language', the following propositions were taken to be self-evident:

1. Words are signs of natural facts.
2. Particular natural facts are symbols of particular spiritual facts.
3. Nature is the symbol of spirit.

David Thoreau, another Transcendentalist, held that letters had things as their roots.[63] Emerson could see and feel the divine nature of the universe:

> A subtle chain of countless rings
> The next unto the farthest brings;
> The eye reads omens where it goes,
> And speaks all languages the rose.[64]

In the years during which Emerson was formulating his theories of nature, symbols and language, Melville perforce saw something altogether different. *Pierre, or the Ambiguities* is a novel that met with a distressingly poor response from his contemporaries. The novel stages the opposition between Pierre's life in the country and in New York and represents a tragic questioning of all transcendentalist optimism. Nature is compared in it to an alphabet, and is not held to be the gentle interpreter of itself, nor does the rose speak all languages. Nature is merely the agency that furnishes us with this 'surprising alphabet' in which each of us may study our own particular lesson, choosing and combining as we fancy, depending upon our mood and specific temperament.[65] Metaphorically and literally, the organic is to be dissolved into what does not resemble it, namely language considered as artifice or alphabetic construction, where we choose and combine various little symbols.

In the essay 'History', Emerson thought that:

> It is the universal nature which gives worth to particular men and things. Human life, as containing this, is mysterious and inviolable,

and we hedge it round with penalties and laws. All laws derive hence their ultimate reason, all express more or less distinctly some command of this supreme, illimitable essence.[66]

In *Pierre*, on the contrary, Melville makes the case for a type of probabilism that banishes idealist theology. The protagonist of the novel realizes that the crude reality of metropolitan life is not 'the will of God', but merely a play of possibilities. Out of this evidence, Melville built a tragedy, replacing transcendentalist optimism by pessimism. He wrote *Pierre* after reading Schopenhauer, just as he wrote *Moby Dick* after studying Shakespeare. Poe, on the other hand, took artifice as the starting-point, and was not concerned with the overall human tragedy but with the game in which each individual mental activity is implicated. As his haunted characters respond to his theory of the effect on the reader, Poe constructs the drama not of the will but, rather, of the combination of circumstances in which both intelligence and dream operate, since they both need the faculty of imagination.

Emile Benveniste's observation that human beings organize their subjectivity through the use of pronouns is well known. For 'I' has no intrinsic nature; it is a linguistic convention that, together with 'you', organizes utterances and the other personal pronouns (in a large number of languages). The protagonist of 'The Tell-Tale Heart', the character who speaks in the first person, has no name, and remains nameless, as the interlocutor or interlocutors 'you' remain nameless. The tale that develops on the phonetic resemblance of 'I' and 'eye' is also constructed on the pronominal symmetry of 'I', the narrator, 'you', the mysterious interlocutor, and 'he', the old man. Poe found immense suggestive power in proper names, yet in 'The Tell-Tale Heart', he resisted any temptation to give names to his characters: he relies upon the barest linguistic elements – the use of pronouns and the similarity of sounds.

The first person is usual in the *Tales of Mystery and Imagination* and in the *Tales of Horror*. Indeed, Poe invariably wrote fiction in the first person. Critics have often observed that the characters in his stories are never much developed psychologically. Poe's fictions tend not to hinge upon studies of individuals and their personalities. His protagonists never live out that opposition between individual and society, which is typical of the nineteenth century – an opposition which was so important within American culture. An example among many is provided by the socio-psychological investigations of Nathaniel Hawthorne in his celebrated novel *The Scarlet Letter*, in which the protagonist is torn between her desire and her duty. But Poe conceived his stories according to the poetic principle: in poetry one cannot separate emotion and mood from its linguistic form and rhythm. The word and its phonetic and expressive implications are the material upon which the poet or the story-teller constructs his composition. Grammar, syntax, words, meter and rhyme, all belong to the rationality of versification.

Thus, long before Benveniste had developed the theory of grammatical persons, Poe's texts, 'The Tell-Tale Heart' in particular, expressed the polarity of 'I' and 'you'. These two pronouns define the act of speech, are opposed to one another and yet are complementary. We cannot conceive of one without the other, and they are wholly reversible, so that the one that is 'you' at the moment 'I' speak, becomes 'I' the moment 'I' listen. But 'I' and 'you' need a the third term, 'he', the pronoun for the one who does not take part in the act of speech. Could not a tale tell the story of the general linguistic situation in which utterances take place? Could not a story stage the act of speaking, of telling a story? *I* tell the tale, *I* am the tell-tale heart. *I* am all voice, all sonority, yet *I* do not adhere to a voice but pass from one person to another, from one mouth to another. *I* is a vocal mask, a sound, a cry, as at the very beginning of Poe's tale, with the words emphasized in the text: 'True! – nervous – very, very dreadfully nervous I had been and am; but why *will* you say that I am mad?'

Those who know the power of words are capable of working on them as objects or forms in themselves. Poe speaks often of his belief in the 'power of words' meaning that language can give shape to any thought, even to 'the evanescence' of the most delicate fancies.[67] If the Transcendentalists saw words as the signs of the divine Truth, Poe himself never tired of repeating in a provoking way that art has nothing to do with the truth, and that it is not didactic. As he suggested in 'The Poetic Principle', his contemporaries harboured a misunderstanding: 'I allude to the heresy of *The Didactic*. It has been assumed, tacitly and avowedly, directly and indirectly, that the ultimate object of all Poetry is Truth.'[68] Poetry has to do with beauty and all the artifice used to achieve it. Poetry has to do with the most mathematical calculation. The power of words is the possibility of expressing everything through them, even what seems almost impossible to say, such as the depth and the mystery of Ligeia's eyes, or the most unexpected feelings of horror, terror, and criminal impulses.

But to be aware of the power of words is also, as *Berenice* shows, to be sensitive to the ineffable, the vague, what Poe called the 'suggestion' of words or of images. Some readers of Poe, like Georges Poulet, for example, posited an opposition between the rational power of words and the ineffable, between logic and reverie, as if they were incompatible.[69] Nevertheless, as it has already been suggested, for Poe, it is not a question of an opposition but of complementarity: the all-powerfulness of words verges on the ineffable and finally succeeds in suggesting it.

'The Tell-Tale Heart' conjugates the double face of words up to the point that the suggestive power of the sentence, 'it was his eye, his veiled eye', becomes an obsessive image, creates the decision to kill and the action. (Agathos tells Oinos in the dialogue entitled 'The Power of Words': 'And ... did there not cross your mind some thought of the *physical power of words*? Is not every word an impulse on the air?'[70]) Everything is very carefully performed until finally one night the protagonist can see the light illuminating just the eye of the old man: the eye appears alone, separated from the body of the person, from his being, and finally the narrator kills the old man, cuts him into pieces, hides these pieces under the floor, until the police come to investigate. The police do not even perceive the crime, until finally the narrator declares it, haunted by what he thought he was hearing: the beating of the old man's heart.

The story concentrates on just a single event, and not on a sequence of episodes nor in the development of the psychology of the characters. There is here no contradiction external to the crime and no personal conflict between the old man and the narrator. Moreover, the decision to kill the old man arises out of a trifle, the veiled eye, for there was no reason for the crime: 'Object there was none.'

It would, however, be incorrect to say that Poe's tales have no narrative structure, even if they do not tell of a hero over an expanse of time corresponding to the development of a consciousness. A story exists but it is a detailed story or, rather, the story of a detail, of a single event. An episode is analysed like a fragment with a magnifying glass, in the same way that a word or a phoneme, separated from the linguistic chain, can dictate a series of suggestions. Poe explained this procedure at great lengths in 'The Poetic Principle' and named it 'the unity of effect'. Another tale, 'The Sphinx', is an allegory for this mechanism, which consists in concentrating on a single episode and analysing it in detail – and corresponds to what can happen with the letters of the alphabet or with passages from books. The narrator is obsessed by a huge and terrible monster, every part of which is described in minute detail. Only at the end do we discover that this monster is simply a tiny insect as seen through a pane of glass and therefore enlarged out of all proportion.

Such attention to detail was the monomania of Egaeus, totally concentrated upon the whiteness of Berenice's teeth. Indeed, the density
of many of Poe's stories and the intensity of the vision derive neither
from the relation between character and time, nor from the ordered
sequence of a beginning, middle and end. The end in a tale by Poe is
almost never a conclusion, but can bring us back to the beginning. In
'The Philosophy of Composition', he actually maintained that a work
of art only begins at the end. Eventually, we know from the start what
is to happen in the narrative. Thus, from the beginning of 'The Tell-
Tale Heart', we know that the protagonist has committed a crime.
There is no element of surprise. Poe pointed out the shortcomings of a
form of writing that tends to use surprise as the main element to hold
the attention of readers. The writer has to involve the readers, but
ought not to employ for this purpose vulgar means, such as surprise. In
the Dupin's stories, it is immediately made clear that Dupin has solved
the case. There is no revelation unfolding as the tale proceeds. What
should interest the reader is the way in which things connect and are
built up, with priority being given to the construction and not to the
outcome of the analysis. The stages in Dupin's analysis are clearly set
out, like an argument. As Poe remarks in his 'Marginalia': 'It is the
curse of a certain order of mind, that it can never rest satisfied with the
consciousness of its ability to do a thing. Still less is it content with
doing it. It must both know and show how it was done.'[71]

Writing and reading are thus two aspects of the same activity. Poe
attacked his Romantic contemporaries for concealing the resources
they drew upon, and for talking always of inspiration and creation. Art
is a technique, and writers or artists are not a class of especially privileged people touched by divine grace, but artisans who work with the
letters of the alphabet, with words and with quotations, rather than
confused metaphysical ideas. Metaphysics was, in his view, an obstacle
to good poetic work. He espoused an ostensibly rationalist and analytic
attitude, which served to stave off the inextricable chaos, the lack of
precision and the preoccupation with essence so characteristic of the
metaphysics of his time:

> 'What is Poetry?' notwithstanding Leigh Hunt's rigmarolic attempt
> at answering it, is a query that, with great care and deliberate agree-
> ment beforehand on the exact value of certain leading words, *may*,
> possibly, be settled to the partial satisfaction of a few analytical
> intellects, but which, in the existing condition of metaphysics,
> never *can* be settled to the satisfaction of the majority.[72]

According to Poe, contemporary metaphysics could not adequately define poetry, for two-thirds of the domain of versification pertained to mathematics. How can one fail to note a polemical attitude against those who, like Emerson, thought that the poet is almost divine? The poet, writes Emerson, is 'the sayer, the namer, and represents beauty. He is a sovereign, and stands on the centre.'[73] The poet for transcendentalist metaphysics is an individual with a mission to perform, capable of responding to the will of God: 'For poetry was all written before time was.'[74] The poet would be the one who was sent into the world 'to the end of expression'. He has to name and express to the others what exists before him. In Emerson's essays, the poet is described in terms of sight and the eye:

> This *insight*, which expresses itself by what is called Imagination, is a very high sort of *seeing*, which does not come by study, but by the intellect being where and what it *sees*, by sharing the path or circuit of things through forms, and so making them *translucid* to others.[75]

Poe's criticism did not spare some of the most well-regarded Romantic poets, such as Shelley, whom he considered utterly obscure:

> His rhapsodies are but the rough notes – the stenographic memoranda of poems – memoranda which, because they were all-sufficient for his own intelligence, he cared not to be at the trouble of writing out in full for mankind. In his whole life he wrought not thoroughly out a single conception. For this reason it is that he is the most fatiguing of poets. Yet he wearies in having done too little, rather than too much; what seems in him the diffuseness of one idea, is the conglomerate concision of many; – and this concision it is which renders him obscure.[76]

Emerson stressed the key words defining the activity of the poet: 'The condition of true naming, on the poet's part, is his resigning himself to the divine *aura* which breathes through forms, and accompanying that.'[77] The poet bathes in a divine aura.

If, for the Transcendentalist, 'the poet did not stop at the color or the form, but read their meaning', for Poe, the word 'genius' meant 'ingenuous' – endowed with *genius* – and the men of genius were far more numerous than was commonly supposed. In order to be a man of genius, one has to have an ability that might be termed constructive ability. It is the capacity for analysis that enables the artist to compose.

Several virtues are required for the work of genius, which, in Poe's opinion, do not derive from the divine aura:

> This ability [of the man of genius] is based, to be sure, in great part, upon the faculty of analysis, enabling the artist to get full view of the machinery of his proposed effect, and thus work it and regulate it at will; but a great deal depends also upon properties strictly moral – for example, upon patience, upon concentrativeness, or the power of holding the attention steadily to the one purpose, upon self-dependence and contempt for all opinion which is opinion and no more – in especial, upon energy or industry.[78]

And he liked to say that the highest praise a Roman could give to a poem would be to say that it was 'written *industria mirabili* or *incredibili industria*'.[79]

The genius is somebody who has developed his mental features, who has focused on the analytical skill, which, as stated in 'The Murders in the Rue Morgue', is 'much invigorated by mathematical study'.[80] Since poetry has a lot to do with mathematics, the poet and the analyst have much in common. The good analyst, like Dupin, can retrace the pieces of a composition and likes to exercise what Poe identifies as 'that moral activity which *disentangles*'. The good reader, the good writer is a true analyst:

> He is fond of enigmas, of conundrums, hieroglyphics; exhibiting in his solutions of each a degree of *acumen* which appears to the ordinary apprehension preternatural. His results, brought about by the very soul and essence of method, have, in truth, the whole air of intuition.[81]

Attention and intuition constitute therefore two essential mental qualities – as Poe argues at length in the famous first part of 'The Murders in the Rue Morgue', where he distinguishes between chess and draughts – the first one requiring powerful attention, and the second one calling for *acumen* (intelligence, intuition).

Finally, just as a character in Poe's narratives is not a psychological whole but an enhanced mental faculty, so the author is no longer a prophetic figure but a condensation of certain forces, namely concentration, industry and analytical skill. As I have said, classical or eighteenth-century rhetorical values allowed Poe to escape the Romantic myth of prophetic inspiration. These views of authorship anticipated Paul Valéry's *Monsieur Teste*: 'I was affected by the acute illness of precision. I pushed to an extreme degree the maddening urge to understand, and I sought within myself the critical points of my faculty of attention.'[82] In this famous fiction, Monsieur Teste is nothing but the architect of the literary text, almost an anonymous force, capable of manipulating words and sentences with, and of purifying language from the deterioration of its everyday use. The author is serving the cause of Art, 'while exterminating all the illusions of the artist',[83] and is the untiring observer of the power of words. For it is industry that actually makes a work. As he wrote in his 'Marginalia', Poe is convinced that:

> In the hands of the *true* artist the theme, or 'work', is but a mass of clay, of which anything (within the compass of the mass and quality of the clay) may be fashioned at will, or according to the skill of the workman.[84]

The unity of effect

Poe's insistence on the value of the short story as against the novel is part of a polemic directed against his contemporaries. A 'short prose narrative', like a poem, can be read in a continuous, short amount of time, 'requiring from a half-hour to one or two hours in its perusal'; therefore its length corresponds to its effect, to the unity of effect, 'the immense force derivable from *totality*'.[85] Poe developed this idea in his 1842 review of Hawthorne's *Twice-Told Tales*:

> Were we bidden to say how the highest genius could be most advantageously employed for the best display of its own powers, we should answer, without hesitation – in the composition of a rhymed poem, not to exceed in length what might be perused in an hour. Within this limit alone can the highest order of true poetry exist. We need only here to say, upon this topic, that, in almost all classes of composition, the unity of effect or impression is a point of the greatest importance. It is clear, moreover, that this unity cannot be thoroughly preserved in productions whose perusal cannot be completed at one sitting.[86]

It was not really a matter of genres, even if a novel 'cannot be read in one sitting' – for Poe had himself written a novel, *Gordon Pym* – but of theoretical position. Romantic writers in Britain and in the United States were concerned with a question that may be traced back to Coleridge, namely the organic principle. This principle also featured in German Romanticism, especially in Schlegel (whom Morella read assiduously). In his discussion of Shakespeare, Coleridge spoke of a quality amounting to genius that had little in common with Poe's *industria*. As F. O. Matthiessen argued in his *American Renaissance*, Coleridge allowed that genius could not be 'lawless', but that his laws represented the capacity for 'acting creatively', where this capacity was a happy correspondence between the creator (genius, artist) and the material that he worked. Without such harmony, the outcome would be a mechanical form: 'The form is mechanic, when on any given material we impress a predetermined form, not necessarily arising out of the properties of the material.'[87] Work, industry, according to the Romantic view of creation, was contemptible, for skill in constructing was the attribute of machines, not men. The nostalgic ideologies of the period held mechanism to be in opposition to the organism. A mechanism was deemed a shameful, impoverished variation that violated the laws of nature. According to Coleridge, what the artist should seek was the organic form: 'The organic form, on the other hand, is innate; it shapes as it develops itself from within, and the fullness of the development is one and the same with the perfection of its outward form – such as the life is, such is the form.'[88] Coleridge's conclusion, largely indebted to Goethe, was of a sort that would delight Emerson, Thoreau and the American Transcendentalist group: 'Nature, the prime genial artist, inexhaustible in diverse powers, is equally inexhaustible in forms.'[89] The love for Nature fostered the use of natural comparisons. Thus, Thoreau wrote that man bears a poem 'as naturally as the oak bears an acorn, and the wine a gourd',[90] and readily spoke of a poem as if it were a natural fruit. The most developed expression of the organic principle is the work of Walt Whitman, and, as Matthiessen pointed out, his *Leaves of Grass* served as its manifesto. For Whitman, even prosody has a natural liberty, and poems grow like the buds of lilies, roses, melons or pears.

Poe clearly rejected any such idea of nature, and, in order to assert his difference, he praised 'a skilful literary artist' like Hawthorne who, 'having conceived, with deliberate care, a certain unique or single *effect* to be wrought out', composed the events according to his 'pre-established design'.[91] Poe preferred 'arabesques' or 'devices' to roses and plants. The narrator of 'Ligeia' enjoys the haunting metamorphosis of the tapestry he had chosen for his chamber: the dreamy pattern of arabesque is the final and most exquisite touch of a man whose architectural taste goes back to ancient cultures and decorating techniques:

The material [of the tapestry] was the richest cloth of gold. It was spotted all over, at irregular intervals, with arabesque figures, about a foot in diameter, and wrought upon the cloth in patterns of the most jetty black. But these figures partook of the true character of the arabesque only when regarded from a single point of view. By a contrivance now common, and indeed traceable to a very remote period of antiquity, they were made changeable in aspect. To one entering the room, they bore the appearance of simple monstrosities; but upon a further advance, this appearance gradually departed; and, step by step, as the visitor moved his station in the chamber, he saw himself surrounded by an endless succession of the ghastly forms which belong to the superstition of the Normand, or arise in the guilty slumbers of the monk.[92]

What attracts Poe is artifice, and not only in the interior decoration of old mansions. As we see in 'The Domain of Arnheim', even nature, or physis, is an artificial construction. Thus, the gardens in Poe's tales are works of architecture realized according to a very precise plan. Mr Ellison reckons that even the happiness of human beings can be the outcome of a preconceived design. Decision, project and construction are pitted against organic development. As far as Poe is concerned, nothing is organic or natural – neither the characters in a novel, nor the writer, nor the work, nor language, nor nature. Neither death nor life are natural either. If Poe's tales place so much emphasis upon a life that is not life – as in 'The Facts in the Case of M. Valdemar' – and upon a death that is not death – such as in 'Ligeia' or 'Berenice' – it is because the organic is in his opinion invariably false, an illusion. What is called organic is in fact a mechanism. As in a mechanism, all you have are pieces that need to be put together, to be assembled, and that can always be dismantled. This holds even for the human body. Thus, 'Loss of Breath' and 'The Angel of the Odd' turn out to be tales of the dismantling of the body. Poe clearly had something of a taste for irony and for strangeness: little in these two stories is clear, save the fact that a person has been cut up, a piece here and a piece there. This calls to mind Kleist's *Käthchen von Heilbronn*, in which the lovely mechanical woman, as she undresses, removes a leg or an arm. Mechanical forms flourished alongside the organic principle, and the nineteenth century was an age of dolls as beautiful as women of flesh and blood.

E. T. A. Hoffmann, with whose work Poe was probably familiar, wrote a famous tale, 'The Sand Man', which tells the story of a man who falls in love with a mechanical woman, Olympia. This is a case of a true reversal of stereotypes. Thus, whereas it is generally machines that are regarded as cold and steely, here it is men who are cold, for they do not understand the love Nathaniel feels for Olympia. A good-hearted friend tries to put the lover on his guard. For Olympia seems very odd, both too quiet and too rigid: 'She has appeared to us in a strange way rigid and soulless ... She might be called beautiful if her eyes were not so completely lifeless. I could even say sightless.'[93] In short, the great problem with the machine is that it does not see; it does not possess the divine attribute of mankind, which is sight. Sigmund, Nathaniel's friend, realizes that the girl's step is peculiarly measured, so that each movement seems determined by the turning of a wound-up cogwheel. There is something about Olympia that is not consistent with an organic, living being: she has the monotonous, soulless precision of a machine. But Nathaniel is in love with the machine and when he discovers his insane error he can do nothing but hurl himself over the balustrade of the Town Hall tower, shrieking, and still searching for the eyes of the mechanical woman. What madness is it that causes this young man to fall in love with a machine? Man finds himself in a machine. In spite of transcendentalism, the human being can be explained in terms of a mechanism – and not in terms of Nature and God. Nathaniel explains his attraction to Olympia thus: 'It is only to the poetic heart that the like unfolds itself.'[94]

Once one had known the beauty of machines, one could no longer believe in nature or in the myth of the organic. The same phenomenon had also fascinated Hawthorne, the contemporary author most admired by Poe. Hawthorne's 'Rappaccini's Daughter' is the story of a girl who is the product of a laboratory, of the most advanced scientific experiment. It is often said, with good reason, that Poe invented science fiction. This invention was made possible by his rejection of the organic, a rejection which he took to its furthest limit.

From Coleridge, Wordsworth and the English Romantics, to Heidegger, the cult of poetry has fled the towns for the countryside, the mountains, the forests and the pure air. Poe, on the other hand, adored cities, the metropolis, Paris, London and the haunting urban crowds. A town is wholly constructed, artificial, designed by human beings; an inextricable mixture of the rational and the irrational, of order and disorder, of that which is planned and that which is incalculable. This process is endless in the life of a big city, and seems to know no respite, like the old man in 'The Man of the Crowd' who, night and day never stops walking, down boulevards and along alleyways, through crowds and in gloomy, secluded corners. He is both decrepit and lithe, poor and rich, for beneath his shabby clothes we can catch a glimpse of a very fine fabric and the sparkle of a diamond. Who is this altogether elusive old man, forever walking and walking? 'Yet', declares the narrator of the story, 'he did not hesitate in his career, but, with a mad energy, retraced his steps at once, to the heart of the mighty London.'[95] Where does the great city begin, and where does it end?

Building are constructed, demolished, reconstructed, and there is accumulation of different historical periods and styles, different visions from different points of view, in an endless phantasmagoria, as if the arabesques of 'Ligeia's narrator were magnified on a huge scale. Stories are intersected, interlocked, sunken into an abyss whose beginning or end it would be quite senseless to seek. The mystery of the city, of the man of the crowd, is the same as the story of Isabel that, in Melville's *Pierre*, the protagonist, hoping to leave his New England village and to live in New York, never manages either to know or to write about in the form of a classical novel. Poe's man of the crowd, the allegory of the metropolis, is like a book that does not allow itself to be read:

'This old man', I said at length, 'is the type and the genius of deep crime. He refuses to be alone. *He is the man of the crowd.* It will be in vain to follow; for I shall learn no more of him, nor of his deeds. The worst heart of the world is a grosser book than the 'Hortulus Animae', and perhaps it is but one of the great mercies of God that *"er lässt sich nicht lesen"*.'[96]

This old man, who is 'the worst heart of the world', is no more transparent than the old man in 'The Tell-Tale Heart', whose eye was covered by a hideous film. In the streets of the great modern cities, there are as many different stories as there were types perceived by the narrator at the beginning of 'The Man of the Crowd'. Simply following them for a moment implies a collage of fragments from stories. A piece here and a piece there, like a fragmented body, or organism. Suggestion and logic are both involved in the cutting-up. And the cutting-up is indispensable for the analysis which is at the root of the detective story, of Dupin's conjectures in 'The Purloined Letter' or in 'The Murders in the Rue Morgue'.

Narrating

Edgar Allan Poe uses various narrative modes in his tales. Three different routes may be mapped out:

1. elimination of the fantastic;
2. merging of plot and of analysis;
3. narrative-as-confession in front of the law.

1. The tales are clearly in the fictional mode. Poe rejected third-person narrative, and refused what can be called the illusion of realist objectivity. Yet he also disdained one of the, so to speak, extreme forms of fiction, namely the fantastic. In fact, fancy, a key term in the English literature of the period, is one that he almost invariably rejects. Thus, although he retains Coleridge's distinction between fancy and imagination, he does not build a Kantian metaphysical theory upon either the one or the other. Coleridge had himself complained of the linguistic confusion between the two terms, and said that no more inappropriate translation for the Greek *phantasia* could have been found than the Latin *imaginatio*. Coleridge considered the distinction between fancy and imagination akin to that between delirium and mania: 'You may conceive the difference in kind between the Fancy and the Imagination in this way; that, if the check of the senses and the reason were withdrawn, the first would become delirium and the last mania.'[97] Fancy is the capacity to combine images that 'have no connection natural or moral, but are yoked together by the poet by means of some accidental coincidence'.[98] Conversely, imagination respects the natural and moral connection between images: '[It] modifies images, and gives unity to variety, it sees all things in one, *il più nell'uno.'*[99]

Coleridge defined imagination 'esemplastic power', and distinguished between productive and reproductive imagination, or primary imagination and secondary imagination. The former is 'the living power and prime agent of all human perceptions, and is a repetition in the finite mind of the eternal act of creation in the infinite *I am'.*[100] Secondary imagination, for its part, is an echo of primary imagination, different in degree and in its mode of operation. 'It dissolves, diffuses, dissipates in order to recreate: or where this process is rendered impossible, yet still at all events, it struggles to idealize and to unify.'[101] Secondary imagination is therefore the law of association, whereas fancy is simply 'a mode of memory emancipated from the order of time and space'. Poe could not accept this idealist discussion of imagination and fantasy, although he was willing to preserve its associationist quality. He never spoke of natural and moral connection, since for him ethics is a heresy, at any rate in artistic matters, and nature is simply an artifice. In his critical discussion of imagination, Poe repeated what he had made Mr Ellison say on landscape and original beauty: 'Thus, the range of Imagination is unlimited. Its material extend throughout the universe. Even out of deformities it fabricates that *Beauty* which is at once its sole object and its inevitable test.'[102]

Poe even goes so far as to assert that the distinction between fancy and imagination is 'one without a difference; without even a difference of *degree*. The fancy as nearly creates as the imagination; and neither creates in any respect. All novel conceptions are merely unusual combinations.'[103] Poe treated the two terms of fancy and imagination as interchangeable because he was mainly interested in the material aspect of the act of composition: the extreme limit to imaginative activity would be set by the industria of the artist, the artist's pure artisanal skill. Consequently, he stated, in 'The Murders in the Rue Morgue' for example, that the difference between ingenuity and the capacity for analysis is much greater than, although similar to, the difference between fancy and imagination. By eliminating Coleridge's difference, Poe ended up erasing fancy and its consequence, the fantastic, since everything is included in the alchemical work of artistic composition.

With 'The Thousand-and-Second Tale of Scheherezade' Poe proceeded to eliminate the fantastic, paradoxically adopting the title of the famous Arabian tale. Poe's Schehrezade has at her disposal one more night than Eastern tradition allowed. The fabulous stories that the young woman tells in order to avoid the death sentence are no longer fantastic, but, rather, true accounts of real marvels actually occurring in the world, and directly linked to science. The king thus hears of the laws of physics, of velocity, the eruption of volcanoes, the morphology of insects, the electric telegraph, and the astonishing details that could only be seen through a microscope. Science and technique have become the stuff of story-telling. The fantastic no longer exists since fiction has already become reality.

2. The second mode in which Poe constructs many of his stories can be defined as a fusion between the narrative and the analysis of the data comprising a particular fact (especially in the case of the 'ratiocinative tales'); or, to put it another way, the narration is simply the account of the analysis of a fact. It is therefore not so much the fact in itself that is essential as the way, or ways, in which a fact is read, cut into pieces, analysed, and interpreted. Dupin is a man who carries out good analyses, capable of yielding good results. Poe formulated, at the start of 'The Murders in the Rue Morgue', the famous distinction between the chess player and the draughts player. The game of chess, which allows for a wide variety of moves, only needs ingenuity. One requires a great capacity for concentration, for 'to observe attentively is to remember distinctly'.[104] But an analyst's skill transcends any system of rules. An analyst is silent, capable of reading between the lines, and of paying heed to things that would appear to have no bearing upon

the game: 'He makes, in silence, a host of observations and inferences. So, perhaps, do his companions; and the difference in the extent of the information obtained, lies not so much in the validity of the inference as in the quality of the observation.'[105] What one must know is what to observe: 'Our player confines himself not at all; nor, because the game is the object, does he reject deductions from things external to the game.'[106] It is a question of seeing, or rather of listening: 'He examines the countenance of his partner, comparing it carefully with that of each of his opponents. He considers the mode of assorting the cards in each hand.' To the analyst every gesture means something, and nothing must escape him: 'He notes every variation of face as the play progresses, gathering a fund of thought from the differences in the expression of certainty, of surprise, of triumph or chagrin.'[107]

The analyst carries out a genuine operation of dismantling, to be followed by editing. Small pieces have to be cut up and reconstructed, in a work of montage. That is precisely what the plot consists of. Narrative is simply the composition of different parts so that they may acquire a fictional unity. Dupin's analyses constitute the plot, in which we may discern a method at work, a modus operandi that becomes the actual subject of the tale. Narrating means surveying the steps in an analysis, describing the pieces that are to be put in place. Narrating also means knowing how to read, and a good narrator, or a good analyst, is a good reader.

Dupin is endowed with a remarkably acute analytic mind but, not unexpectedly, he has something in common with Ligeia. For he too belongs to an old family, and is in even more distressing circumstances than Ligeia, since he does not have much money and has to make the most stringent economies in order to get by. He lives abstemiously: 'Books, indeed, were his sole luxuries, and in Paris these are easily obtained.'[108] As was the case with Ligeia and Morella, his dominant passion is for books. Furthermore, he met the narrator in an obscure bookstore on the rue Montmartre, when seeking a rare item. Dupin likes to tell stories and to display his analytic skill. He is blasé, eccentric, and a worshipper of the night, a creature of the big city and a *flâneur*. He loves books, exercises his analytic skills, and works for cash, not out of pure heroism. Money, the letters of the alphabet, chess, draughts, and the stages in an analysis are all systems of forms or of symbols that have little to do with Nature and its transcendental meanings.

3. The third mode of narration used by Poe in his fictions is constructed on a paradoxical motif such as in 'The Imp of the Perverse', 'The Black Cat' and 'The Tell-Tale Heart'. Here the confession of the

narrator is dramatically staged at an extreme moment. These tales, which form a sort of cycle, are set just prior to a condemnation to death, and enact a very particular situation, in which the narrator feels a compelling need to tell his own story. This is not in fact for the pleasure of telling, as with Dupin, but in the hope of gaining relief; as the narrator of 'The Black Cat' says: 'But to-morrow I die, and to-day I would unburden my soul.'[109]

The action of the crime is always described with great precision, in terms of feelings and gestures. Everything can be named, even the most terrifying things, such as the coagulated blood of the corpse, the eye torn out of the cat's head, the physical terror and the mental horror. We learn, therefore, of the decision to act, of the rigorous logic underpinning the plan, or of the violent impulse to act. In 'The Imp of the Perverse', the assassin lays stress upon the premeditated nature of his deed: 'For weeks, for months, I pondered upon the means of the murder. I rejected a thousand schemes, because their accomplishment involved a *chance* of detection.'[110] It was a book, and the reading of it, that gave him the idea: 'in reading some French memoirs, I found an account of a nearly fatal illness that occurred to Madame Pilau, through the agency of a candle accidentally poisoned.'[111] In 'The Black Cat', the narrator, having tried to kill his much-hated cat, and having been thwarted in this by his wife, finds that he cannot curb his fury, and slays his wife instead: 'Goaded by the interference into a rage more than demoniacal, I withdrew my arm from her grasp and buried the axe in her brain. She fell dead upon the spot without a groan.'[112] In a similar way, in 'The Tell-Tale Heart', the protagonist insists from the beginning upon the force of his logic and patient work during the whole course of events.

'The Imp of the Perverse' supplies the key to a reading of the three tales. It begins with a long psychological and philosophical discussion of perversity:

> Induction, *a posteriori*, would have brought phrenology to admit, as an innate and primitive principle of human action, a paradoxical something, which we may call *perverseness*, for want of a more characteristic term. In the sense I intend, it is, in fact, a *mobile* without motive, a motive not *motiviert*. Through its promptings we act without comprehensible object; or, if this shall be understood as a contradiction in terms, we may so far modify the proposition as to say, that through its promptings we act, for the reason that we should *not*.[113]

Driven by this inner force, the narrator, who has committed a perfect crime, feels impelled to betray himself and speak out about his actions. The story analyses each stage in the progress of this urge towards self-destruction, this compulsion that causes a reasonable human being to act for no comprehensible reason or for an irresistible 'unreasonable' reason; a few words at the end make it clear that the whole narration in the first person has been given in a very precise setting, that of a prison: 'I have said thus much, that in some measure I may answer your question ... that I may assign to you something that shall have at least the faint aspect of a cause for my wearing these fetters, and for my tenanting this cell of the condemned.'[114] The narrator is, then, in his cell. He declares himself the victim, 'one of the many uncounted victims', of the imp of perversity: driven by an invincible force, the subject yields to the law. He must tell of his crime precisely because he should not. His madness does not lie in having committed the crime but in feeling compelled to speak out about it.

Indeed, this is precisely what happens in 'The Black Cat' and in 'The Tell-Tale Heart'. All three tales are in their various ways concerned with the predicament of a narrator who is telling or writing his story immediately before being condemned to death. Whereas in 'The Imp of the Perverse' the narrator confesses halfway through the tale that the place where he is recounting his deeds is his cell, in 'The Black Cat' he declares, right from the start, that he is engaged in the writing of his own story: 'For the most wild yet most homely narrative which I am about to pen, I neither expect nor solicit belief.'[115]

Once again the narrator is in his prison cell, and there he writes of his crime. He has killed his wife because of his hatred for the black cat. After the murder, he hid her corpse in the cellar, and finally showed it to the police, just when he was out of danger. No one had discovered his crime, nor could anyone have discovered it. It was he who, prey to 'the imp of the perverse', wished to prove to the police how solid the walls of his house were, and, in so doing, struck with a cane precisely where the corpse had been for several days. An inhuman, terrifying cry was heard. The wall collapsed to reveal the already decomposed body of the woman and the hideous cat, with just one eye, still alive, seated on her head: 'with red extended mouth and solitary eye of fire, sat the hideous beast whose craft had seduced me into murder, and whose informing voice had consigned me to the hangman.'[116]

So the prison may appear at the beginning or in the middle or at the end of the story, which may be spoken or written. Whereas the scene of the crime, and of its consequences, is described in great detail, the place where the narrator confesses is merely alluded to in a sentence at the beginning, at the end or in the middle of the tale. The allusion is brief, sharp, and without description. It is not the specific but the generic that dominates: the non-identified cell of the condemned man; the anonymous, faceless agents of the law and the executioner; the use of the second person, 'you', to indicate interlocutors, judges or policemen who do not utter so much as a single word in the course of the whole story. The entire confession is internalized, and not because of some Kantian interior morality. The murderer does not exactly feel guilty, nor is he eaten up by remorse. Rather, impelled by the whim to which he has fallen victim, he is led to follow in reverse the course of his acts, decisions and impulses. Thus, in relation to the crime, the subject plays two parts. The crime was perfect in its execution, and the narrator knew exactly how to hide it; but, once the deed is done, a perverse impulse destroys the whole thing.

The Tell-Tale Heart

The Tell-Tale Heart' can therefore be read as a variation on the perversity motif, around the paradox of the narrator who betrays himself, revealing his own crime. The three tales were all written between 1843 and 1845. Nevertheless, while in 'The Imp of the Perverse' and 'The Black Cat' the prison cell from which the narrator speaks or writes is actually mentioned, in 'The Tell-Tale Heart' the place in which the narrator tells the story is not defined, so that it could be the house where he committed the crime, or the court, or the prison, as if this tale were designed to represent an extreme case of the imp motif.

In the three tales, the narrator remains nameless: 'I', in English, is a letter of the alphabet, a sound that appears in all sentences where the subject speaks about himself; it is a pronoun, a linguistic function. 'I' is one of the letters Poe loved, that resounds in the much-cherished name of Ligeia. 'I' conjugates with 'you' and declines with the tenses of verbs – the verb 'to be' for example: 'I had been and am ... ' The past and the present of the verb to be in the first person appear in the first lines of the tale, and then the future of the second person: ' ... will you say'.

The narrator longs to tell, and merges with 'you', because this unidentified interlocutor could also be he himself, because that same doubt that might have gripped 'you' could also haunt the 'I': am I mad? No, do not think that I am mad since I am going to show you how logically I proceeded: 'Now this is the point. You fancy me mad. Madmen know nothing. But you should have seen *me*. You should have seen how wisely I proceeded – with what caution – with what foresight – with what dissimulation I went to work!'[117]

But the sound designating the first person singular can also be written 'eye', like the old man's 'vulture eye', 'his Evil Eye' that haunts the narrator. I have committed the perfect crime – suggests the narrator – even if 'object there was none'. And here it comes, the imp of the perverse that causes one to act for a trifle, 'a mobile without *motive*, a motive not *motiviert*'. Like the ticking of a watch, or the beating of a heart, the sentences follow on one after the other: 'Object there was none. Passion there was none. I loved the old man. He had never wronged me. He had never given me insult. For his gold I had no desire.'[118] The short, cutting sentences follow until: 'I think it was his eye!' One must read this sentence aloud, hear it, hear it with what was the most well-developed sense in the narrator: hearing. One must listen to the sound occurring at both the beginning and the end of the sentence: 'I', 'eye'. The story told at the first person, is the story of the 'eye': as suggested at the beginning of this chapter, it is similar to Bataille's story, since it is the story of an object, the eye, and a linguistic game based on the homophony between two words in English.

'I think it was his eye': the brevity of the sentence, with its jerky rhythm hinging on the letter *i*, is such that it resembles a line of verse or a motto, and it is thereby turned into a single word, in the breath of diction: 'eye'. Unlike 'eyes' at the plural, 'eye' in the singular, by itself, isolated, does not hint at a human face, at a whole person: it is a substantive designating an object. 'Eye' is the term as found in the dictionary, open to every occurrence, but almost unreal, abstract, cut off from the life of a whole sentence. It can easily become an obsessive sound, and, like in Bataille's 'Story of the Eye', it can lead to crime.

'I' is the subject and 'eye' is the object, but the homophony opens up to the undercurrent of suggestion, and dilutes the difference. 'The Tell-Tale Heart' has as its subject – or object – an object, the eye; the object of the crime is the eye, but 'eye' sounds like 'I', namely the subject in the first person that tells the story. Sounds, words, meanings are the matter of poetry and prose. As we know, Poe believed in both the logical power and the suggestive power of words:

> I do not believe that any thought, properly so called, is out of the reach of language ... There is, however, a class of fancies, of exquisite delicacy, which are *not* thoughts, and to which, *as yet*, I have found it absolutely impossible to adapt language. I use the word *fancies* at random, and merely because I must use *some* word.[119]

The analyst, not unlike the poet, likes rebuses, enigmas, hieroglyphs, conundrums: 'He derives pleasure from even the most trivial occupations bringing his talent into play.'[120] Words and sounds, grammar and syntax offer many possibilities of games and suggestions. What if one could eliminate the grammatical persons, or decline pronouns: 'I', 'he', 'it'? The narrator of 'The Tell-Tale Heart' accumulates short sentences where the personal pronouns resound with all their suggestive power:

> *I* loved the old man. *He* had never wronged *me*. *He* had never given *me* insult. For his gold *I* had no desire. *I* think *it* was his *eye*! yes, *it* was this! One of his *eyes* resembled that of a vulture – a pale blue *eye* with a film over *it*. Whenever *it* fell upon me, my blood ran cold; and so by degrees – very gradually – *I* made up my mind to take the life of the old man, and thus rid *myself* of the *eye* for ever?[121]

'*I* think *it* was his *eye*.' 'It' is the neuter; 'it' is in the middle of the short sentence. It designates the thing, whatever object might be familiar. It, the eye of the old man, is veiled. 'It' is the neuter, a trifle, or a film on the eye.

One should perform a chemical analysis of Poe's tales and identify the elements, as Poe himself suggested. Ciphering and deciphering, that is the continuous work of the skilful reader and the skilful writer, constantly manipulating words, letters and sounds, endlessly composing them, always aiming at the unity of effect. Where an operation succeeds, the calculation must have been right, the intuition must be correct. The heart appears in 'The Man of the Crowd' as in 'The Tell-Tale Heart', since the old man in 'The Man of the Crowd' is 'the type and genius of deep crime', and also 'the worst *heart* of the world [my emphasis]'. He is 'a grosser book than the "Hortolus Animae"', a book that *lässt sich nicht lesen*. Through the arabesque of words and sounds, one can neutralize or hold together opposite meanings. So, secret, as in 'The Man of the Crowd', and revelation, as in 'The Tell-Tale Heart', cease to be mutually exclusive, but lie rather on the same axis, like to say, or to tell, and to read, *lesen* in German, for *legein* in ancient Greek means to say.

Thus 'The Man of the Crowd', probably written in 1840, is to a certain extent the photographic negative of 'The Tell-Tale Heart'. The former takes place in London, in wide open metropolitan places, in the streets and in the midst of the crowd of a real city, the latter in the close space of an apartment and mainly in the old man's bedroom. In one tale the scene is set with a very small number of architectural elements, a bedroom, a door, a bed, the floorboards, whereas in the other there is all the variety of the big city. In 'The Man of the Crowd', everything is traffic, movement, speed, shortness of breath and, indeed, chance, for the narrator begins to follow the unknown old man out of curiosity and without any precise plan. He follows him for a whole night and a day, leaving him only on the second evening, for the time experienced is infinite, and perpetual recommencement takes place. Conversely, in 'The Tell-Tale Heart', the narrator knows the old man, lives with him, and the action is unique, predetermined, slow and studied, unfolding within the well-defined timescale of eight nights.

Yet the two tales are linked by the genius of 'deep crime', or the demon, the imp of perversity. The narrator of 'The Man of the Crowd' saw the neutral, empty gaze of the mysterious old man: 'And, as the shades of the second evening came on, I grew wearied unto death, and, stopping fully in front of the wanderer, gazed at him steadfastly in the face. He noticed me not.'[122] The old man in the other tale also has an eye without a gaze; and, because it is veiled, the narrator never knows if it is looking at him or not. It haunts him. 'I think it was his eye! yes, it was this.' *This*, *th*, *teeth*: the narrator of Berenice, for his part, was haunted by tee*th*: 'The teeth! – the teeth! – they were here, and there, and everywhere, and visibly and palpably before me... . They – they alone were present to my mental eye, and they, in their sole individuality, became the essence of my mental life.'[123] In this stream of rhymed terms and alliterations of *th*, it is the eye, the mental eye, that constantly sees the teeth. Those of Berenice were 'long narrow, and excessively white, with the pale lips writhing about them'. Likewise, the old man's eye in 'The Tell-Tale Heart' was 'a pale blue eye, with a film over it'. The horrible eye that haunts the narrator is pale in colour. After her illness, Berenice too had eyes without a gaze, and without light: 'The eyes were lifeless, and lustreless, and seemingly pupilless.'[124] The cycle of obsession is infinite, following the movement of suggestion. Berenice then resembles Poe's old man, just as Ligeia had done, since the indescribable effect of her eyes' expression was comparable to that of the eyes of old people: 'I have felt it in the glances of unusually aged people.'[125]

The alchemy of the mind demands equations between some fragments of the tales: refrains, neutralizing effects, contrasts as in the rhymes of a poem, arise out of such a chemistry. Words, sounds and images turn in a kaleidoscope.

When chemical elements are combined, one should see the outcome, which can be unexpected. Thus, the old man in 'The Man of the Crowd' is the genius of crime, 'the worst heart', while in 'The

Tell-Tale Heart' the old man becomes 'his Evil eye', but 'eye' sounds like 'I', and the gaze I cannot meet is above all my own gaze. So it is 'I' that am the old man; 'I' is the 'Evil eye', and in that respect something wicked, impish, namely the genius of crime, the one 'I' have committed and 'I' tell. Or else 'the worst heart in the world' is the one that tells, or 'the tell-tale heart'. It is the heart that corresponds to the crime; it is there under the floorboards, it is the *corpus delicti*, the body of the old man cut up into pieces, the beating heart. But of whom? 'I' and 'eye', the subject of the crime and the object of it, are merged through the hallucination of the same sound. The first-person narrator of 'The Tell-Tale Heart' undergoes a process of identification with the old man. The old man had been completely identified with the unbearable image of his veiled eye. He will be ultimately destroyed because of the enormity of a detail, as it happens to the narrator at the very end, when, after the crime, he cannot stop hearing the beating of the heart. Everything merges, as if 'I' and 'eye' were finally the same body.

The murderer is wholly comparable to his victim, being himself the victim of the demon of perversity that is pushing him to betray himself. The execution of the crime is slow and precise. Seven nights pass before the narrator can perform the deed, the old man's eye being not open; because, as we know, it was not the old man who annoyed him 'but his Evil eye'. The narrator has to wait until the eighth night, when the old man hears a noise, wakes up and yells: 'Who is there?' And then, the narrator explains: 'He was still sitting up in the bed listening; – just as I have done, night after night.'[126] Then a moan went up. Which the narrator knew only too well:

> I knew the sound well. Many a night, just at midnight, when all the world slept, it has welled up from my bosom, deepening, with its dreadful echo, the terrors that distracted me. I say I knew it well. I knew what the old man felt ... [127]

How, at this stage, can one distinguish the narrator's terror from that of the old man? 'His fears had been ever since growing upon him. He had been trying to fancy them causeless, but could not. He had been saying to himself – "It is nothing but the wind in the chimney".'[128] The narrator can feel exactly what the old man feels.

The old man is terrified, and his heart beats loudly. Indeed, it beats too loudly, and the neighbours might hear it. There is therefore no time to lose, and the old man must be killed at once. Yet when the deed is finally done, the identification with the old man, now dead, cut into pieces, and well hidden, becomes unbearable. The pieces of his body are under the floorboards, and the murderer plants his chair on the self-same spot, in order to chat with the policemen. He then hears the beating of the heart, very loud, too loud, ever louder, until at last, goaded beyond measure, convinced that the noise is coming from beneath the floor-boards, from the old man heart, he has to confess his crime.

One can be very logical, master everything, and finally become the victim of an idea, a sensation that comes from the body, from one of its senses, namely hearing. The story of the eye is also the story of hearing, for the beating of the heart is clipped and rhythmical, like all the short sentences resounding in the tale.

Poe rejected the belief in Nature and the organic principle. Yet the organic would reappear from a very different angle as organ – be it the eye, or ears, an acoustic sense that is only too acute, or the heart that beats as if it would never stop. And the body is cut into pieces. In Poe's tale, detail and fragment assert themselves against the whole, against the Emersonian idea of 'each and all'. The eye is an isolated organ, separated from the whole, and such is the heart – an isolated organ.

'Funes or Memory' is the tale by Borges which the author himself has described as the metaphor for insomnia – a sort of expanded faculty of attention that allows the protagonist to see everything in the most perfect detail from all possible perspectives. It is the story of the detail that kills, becomes the whole world and a true obsession. 'The Tell-Tale Heart' may likewise be read as a metaphor for the heart. For finally the whole story is, as Barthes said of Bataille's 'Story of the Eye', a sequence of migrations of the eye as an object and a linguistic artifice that reverses the terms and the most common figures of speech. From sequence to sequence, 'The Tell-tale Heart' finally concentrates at the end on one thing, an organ called heart, with a final 't', and the letter 't' features in 'it', in the title of the story, 'The *T*ell-*t*ale hear*t*, and likewise in the beating of the heart. The letter 't' beats like a hammer, contributing to the unity of effect that is quite the opposite of the transcendentalist unity. Poe, who loved Nathaniel Hawthorne's tales, knows the importance of that hammering in order to induce 'an exaltation of the soul which cannot be long sustained'. The short narrative, like a poem, has to hammer in the reader's mind: 'Without a certain continuity of effort – without a certain duration or repetition of purpose – the soul is never deeply moved. There must be the dropping of the water upon the rock.'[129]

'The Tell-Tale Heart' was written at the end of 1842. In the spring of the same year, Edgar Allan Poe had a heart attack. His stepfather, John Allan, suffered from a weak heart.[130] Edgar Allan Poe could never quite bring himself to accept the name of his stepfather, so he dropped Allan or, rather, only kept the initial letter, the first in the alphabet, and he always wrote Edgar 'A.' Poe. 'A', as in Ligei*a*, and at the very heart of he*a*rt.

Ciphering and deciphering are, for Poe, the work of the writer and of the reader. Letters and sounds are for Poe, as for Bataille, the domain of literature. They constitute the basis of a poetic or narrative composition; like an arabesque, they develop a motif or a theme, aiming to the unity of effect. The writer and the reader should both have the faculty of attention that characterizes many of Poe's protagonists – Egaeus, Dupin and the narrator in the first person of the 'The Tell-Tale Heart'.

2
Van Gogh and Hofmannsthal: Colours and Silence

This chapter will treat, from a Baudelairean perspective, the unexpected link between Hugo von Hofmannsthal and Vincent Van Gogh as pointing to some crucial questions in modern art: the interplay between the past and the present, the discrepancy between reality and language, and the attempt to express this very discrepancy through the link between literature and painting.[1]

The term 'modern' can be understood in two different ways. On the one hand it implies a belief in the totally new, in the breaking off of tradition – typical of avant-gardes; on the other, the modern is apprehended as weighed down by culture, by the past, capable of becoming classical or even decadent. Baudelaire demonstrated both aspects of modernity. In his long poem 'Le Voyage', he invites anyone who loves spiritual adventures to strive for the new: 'Let's plunge to the bottom of the Unknown, to discover something *new*!'[2] But in *Le Peintre de la vie moderne*, where he investigated the question of contemporary art and aesthetics through the sketches of Constantin Guys, Baudelaire stated the equal value of the past and the present:

> The past is interesting not only by reason of the beauty which could be distilled from it by those artists for whom it was the present, but also precisely because it is the past, for its historical value. It is the same with the present. The pleasure which we derive from the representation of the present is due not only to the beauty with which it can be invested, but also to its essential quality of being present.[3]

While discussing the concept of 'modernity', he suggested that the modern should deserve to become ancient: 'In short, for any "modernity" to be worthy of one day taking its place as "antiquity", it is necessary for the mysterious beauty which human life accidentally puts into it to be distilled from it.'[4]

Baudelaire constantly affirms that Delacroix is the 'most original painter of ancient or of modern times'.[5] He is both ancient and modern, since he excels both in the grandeur of composition typical of the ancient masters and in the expression of the melancholy feeling characterizing modern sensitivity. Delacroix's art makes a deep impression on the soul and 'quickly enough guides our thoughts towards the fathomless limbo of sadness.'[6]

In one of his first enthusiastic comments on Delacroix (*Salon de 1845*), Baudelaire praised *La Mort de Marc Aurèle* (*The Death of Marcus Aurelius*), a painting which had not been appreciated by contemporary critics: Marcus Aurelius is dying and his son Commode appears light-hearted as if he were thinking about something else. The vision of Roman decadence is depicted with the modern use of colour and with the modern feeling par excellence, melancholy: for Baudelaire, past and melancholy are tied together in the representation of that Roman scene. Perhaps, ever since Baudelaire there has been an inexhaustible complicity between the modern and the decadent – a feature which characterized the endeavours of a host of artists of the turn of the century in Vienna. A line of Rilke's *Der Letzte* expresses the feeling that haunted so many writers: 'And I feel myself to be the heir of something that transcends today.' The same mood is evident in Georg Trakl's *Amen*: 'Corruption gliding through the crumbled room; Shadows on yellow hangings; in dark mirrors the ivory sorrow of our hands is arched. Brown beads trickle through fingers that have died ... '[7]

The connection between Hofmannsthal, who has that Viennese frame of mind, and Van Gogh, whose works made such an impact on the Viennese writer, shows that the relationship between literature and painting does something more than respond to the classical wish of Horace: *ut pictura poesis*. It corresponds to the attempt to express modernity, modern life, the one art being a continuation of the other, as suggested by Baudelaire. In his essay 'The Life and Work of Eugène Delacroix', he defined the 'strange, mysterious quality' of Delacroix as 'the invisible, the impalpable, the dream, the nerves, the *soul*' that the artist was able to interpret 'with the perfection of a consummate painter, with the exactitude of a subtle writer, with the eloquence of an impassioned musician.'[8] But, in addition to this praise which both summarizes and blends the qualities of the various arts, Baudelaire stated an essential feature of modern aesthetics: 'It is moreover one of the characteristic symptoms of the spiritual condition of our age that the arts aspire if not to take one another's place, at least reciprocally to lend one another new powers.'[9] Van Gogh, not unlike Delacroix, was aware of the importance of literature for painting. No sooner had Van Gogh resolved to become a painter than he began to read:

> So I studied fairly seriously the books within my reach, like the *Bible* and *French Revolution* by Michelet, and last winter Shakespeare and a few by Victor Hugo and Charles Dickens ... So you would be wrong to persist in the belief that, for instance, I should now be less enthusiastic for Rembrandt, or Millet, or Delacroix, or whoever it may be, for the contrary is true. But you see, there are many things which one must believe and love. There is something of Rembrandt in Shakespeare, and of Correggio in Michelet ... If now you can forgive a man for making a thorough study of pictures, admit also that the love of books is as sacred as the love of Rembrandt, and I even think the two complete each other.[10]

Deeply impressed by Van Gogh, Hofmannsthal believed that painting starts where literature becomes silence, and lends new powers to literature.

My method here will be to present the reader with a montage of literary and figurative passages showing the struggle of those who considered words to be inadequate to express the modernity of 1900. A new language was necessary.

One can see a threefold link between Van Gogh and Hofmannsthal. To begin with, there was the violence of the landscape of Provence, of the south of France, Van Gogh's best-loved place, which captured Hofmannsthal's imagination during his first journey through France in 1892. Secondly, when the Viennese poet stayed in Paris in 1900, he became acquainted with Mallarmé, Manet and Rodin, and also with Gauguin, who had been Van Gogh's friend. Hofmannsthal saw some of Van Gogh's pictures. Finally, and most important of all, there is a text by Hofmannsthal, *Die Briefe des Zurückgekehrten* (*The Letters of a Man Who Returned*; published in 1907, but dated 1901). Hofmannsthal's traveller, having returned to Germany and to Austria after an absence of several years, has been forcefully struck by the evidence of the European crisis. The gestures of ordinary Germans and Austrians remind him of automata, while he senses their inner emptiness. He too is afflicted by a sort of inner sickness, which leads him to perceive objects, trees, houses as if everything were 'filled with inner uncer-

tainty, malicious unreality', 'a breath not of death but of Not-life, indescribable'. When this condition has all but overwhelmed the traveller,
so that he can no longer contemplate even walking slowly up and
down the avenues or sitting in a café and reading the newspaper, he
stops in front of a gallery:

> My dear friend, there's no such thing as chance; I was meant to see
> these pictures, was meant to see them at this hour, in this agitated
> condition, in this sequence. There were in all about sixty paintings,
> middle-sized and small, a few portraits, otherwise mostly land-
> scapes; in only very few was the human figure important; on most
> of them it was the trees, meadows, ravines, rocks, ploughed fields,
> roofs, garden plots. As to how they were painted I cannot offer any
> information ... Nevertheless, I remember ... frequently having seen
> [in Paris] in studios and in exhibitions things which bore a certain
> resemblance to these – very bright, almost like posters, in any case
> quite different from paintings in the galleries. At first sight these
> here seemed to me loud and restless, quite crude, quite strange; in
> order to see the first of them as pictures at all, as a unity, I had to
> prepare myself – but then, then I saw, then I saw them all thus, each
> single one, and all together, and Nature in them, and the strength
> of the human soul in them which here had transformed Nature, and
> tree and bush and field and slope which were painted here, and also
> that other strength, that which was behind the paint, that essence,
> that indescribable sense of fate – all this I saw, so that I lost the sen-
> sation of myself to these pictures, and got it back powerfully, and
> lost it again![11]

As revealed by a postscript at the end of Hofmannsthal's text, those
extraordinary paintings were Van Gogh's. Hofmannsthal had thus
spoken of Van Gogh, and had grasped the sense in which he was a
painter of modern life, and that in a highly Baudelairean fashion, in
accordance with the formula that 'the best account of a picture may
well be a sonnet or an elegy'.[12] These pages by Hofmannsthal, to my
knowledge the best criticism of Van Gogh before Antonin Artaud's *Van
Gogh, ou le suicidé de la société*, form a narrative, a prose elegy, which
insists upon the value of expressive colour. This prose elegy shows an
understanding of painting very similar to Baudelaire's vision of
Delacroix's use of colour as expressive of feelings and thoughts.

Hofmannsthal gives a description of the paintings not at the beginning
but at the end of his letter, as if Van Gogh's colours were the solution, the

point of arrival that would serve to assuage the anxiety, the sense of a loss of reality experienced by his traveller. The traveller in effect recovers through the pictures the reality he lacked: the violence of the art enables a dumb reality to speak; it is a substitute for the unreality of the real and, finally, it overcomes the sense of loss. Thus, the traveller, after looking at the pictures, goes on to a business appointment, where he manages to obtain for his firm 'more than the board of directors, in their wildest hopes, had expected from me, and I procured it as in a dream one picks flowers from a bare wall.'[13]

Hofmannsthal's traveller recovers precisely what the colours had been for the painter himself, who, once the most tormented pictures were finished, wrote to his brother Theo as follows: 'these canvasses will tell you what I cannot say in words, what I see as healthy and invigorating in the countryside.' The sense of reality regained by the traveller – his vision of the pictures, his success in business – like the health of the countryside invoked by Van Gogh, serves to scotch the romantic myth of the mad, tormented painter. By the same token, it reveals his artistic mastery, which is not so different from Hofmannsthal's mastery of words, and the power of art, which not only restores meaning to objects but also helps toward an understanding of reality itself – be it a painting, a poem or a political or financial deal. All avant-gardes trusted in this power of art.

If there is a link between Van Gogh, a towering but solitary figure, and the notion of the avant-garde, it is one of solitude, exile and foresight. It is sometimes said that Cézanne paved the way for cubism, and Van Gogh for expressionism. Van Gogh, who could not sell his canvases when he was alive, forms part of the artistic avant-garde after the event, given a historical perspective whereby the future is encompassed by the past. It is as if Van Gogh foresaw the painting that was to come.

As for Hofmannsthal, a Viennese aristocrat best known as the librettist of Richard Strauss and as a supporter of the idea of conservative revolution in his patriotic essays of the 1920s, it seems a little wayward to associate him with the avant-garde. Hofmannsthal had belonged to the literary group *Jung-Wien*, around Hermann Bahr (*Die Jungen* were originally, that is, towards the end of the 1870s, the new left of the Constitutional Party). The young practitioners of the decorative arts, Gustav Klimt at their head, founded the Secession, which was an avant-garde for a few years at least, and Hofmannsthal contributed for a time to the Secessionist review, *Ver Sacrum*.

Hofmannsthal may be said to embody the intrinsic ambiguity of the Secession, which combined old and new, progressive taste and conservative taste, and which would ultimately fall apart, thus facilitating the rise of the other Viennese avant-garde, which was tougher and rejected any idealized notion of the work of art and its unique character. By contrast, then, with Oskar Kokoschka, Karl Kraus and Adolph Loos, the great negative spirits of the epoch, Hofmannsthal, together with Klimt, represented the backward-looking dream of the Secession, the lovely illusion that art would not only not lose its aura of the ideal but would further intensify it, covering it with a golden veneer of nostalgia – witness the golden colours of some of Klimt's best-known paintings.

The poster for the first exhibition, in 1897, of the Secession shows an asymmetrical frame around a blank space given shape by drawings in linear perspective of Athena and of Theseus battling with the Minotaur. One can regard this blank space in the centre of the composition as at once an interrogation, a suspension and a possibility. This void is a suspension of representation and of judgement; it is therefore expectation or silence, and is thus akin to a mirror that reflects no image, like the empty mirror that *Nuda Veritas* holds in her hand in the 1898 poster by Klimt. Therefore, *Ver Sacrum* begins its Spring in this fashion, with a void, which is the opposite of a manifesto.

This blank space in the poster questions modernity itself, and shows it waiting for answers; in this regard it reflects very accurately the actual programme of the Secession, as formulated by the architect Otto Wagner, who spoke of the need to show modern man his true face. Another version of the same project was inscribed on the door of the house of the Secession – the building, or rather the temple, of Josef Olbrich – in the words, *Der Zeit ihre Kunst. Der Kunst ihre Freiheit* ('An art fit for the times, and liberty for art'). In the poster representing Theseus, the new possibilities are indicated through the use of linear perspective, and through geometrical retrenchments that would prove to be more symbolic and more expressive than academic painting, whether realist or impressionist. Indeed, if one disregards the representational aspect and concentrates on the lines and the large blank square of Klimt's drawing, one can almost see it as anticipating Mondrian's use of space. This poster seems to mark the end of Klimt's first period, as painter and decorator of the Ringstrasse, a period framed, so to speak, by academic realism and by a sort of historical impressionism. Carl Schorske[14] commented that that which is repressed invariably returns, and it is true that Klimt's paintings would in his last period be characterized by the most extreme pleasures of the eye, by the most vibrant portrayal of light and by a gilded geometricism transfiguring reality. Such works call to mind the *joie de vivre* of *Der*

Rosenkavalier, the melancholic waltz and languorous vertigo of Hofmannsthal, several of whose comedies are set in Venice, the quintessential impressionist city.

I shall not concern myself here with the refined use of colour and the diffused sensuality of Klimt's maturity, since these are attributes belonging to another moment in history. I want to concentrate upon the poster of the Secession, taking into account a short period to be treated here not in a historiographic, Hegelian fashion, but photographically, in the manner of the photograph that, as Walter Benjamin put it, captures the *hic et nunc* of the thing, or, as Roland Barthes expressed it, the 'that has been', the contingency of the event.

The event in this case is the 1897 poster and the hole, void, or silence at its centre, which can be compared, in visual terms, to another event, which is not figurative but literary, namely, a short text by Hofmannsthal of very nearly the same date. In *Lord Chandos's Letter* (1901–2), the English lord explains to his friend Francis Bacon that he has found it increasingly impossible to write, to pursue literary projects conceived at an earlier date, to believe in words, in language, or in the perfection of adjectives. The earlier projects rested upon harmonious correspondences between nature, science and the self. Now, for no definable reason, with no external fact having precipitated a crisis, all of that was no longer possible. Thus, Lord Chandos could no longer bring himself to utter abstract words, to carry on a normal conversation, or use such words as 'nature', 'soul' and 'body'. It was the end of an era, and the crisis of the old order, and here the England of 1603, the year of Queen Elizabeth's death and of the solar eclipse, becomes an allegory for Hapsburg Austria at the beginning of the twentieth century.

Lord Chandos's Letter marks the moment at which Hofmannsthal's impressionist period abruptly ended, for after that he stopped using the signature 'Loris'. This name had been used as a pseudonym of an unabashed aesthete, who had been enamoured of forms colours and sensations, and who had known the pleasure, both fresh and nostalgic, to be derived from the ephemeral, from the magic of words, from the dance of words, and from the fascination and absorption of the external world. Loris could accumulate impressions and his language could express all of them in a rich and sensual tongue, while Chandos suffered such a devastating spiritual collapse that no existing language could help him. Words, which had Loris so much in thrall, floated around Chandos, isolated and threatening, empty of meaning and heavy as objects – and no longer sounding like a most lovely and continuous stream of music. Lord Chandos could no longer write in any language, whether it were German, Latin, English, French or Italian. Silence, the interruption of any and every production of language, was what Chandos now held to. He did what Karl Kraus, the critic at odds with the *Jung-Wien*, would suggest in 1914: 'Let whoever has something to say, step forward and shut up.'

But one can only fully understand *Lord Chandos's Letter* if one places it alongside the aforementioned letter, which continues and completes it, namely that of *The Letters of a Man Who Returned*, in which Hofmannsthal speaks of Van Gogh. Like Lord Chandos, the traveller is prey to a spiritual vertigo which disturbs his vision of objects, and which makes them appear to him to be as isolated, unreal and threatening as words do to Chandos, who writes to his friend Francis Bacon:

> How shall I try to describe to you these strange spiritual torments, this rebounding of the fruit-branches above my outstretched hands, this recession of the murmuring stream from my thirsting lips?...
>
> My case, in short, is this: I have lost completely the ability to think or to speak anything coherently ...
>
> Single words floated round me; they congealed into eyes which stared at me and into which I was forced to stare back – whirlpools which gave me vertigo and reeling incessantly, led into the void.[15]

The traveller confesses a very similar feeling:

> I felt myself growing ill from within, but it wasn't my body; I know my body too well. It was the crisis of an inner indisposition ... Now and again in the mornings it happened, in these German hotel rooms, that the jug and the wash-basin – or a corner of the room with the table and clothes-rack – appeared to me so non-real, despite their indescribable banality so utterly non-real, ghostly as it were, and at the same time ephemeral, waiting, so to speak temporarily, to take the place of the real jug, the real wash-basin filled with water ... From it there emanated a slight unpleasant vertigo, but not a physical one ... it was like a momentary floating above the abyss, the eternal void.[16]

Klimt's poster and *Lord Chandos's Letter* reveal the shortcomings of impressionism when faced with the violence of the contemporary world, and the limitations of the art used in either case. In the poster, given the fact that it is a sheet of paper and that it belongs to the sphere of the graphic arts, we mourn the painting. The poster lies somewhere between the artisanal product – of the sort to be found in the Viennese workshops, the *Wiener Werkstätte*, established in 1903 by artists from the Secession – and the work of art, which nevertheless could be readily reproduced. The poster, in which Theseus features, has the radical qualities of an anti-picture; it contains almost as many written as drawn signs; it attains the greatest possible economy of representation, even going so far as to give figurative expression to the void – thus lending itself to an infinite number of different interpretations – even opting for a complete rejection of colour, of the positive richness of impressionist colour. Just as, accord-ing to Hofmannsthal, speech was indecorous, it could have been suggested by Klimt that painting was indecent.

Thus, Lord Chandos's text, a letter in narrative form, reproduces the characteristics of the poster, for in the short narrative letter we mourn the poem, or indeed any fully achieved literary form, be it novel, tale, critical essay, play, prose poem or aphorism. The letter is cast in the style of a journalistic feuilleton, which was excoriated by Kraus, and which was the most popular literary genre of the period, just as the poster was the most prominent form in the visual arts. Hofmannsthal's story uses the fewest possible words to say what it has to say, seeming almost to lapse into silence at times. He likewise espoused the principle of economy when writing for the stage, and this well before he had begun to collaborate with Strauss. In his 1903 essay, 'Die Bühne als Traumbild' ('The Stage as Dream-image'), ornamentation seems akin to a crime, much as it does in the famous essay by the architect Adolf Loos, *Ornament und Verbrechen* (*Ornament and Crime*), which is perhaps the loveliest and most poetic formulation of an essentialist approach to the question of ornamentation. Where the task is to produce a design for the stage, Hofmannsthal suggests sacrificing all ornament and stylistic refinement:

[The stage designer's] eye should be creative in much the same fashion as is the eye of the dreamer who perceives nothing that is without meaning ... Dreams are indescribably economical. Who can overlook the tremendous violence they contain, combined with an astonishing barrenness and nakedness?[17]

To pass from the liveliness of impressionism to stubborn silence, from trust in sensations to the sickness that sunders the ties between the self and the world, between thought and language, is equivalent to lifting the veil from truth, to seeing it naked: this indeed is the index of the modern. I am not concerned here with what Klimt and Hofmannsthal would subsequently do, but rather with these particular intellectual events, Hofmannsthal's two letters and Klimt's two posters for the Secession, and I like to would focus upon them as if they were two photographs. I am not concerned here with what Benjamin quite rightly takes objection to, but with the very moment at which he points out to Adorno the significance of *Lord Chandos's Letter*:

> Julian [in Hofmannsthal's *Die Turm* (*The Tower*)] betrays the Prince: Hofmansthal has turned aside from the task he had identified in *Lord Chandos's Letter*. His falling silent was a kind of punishment. The language that was withdrawn from Hofmannsthal could be the very same one that was at that same period given to Kafka. For Kafka took upon himself the task that Hofmannsthal had embraced morally and therefore politically.[18]

Warheit ist Feuer und Warheit reden heisst leuchten und brennen ('Truth is fire and telling the truth means shining and burning') reads the *Nuda Veritas* poster by Klimt. In referring to the fire of truth, the text might be taken to mean that silence had to be made to speak its terrifying language, so that, by means of fire, another language and another use of colour, that of violence, might be found.

Van Gogh, who is known to have been deeply influenced by the impressionists, sensed the shortcomings of impressionism, and therefore the need to discover another colourism, that of *expressing* through colour:

> And I should not be surprised if the impressionists soon find fault with my way of working, for it has been fertilized by the ideas of Delacroix rather than by theirs. Because, instead of trying to reproduce exactly what I have before my eyes [realist trompe-l'oeil, as he puts it in another passage], I use colour more arbitrarily so as to express myself more forcibly.[19]

Sight becomes an organ aiming to distort the real, doing violence to objects and to perspective, in order to express inner feelings, as in the famous poem 'Le Cygne', where Baudelaire defines the sky as being '*cruellement bleu*' ('cruelly blue'), as, too, in Van Gogh's picture of the cornfield with the black crows, in which the blue is 'terrible' – as terrible as Delacroix's blue is for Van Gogh:

> When Paul Mantz saw at the exhibition the violent and inspired sketch by Delacroix that we saw at the Champs Elysées – *The Bark of*

Christ – he turned away from it, exclaiming in his article: 'I did not know that one could be so terrible with a little blue and green.'

Elsewhere Van Gogh speaks of an 'absolutely harrowing malachite'.[20] He dreams of a colour that would express the truth of being, the fire of truth:

> I want to paint men and women with that something of the eternal which the halo used to symbolize, and which we seek to confer by the actual radiance and vibration of our colourings. Portraiture so understood...would be more in harmony with what Eug. Delacroix attempted and brought off in his *Tasso in Prison*, and many other pictures, representing a *real* man. Ah! Portraiture, portraiture with thought, the soul of the model in it, that is what I think must come.[21]

Hofmannsthal's traveller understood that Van Gogh's blue, green and yellow, his landscapes and his portraits were truly terrifying. He could sense all this because he too had inside himself the brutality of the real or, indeed, the unreality of the real, all those objects that appeared to him so 'un-real despite their indescribable banality, so utterly not real' as if they were ghosts. What is awaited is expression, or rather expressionism capable of giving to colours the power of signifying 'more forcibly', as suggested by Van Gogh. Hofmannsthal, at the moment of crisis, when, through Chandos and the traveller, he contemplated silence and the possibility of the loss of meaning, when he brushed against the language of Kafka, understood the strength of expressionism which, like the interiorization of the shocks of metropolitan life, is both the presence of anxiety and the actual mastery of it:

> It was in a storm that these trees were born under my eyes, were born for my sake, their roots stretching into the earth, their branches stretching against the clouds; in a storm these earth rifts, these valleys between hills, surrendered themselves; even in the bulk of the rock blocks was frozen storm. And now I could from picture to picture, feel a Something, could feel the mingling, the merging of formation, how the innermost life broke forth into colour and how the colours lived one for the sake of the others, and how one, mysteriously powerful, carried all the others; and in all this could sense a heart, the soul of the man who had created it, who with this vision did himself answer the spasm of his own most

dreadful doubt. I could feel, could know, could fathom, could enjoy abyss and summit, without and within, one and all in a ten-thousandth part of the time I take to write these words – and it was as though two men, were master over my life, master over my strength, my intellect, felt the time pass, knew there were now only twenty minutes left, now ten, now five, and stood outside, hailed a carriage, and drove away.[22]

In like fashion, Van Gogh knew what was healthy and invigorating about the countryside.

Lord Chandos's Letter and the traveller's letters exemplify two different expressionist modes. The first mode is stasis, like the reified words and the objects seen by the traveller, which are somehow detached from the space around them, condensed and isolated, and which seem to be fragments of an impossible continuity, cut away from their function, things perpetuated in their actual nature as things, like the bare words that so obsessed Lord Chandos. The literary equivalent would be the spectral classicism of Trakl, or the spare, geometrical and petrified language of Kafka. The second mode is dynamic and spasmodic, as is exemplified by number of Van Gogh's canvases or Munch's *The Scream*. It is in this mode that the dying rats appear; they are not seen by Lord Chandos with his actual eyes, with the realist or impressionist optic nerves responding to the external world in front of them, but with the mental eye, since Lord Chandos imagines the scene. All of a sudden, as he moves forward on his horse and sees nothing but a freshly ploughed field and a quail, Lord Chandos is assailed by the vision of dying rats in a cellar in which he had ordered poison to be put down:

> As I was trotting along over the fresh-ploughed land ... there suddenly loomed up before me the vision of that cellar, resounding with the death-struggle of a mob of rats. I felt everything within me: the cool, musty air of the cellar filled with the sweet and pungent reek of poison, and the yelling of the death-cries breaking against the mouldering walls; the vain convulsions of those convoluted bodies as they tear about in confusion and despair; their frenzied search for escape, and the grimace of icy rage when a couple collided with one another at a blocked-up crevice.[23]

As he narrates this scene, Lord Chandos compares it to scenes in battles described by Livy; for example, in the hours preceding the

destruction of Alba Longa. This scene aroused a feeling which is close
to the pietas of the Ancients, although it is not exactly pity:

> Forgive this description, but do not think that it was pity I felt. For
> if you did, my example would have been poorly chosen. It was far
> more and far less than pity: an immense sympathy, a flowing over
> into these creatures, or a feeling that an aura of life and death, of
> dream and wakefulness, had flowed for a moment into them – but
> whence?[24]

Perhaps, the best figurative equivalent for the state described by
Hofmannsthal would be Kokoschka's *Pity*, for there too we sense an
immense sympathy, an aura of life and death. The painting does not
represent the external world, it expresses its effect on the mind; as if
things and words were bare in front of astonished eyes, of mouths
incapable of any utterance.

Once impressionism, and with it the simple reproduction of the
outside world, has been superseded, both reality and sight became
quite alien one to the other. Where an earlier language had given
promise of correspondences, in the balance between joy and melancholy, the new language was expected to express that gap between
reality and vision, words and meanings. The world is internalized,
anxiety colours any feeling, expression is taken to its furthest limits.
The Viennese had been influenced by Mach's theories and, in particular, the idea that the subject is a knot of feeling (*Einfühlung*). If
Hofmannsthal's traveller is so moved by Van Gogh's paintings, it is
because he already feels that intensity within himself. 'But what
are colours if the innermost life of objects doesn't break through
them!':[25] the traveller writes, and Van Gogh wrote in a similar vein to
Theo: 'It is colour not locally true from the point of view of the
trompe-l'oeil realist, but colour to suggest some emotion of an ardent
temperament.'

In 1900, modernity could only be grasped with an intellectual intensity that combines thought and feeling. It could only be expressed
without sentimentalism, by the raw endeavour of expressionism,
understood not only as historical movement but also as the tension
and the strong need to express emotions. In one of his letters Van
Gogh told Theo that he sought to 'express not something sentiment-
ally melancholic, but a deep sorrow', and Hofmannsthal's traveller
asked: 'why colours could ... not be sisters of sorrow, since both
colours and sorrows draw us into eternity.' Lord Chandos formulates

the basic principle of Viennese philosophy, and of modernity (and of what would later in the century be the novel of the modern man, Robert Musil's *Der Mann ohne Eigenschaften*), namely, the chiasma of thought and feeling: 'we could enter into a new and hopeful relationship with the whole of existence universe, if only we begin to think with the heart.'[26]

And to feel with the brain, one should perhaps add, as Ulrich, in Musil's novel, believes, when he writes the treatise on feeling, discovered by his sister Agathe. There is an interpenetration of reason and emotions, according to a strongly held principle of Austrian philosophy, reacting against the Kantian division between the soul and the intellect. This might well be what was meant by Klimt's poster, in which Athena, or intelligence, and the Minotaur, or instinct, meet. The modern man would have to know the tragic, violent aspect of modern existence, but would also need to win his or her inner battles, and to master life with a new language that would be equal to the new reality. The modern man would finally have to search out a language with the power to express the nuances of feelings. While looking at a beetle in the murky water of a watering-can, Lord Chandos says: 'what was that made me want to break into words which, I know, that, were I to find them, would force to their knees those cherubim in whom I do not believe?'[27] But Chandos believes in new, unsettling objects. Hence the description of the scene that struck Benjamin, and that shows, as Baudelaire wished, that modernity is worthy of being ancient. In the scene in question, which is set in a full meeting of the Senate, Domitius reproaches Crassus, the orator, for having wept at the death of his fish and Crassus answers that he has done what Domitius has not done over the death of his wives. The scene is imprinted in Lord Chandos's mind:

> I know not how oft Crassus with his lamprey enters my mind as a mirrored image of my Self, reflected across the abyss of centuries. But not on account of the answer he gave Domitius. The answer brought the laughs on his side, and the whole affair turned into a jest. I, however, am deeply affected by the affair, which would have remained the same even had Domitius shed bitter tears of sorrow over his wives. For there would still have been Crassus, shedding tears over his lamprey.[28]

Seeing and saying break one against the other. Chandos is faced with the shortcomings of literature, the impossibility of speaking and writing in any language, silence; but Chandos discovers Crassus's feelings for his fish, and the traveller the paintings of Van Gogh:

> How can I make it even half clear to you the way this language talked into my soul, the way it threw toward me the gigantic justification of the strangest indissoluble condition of my inner self, the way it made me understand at once what, in my intolerable stupor, I could hardly bear to feel, and which, nevertheless (so much did I feel it!) I could no longer tear out of myself! And here an unknown soul of incomprehensible power was giving me the answer, by revealing to me a whole world![29]

In marked contrast to the coquettish imitation of one art by the other, or to the famous rivalries of pen and pencil (such as that of the Goncourt brothers), each art shows for the artist the void in its actual essence. Not only does each art wish to be what it is not, one therefore aspiring to be colour and the other words, or music, but also and above all the arts join forces so as not to be blinded by modern reality, so as to allow the language of silence to speak, showing therefore modern man his true face. Such a complicity between the different arts in no way resembles Wagner's notion of the total art-work, that ideal of a cohesive community united in a coherent composition of arts. Art would correspond, rather, to metropolitan reality, to what Hofmannsthal calls, in the wake of Poe and Baudelaire, 'the vast desert of our cities that teem with humanity'.[30] The identification of the modern with the big city is what gave rise to a poetics equal to the nervous life of the great city. Metropolitan life asks of literature that it transcend speech and the harmony of sounds, the pleasure of the eyes and the ears, that it learns to see and to express more deeply. The modern metropolitan artist should know how to open his or her eyes and eschew pity or, at least, classical pity, in favour of the violent pity expressed by Kokoschka, or by Lord Chandos's when thinking about the dying rats. Words in modern literature are now themselves meant to be eyes: 'Individual words swam around me: they melted into eyes, which stared at me, and which I had to stare back at: they are like whirlpools, it gives me vertigo to look up at them, they turn without cease, and transport you into nothingness.'[31]

The emptiness to which Lord Chandos refers, and these words that are eyes, are not dissimilar to the empty gaze of the old man in Poe's famous metropolitan tale 'The Man of the Crowd' (which had been translated by Baudelaire and gave its title to a chapter in Baudelaire's

The Painter of Modern Life). Seeing becomes an uncontrollable obsession. The silence and emptiness of Lord Chandos, and of the traveller upon his return, culminate in a powerful image in the 1907 essay by Hofmannsthal, 'Der Dichter und diese Zeit' ('The Poet and the Present Time'). The poet is described as one whose eyes have no eyelids: 'He [the poet] is there and changes place noiselessly, he is but eyes and ears ... On no being, no thing, no ghost and no spectre engendered by the human mind should he close his eyes. It is as if his eyes had no eyelids.'[32]

The same note is struck by Trakl when he writes in the last stanza of 'Helian': 'O ihr zerbrochenen Augen in schwarzen Mündern' ('O you broken eyes in black mouths'). For Hofmannsthal, the poet is not simply one who writes verses, he is anyone, or no one, an impersonal being that, like a seismograph, records every movement, every vibration of his epoch, a being without eyelids, who never stops seeing, who cannot stop seeing, just as 'The Man of the Crowd' could not stop walking through the city, just as Van Gogh could not stop painting. The poet's eye 'was touched by the living fire', suggests Hofmannsthal. Might it not be the fire of the *Nuda Veritas* of the modern man, a fire that is perhaps the night and enables the expression of emotion. 'It often seems to me,' wrote Van Gogh to Theo on 8 September 1888, 'that the night is much more alive and more richly coloured than the day.'

3
Baudelaire, Haussmann, Fustel de Coulanges: The Modern Metropolis and the Ancient City

> – Tell me, enigmatical man, whom do you love best, your father, your mother, your sister, or your brother?
> – I have neither father, nor mother, nor sister, nor brother.
> – Your friends?
> – Now you use a word whose meaning I have never known.
> – Your country?
> – I do not know in what latitude it lies ...
>
> Baudelaire, *Le Spleen de Paris*

One of the first metropolitan heroes is homeless: the protagonist of Poe's 'The Man of the Crowd' (1840) – terrible, mysterious, decrepit – is an old man who wanders day and night in London. The narrator tries to follow him, day after day, night after night: impossible to see him resting anywhere.[1] 'The big city's genius' is continuously rushing, running, retracing his steps 'with a mad energy'. To the narrator's surprise, there is no rationale in the old man's circuits. Disquieting allegory of the city, the man of the crowd inhabits the streets, condemned to be eternally outside, without a home, without a name. If he gets inside, it is in a public place, in 'one of the huge suburban temples of Intemperance', in 'the most noisome quarter of London, where everything wore the worst impress of the most deplorable poverty, and of the most desperate crime',[2] next to anonymous, wretched people, drinking gin, mixing misery and despair.

Like Poe, Baudelaire characterized the big city as the place of the homeless. 'Les Sept Vieillards' (1859) tells of an hallucination similar to the one of Poe's narrator. The voice speaking in the poem recounts a terrifying encounter in the 'Swarming city, filled with dreams'. The poet-narrator sees an old man multiplying until he finally gets home, sick and exhausted, 'wounded by mystery and absurdity'. 'Les Petites Vieilles' (1859), 'dismembered monsters who once were women', hang about the streets dragging themselves along, exposed to urban traffic, 'like wounded animals'.[3]

For the great writers of modernity, those whom Walter Benjamin chose as the most poignant examples of a new nineteenth-century consciousness and perception, to be homeless is much more a mental than a physical condition. The awareness of this condition is what distinguishes two modes of realism in literature and art: I would call one mode simple, external realism, and the other complex, interiorized realism.

The simple realist writer, the only one whom Georg Lukács would acknowledge, stresses social status, economic condition, visible structures. Balzac's *Illusions perdues* starts with the spectacular change in the mode of production of an old typography, Zola's *Au bonheur des dames* with a swarm of people coming out of the Saint-Lazare train station early in the morning. The state of mind of the characters is directly determined by their material condition. The more dearly, precisely, richly the writer describes people, objects, places, the more successfully he represents his world and his time. Description acts didactically, offering a message that can be either a moral warning or a political explanation. The other type of realism identifies the effects of the new nineteenth-century reality upon the mind. The new material reality of the century becomes a total psychological condition that affects perception and sensibility. Description is almost irrelevant to this type of realism, characterized by an enigmatic allegorical power. In 'Spleen LXXVIII', using one of his favourite rainy urban landscapes associated with anguish and despair, Baudelaire perverts the old Christian allegory of Hope into a violent Piranesi-like sketch:

> When earth is changed into a damp prison cell.
> Hope, like a bat, goes beating at the wall,
> Knocking its head against the rotten ceilings ...[4]

What was once a virtue now suffocates all feelings of expectation into an overwhelming prison formed by the rain and the dark sky. Nature is transformed into the unnatural space of the prison according to the same negative comparison that made Hope similar to a bat. The final headache suggested in the last two lines takes on a universal dimension of pain: 'Atrocious, tyrannical Anguish, /Plants its black flag onto my bent head.' The image remains suspended between literal and metaphorical meaning.

Is the poet's headache – his very physical condition of pain – transfigured into a metaphor of anguish, in the same way that Borges declares 'Funes, or Memory' (*Fictions*) a metaphor of insomnia, or Poe's 'Tell-Tale Heart' can be read as the story of a heart attack? Or is it atrocious, tyrannical Anguish that conquers the body and becomes a headache? This suspension between literal and metaphorical meanings shapes Baudelaire's allegory. This allegory is not the baroque one that embodies the Catholic vision of the world, making clear that under a visible meaning there is another meaning spectacularly staged.[5] Because of this peculiar intertwining of abstract and concrete, observation and hallucination, external and internal, we can speak of another type of realism, actually more realistic than the most obvious realism.

Brecht fought for the breadth and variety of realist writing. Around 1938, he accused of formalism what he called 'the theory of realism', because it was founded on very few 'bourgeois novels of the last century.' Why only novels? What about realism in poetry or in drama?[6] While not rejecting Balzac and Tolstoy, he believed that Lukács was wrong in his determination to consider only the old masters of realism. One should understand, for example, that Dos Passos, who uses the technique of montage extensively, is a realist. This technique, used by Brecht himself, consists of constructing something like 'intersecting and antagonistic actions and reactions.'[7] Montage is far from the mode in which Balzac conceived his plots, around the centrality of the individual, according to an inexhaustible organic principle. Brecht said that Balzac 'writes gigantic genealogies', and 'families are organisms, individuals 'grow' within them.'[8] The technique of montage viewed by Brecht is very similar to Baudelaire's allegory, which cuts and concentrates antagonistic images in the most non-organic way. Even the famous correspondences are anti-organic. Benjamin seemed to think that the theory of correspondences contradicted what he called Baudelaire's 'renunciation of nature.'[9] But in 'Correspondances', Nature is perceived as a temple, as an enigmatic puzzle of words, as language, the symbolic activity *par excellence*:

> Nature is a temple where living pillars
> Sometimes utter confused words;
> Man reaches it through forests of symbols
> That watch him with a familiar gaze.[10]

'Forests of symbols' is an allegory that joins two antagonistic forces: the natural and the symbolic. But the symbolic is stronger the natural, since symbols look at man with 'a familiar gaze'. This image perverts the cliché of nature as a temple, and the balance between the terms of the correspondences: the third and fourth lines of the quatrain twist the allegory towards the world of culture, construction, and artifice. No wonder that the last lines betray nature, expressing what Benjamin called Baudelaire's 'renunciation of nature.' Even though perfumes are involved, those which produce the ecstasy of the spirit and the senses are not the natural and fresh one but the 'corrupted ones.' The first alexandrine is a false correspondence since it cannot be harmoniously divided into two hemistichs respecting the wholeness of a word, since *temple* is the term where the verse is divided into two parts: 'La Nature est un temple où de vivants piliers' (Nature is a temple where living pillars). Similarly a false symmetry links fresh and corrupted perfumes:

> There are perfumes as innocent as children's flesh,
> As sweet as oboes, as green as meadows,
> – And others that are corrupt, rich and triumphant,
>
> They have the vastness of infinite things,
> Such as amber, musk, benjamin and incense,
> Which sing the ecstasies of mind and senses.

Only corrupt perfumes offer transcendental powers, leading to the infinite. Moreover, they resemble opium and *paradis artificiels* more than sacred nature. At the same time poems with titles like 'Le Crépuscule du soir' or 'Le Crépuscule du matin' derive from urban reverie, as Baudelaire himself wrote to Desnoyers who asked him for some verses on Nature. He declared himself incapable of being moved by plants and vegetables. In the woods, he could only think of cathedrals. He could only be moved by urban landscapes, 'by our extraordinary cities', whose 'prodigious music' seemed to him 'the translation of human lamentations'.[11]

In his criticism of simplistic understanding, Brecht reads allegorical poems as powerful examples of realism, like Percy Bysshe Shelley's 'The Mask of Anarchy', a poem written in 1819 immediately after the Manchester riots.

> I met Murder on the way –
> He had a mask like Castlereagh –
> Very smooth he looked, yet grim;
> Seven blood-hounds followed him.[12]

Shelley's poem suggests a broader and deeper notion of realism. Brecht underlined the concreteness of Shelley's allegory: 'We follow anarchy's procession up to London, we see great symbolic images, but, at every line, we know that it was reality that spoke through such images.'[13] The effect of what can be called allegorical realism has an intensity that no detailed description can reach. A little text by Baudelaire of 1855, 'Puisque réalisme il y a', quotes in its title a few words of a letter written by Gustave Courbet to Champfleury while the painter was working on his *L'Atelier du peintre: Allégorie réelle*. In this text Baudelaire attacked Champfleury, the champion of realism: 'Since he studies in minute detail, he believes he is grasping an exterior *reality*. Therefore, he calls it *realism* – he wants to impose what he thinks is his method.'[14] Baudelaire was always aware of the multiple meanings that could be given to the term realism, which after belonging to the philosophical vocabulary, became, during the nineteenth century, an artistic term. In August 1857, at the trial of *Les Fleurs du Mal*, Baudelaire himself was condemned for 'a coarse realism that offended decency'.[15] He relentlessly scorned the 'vulgar people' for whom, as he wrote in his essay on Madame Bovary, the term meant 'a minute description of accessories'.[16] Baudelaire was convinced that true art was capable of renouncing details, as he often said while commenting Delacroix's paintings.[17]

Flaubert can describe beyond the usual sphere of description, not because his style is objective, as a simplistic criticism has pointed out, but because it implies the reification of literature itself. Simple description is founded on the objectification of language.[18] We identify literary modernity with this process because it challenges representation itself. The reification of literature or of language is the symptom of a disturbed relationship between language and reality; Baudelaire spoke of 'confused words' in 'Correspondances'. The old language that relies on description is inadequate to express the formidable new reality of the huge urban crowds, the most disconcerting result of industrialization. This reality affected perception and the awareness of the self. Literary, or artistic, modernity acknowledges the discrepancy between language and reality.[19] The excess of description or the lack of it are two similar modes of dealing with literature's deep realism, while didactic description is limited to realism as a form, as a school.

When art reaches what I call deep realism, or allegorical realism, it always escapes definitions in terms of schools. Is Manet an impressionist? A realist? How can we read the disquieting gaze of some of the men and women he painted? Why, looking at the *Gare Saint- Lazare*, do we notice the lost gaze of the woman in black more than her dress, or the gate, or the black smoke coming from the train at a distance? The simple level of description, in the realistic mode or in the impressionistic mode, is overwhelmed by the 'allegorical' power of those two watery eyes looking in an unidentified direction, following unpredictable dreams, or by the invisible gaze of the little girl whom we see from the back, facing the gate. I would say that realism as form, or as school, helps the reader or the spectator to understand the world, take a position, while allegorical realism pushes our understanding further, refines our thought, forcing it to go in different directions, suspending it between dream and a cruel, almost algebraic logic.

In the cruel realism of *Les Fleurs du Mal* a quick descriptive remark turns into a condensed imagery, where the most brutally physical details encompass the most subtle metaphysical reflections. The famous metropolitan poem, 'To a Passerby' ('A une passante'), begins with a sentence that sounds like a description but is immediately charged with allegory: 'The deafening street screamed round me.'[20] Benjamin commented on this poem suggesting that the crowd is for Baudelaire such an inner reality that we cannot expect him to depict it.[21] After a quick glimpse whereby the reader, like the poet speaking in the first person, catches the movements of a mysterious woman passing by, the sonnet elaborates an interrogation on time and space. But, with a tough sense of reality, of the big city's nervous life, the interrogation is contracted into the spasm of a few lines carrying the marks of solitary, metropolitan eroticism:

> And I, tense and irritable like a wild eccentric,
> Drank in her eyes, sombre stormy sky,
> The sweetness that enthrals, the pleasure that kills.

These lines, as Benjamin pointed out, 'show, in their internal configuration, the marks that love itself receives from the big city'.[22] Issued from the metropolitan experience, the ephemeral moment and eternity are juxtaposed in their interminable disproportion and nevertheless disquieting proximity, since they are both impossible to grasp. And the poems ends with this question: 'Fugitive beauty ... Shall I not see you till eternity?' The descriptive mode, of Balzac or Hugo, even if directed toward the representation of a growing city, needs length and accumulation of details. It lacks what Georg Simmel called 'the intensification of nervous stimulation, which results from the swift and uninterrupted change of outer and inner stimuli',[23] and which implies continuous intellectual activity. Description, in its slowness, misses metropolitan nervousness, that contracted brevity which characterizes the most inner experience of the metropolis. Therefore, paradoxically, the writers of nineteenth-century Paris, of modern life and modern crowds, use a mode of literary construction that corresponds more to country than to city life. The point for Baudelaire's allegorical realism is never to depict what he saw, but to render the big city's physical and psychological rhythm in language itself, in the sentences' spasms, in the lines' pauses, in the jamming together of images belonging to different logical orders. The verb *hurlait* (screamed) applied to the *rue assourdissante* (the deafening street) gives to the first line of 'A une passante' the violence of some expressionist paintings, dehumanizing the human voice, disfiguring architectural structures into devouring monsters. Baudelaire bathed in the crowd; as Benjamin wrote, he let 'the crowd act upon himself'. The poet of Paris could never write as Shelley did in what Benjamin calls a brutal and direct way:

> Hell is a city much like London –
> A populous and smoky city;
> There are all sorts of people undone, ...[24]

Baudelaire's livid urban illumination sparkles abruptly, burning all parallel terms: not a single adjective nor adverb lingers on the comparison between the metropolis and a monster, the comparison on which Balzac or Hugo would have dwelled for pages. The rhythm of the metropolis does not allow the pause of *as* or *like*. In the convulsive rhetoric of the huge capital, associations burst forth – violent, quick, condensed. When Baudelaire expressed his enthusiasm for the sketches of Constantin Guys he was fascinated by the rapidity of their execution: 'in trivial life, in the daily metamorphosis of external things, there is a rapidity of movement which calls for an equal speed of execution from the artist.'[25]

The emergence of the metropolis in the nineteenth century caused different reactions. They can all be read as variations of the sense of fear that, as Benjamin suggested in his essay on Baudelaire, pervaded any one who observed the crowds – the German provincial Engels, as well as Hugo, who introduced the masses into the titles of his novels (*Les Misérables, Les Travailleurs de la mer*). Obviously, in the century of the big city, people developed both urban and anti-urban feelings – more than feelings: whole attitudes and ideologies. We can even trace trends: for example, since the first decades of the nineteenth century, the English literary tradition is strongly anti-urban. The myth of nature in the Romantic poets carries the imprint of the rejection of the city, of industrialization and modern life. Mobs and machines are the horror of modern life. The opposition between the city and the country constitutes an intellectual theme displaying the most stubbornly anti-modern attitudes and the most blunt progressivist hopes. The opposition between city and country becomes the struggle between past and present. If John Stuart Mill embraced the utilitarian philosophy of the present, Thomas Carlyle identified the crisis of his own time in what he called the worship of machinery. Mechanization, according to him, had not only diffused itself into 'the external and physical', but also into 'the internal and spiritual'. In the Mechanical Age, 'nothing follows its spontaneous course, nothing is left to be accomplished by old natural methods'.[26]

For the detractors of the city, country life and closeness to nature bring the sole possibility of salvation for a human race corrupted by modern life. The hatred of the city is strong in the American Transcendentalists. Countless passages by Emerson could be cited to show how the ideology of nature is founded on the rejection of the new metropolitan reality. The best critic of the idealist position is Melville: the novel *Pierre, or The Ambiguities* powerfully stages the opposition between the country and the metropolis. Melville is close to the thought of Baudelaire, in that they both recognize in their own ways that the only truth is the metropolis, its rhythm, its monstrosity. It is useless to be actively nostalgic for an idyllic past, or an idyllic nature. The closest brother to Poe's man of the crowd, or to the many Baudelairean homeless, is Melville's anti-hero of the short story *Bartleby*, the bodiless clerk of Manhattan who, dried up by his repetitive life, knows nothing but his office. We can see in Bartleby a sort of Weberian intuition, whereby Melville identified the city with bureaucracy and administration.[27]

Negative thought, devotion to nature, worship of the past, optimism, pessimism, and a cruel lack of both – all these elements show that the new reality of the nineteenth century never stops inspiring illusions and disillusion. This does not mean that a single author or artist fully embraces just one attitude. Everything is nuanced and complicated. It would be too reductive to see Balzac simply and solely as the writer of modernity because he depicted the metropolis. Again, if Balzac wrote powerful descriptions of Paris, his descriptive mode is nevertheless backward, a literary means of production, closer to the rhythm of the country than to that of the big city.

The dream of total rationalization

Amongst the great variety of attitudes toward the big city stands the triumphal vision of the Baron Haussmann, who made Paris the capital of the nineteenth century, as Benjamin called it in the title of his famous essay. Most of the images of Paris that belong to our repertory of cultural stereotypes – from impressionist painting to the main boulevards, to café life – derive from Haussmann's transformation of Paris. The intention of Napoleon III's protégé, was clear: a total rationalization, cleaning and opening the city, was necessary for the circulation of the thousands of people pouring into Paris by rail every day, as well as to establish a well-organized civic centre in the Ile de la Cité. Haussmann was appointed as the Prefect of Paris in June 1853. Thanks to the Emperor who had endowed him with absolute power of decision, he defeated the strong opposition of the old administration, who were afraid of his grandiose and astronomically expensive projects. He looked down upon the people at the Hôtel de Ville as well-intentioned administrators, incapable of a broad, up-to-date economic vision. The Baron wrote in his *Mémoires* that they were still thinking in terms of the traditional cash economy. They thought they could run the city as a 'good father runs his family business, by following the rules of tight economy, prudent reserve and provident hoarding, that a rich man observes in his private life.'[28]

The Baron, on the contrary, thought that a new economical vision should inform the decisions of the Hôtel de Ville, and that he was the inventor of the economic logic of 'productive expenditures'. Deficit financing, far from being perceived as a danger, represented for him a productive force: taxes had to be increased and the tax revenue of the city would pay the long-term debts contracted for the transformation, or embellishment, as the Baron liked to say, of Paris. The idea of deficit financing was actually not his invention, but a rather common theory among the Saint-Simonians who surrounded the Emperor. Their economist, Michel Chevalier, sat at Napoleon's Conseil d'Etat as soon as it was established in 1851. Haussmann wanted to realize the imperial dream of the Emperor, his state capitalism, and succeeded in bringing together the political conservatism and the economic progressivism of the Second Empire:

> Now, a Big City, especially a Capital, has the duty of keeping up with the role it plays within the country; and when this country is France, when centralization, which is the principle of its strength,

made its own Capital at the same time the head and the heart of the social body, the Capital itself would miss its glorious function, if, in spite of everything, it systematically lingered in the mechanism of an outdated routine.[29]

Haussmann's urban planning included the cutting of new streets through old quarters, with two main axes – one east-west and the other north-south. He liked to recall in his *Mémoires* how Paris was gloomy with narrow streets, and unhealthy because of the lack of a sewer system. He wanted to give the Parisians water, air, shade, and wide streets. The utopia of Haussmann's state capitalism is a big city in which everything can be controlled. This rationalized metropolis pushes the panoptical utopia one step further. Bentham's prison implied perfect visibility and control over a small number of people. The Capital of France would be festive, a panopticon turned into a street festival, a clear-cut metropolis capable of avoiding urban disorder as well as social and political unrest. The astronomical expenditures of the Paris prefect, the rationality of his figures and daring planning, embody the ethos of the Second Empire: Bonaparte's populism and fear of revolutions. The large boulevards would fulfil a doubly healthy function: they 'will permit the circulation not only of air and light but also of troops. Thus by an ingenious combination, the lot of the people will be improved, and they will be rendered less disposed to revolts.'[30]

In his 1938 essay 'Second Empire Paris in Baudelaire', Benjamin connects the phenomenon of *flânerie* to Haussmann's changes of Paris. It was impossible to wander around the city without entering the large boulevards and passages, the arcades filled with shops and people, without seeing all the invention and display of industrial luxury. In a straightforward Marxist way, Benjamin links a cultural phenomenon to the new material condition of life. One cannot understand Baudelaire's lyric, the Baudelairean figure of the *flâneur*, the poet's double, without understanding the Haussmannization of Paris. Baudelaire wrote his poem 'Le Cygne' before Hausmann's interventions but already at the moment the Rue du Carrousel was dismantled. It would be difficult to find a poem that could comment on Paris's transformations more powerfully than 'Le Cygne' (1860): 'Near a dried-up stream the animal, opening its beak/Nervously bathed its wings in the dust.'[31] Wounded allegory of all the homeless, marginal and subalterns, the swan stands as the embodiment of Baudelaire's social awareness,[32] one with no humanitarian sentimentalism, no militant endeavour, no intellectual good will. Just bare allegorical realism. Even more than Courbet's

Atelier du peintre, Baudelaire's swan becomes an *allégorie réelle*, a real allegory. It bathes in dry reality:

> I think of the thin, consumptive negress
> Trampling in the mud, and searching with her haggard eyes
> For the absent palm-trees of splendid Africa,
>
> ...
>
> I think of the prisoners, of the vanquished! ... and of many
> others besides![33]

Baudelaire's vision of sorrow and suffering sounds like a blunt response to Haussmann's triumphant rhetoric claiming that the wide boulevards will improve the lot of people. What I called Baudelaire's negative thought – modern, urban, ironic, disillusioned – is to be read as a radical criticism of Haussmann's imperial vision and faith in rationalization.[34] In fact, the most violent opposition to Haussmann's rationalist utopia was neither the socialist hope in progress, nor the regret for a backward, rustic, pre-industrial world. The most violent rejection of Haussmann 's rationalization was the perception of Paris as the defeat of reason: Paris, haunted reality, with its anguish, its misfits, its grey sky.

The ancient city

Among the many responses to the phenomenon of the metropolis in nineteenth-century France, Haussmann's response represents what can be called the utopia of the present, absolute faith in the metropolis. Balzac, who described Paris as a monster, regretting a previous form of more human life, shows an irresistible attraction for the monster. Baudelaire represents the allegorical-realistic perception of the necessity and at the same time the danger of the metropolis. The English Romantics and the American Transcendentalists opposed the country, the purity of nature, to the horror of big cities. But sometimes the city – the *polis*, or the *urbs* – was erected as the counterpart of the metropolis, the first being human, the latter being inhuman. In the same years in which Haussmann destroyed parts of the old city of Paris in order to open up the modern metropolis, the historian Fustel de Coulanges thought of the ancient city as the beginning of Western civilization, as the place beyond modern contradictions between nature and culture, the individual and the state.

Criticism of the present can take various shapes and political colours. The reactionary might complain about the spirit of the age, like Carlyle in *Past and Present*, the conservative might take shelter in some illusion; the militant might see everywhere the cunning of capital, the trap of ideology. The most peculiar phenomenon of homelessness in the nineteenth century, the beginning of our modernity, is probably a generalized feeling of not being completely at home in the present time. The dialectic of the new and the old, the ambivalent relationship that the nineteenth century, followed by the twentieth, entertains with tradition – what is called today the canon – are symptoms of discomfort with images of the present. On one hand a tradition seems to suffocate any new crisis, on the other any new form institutes a habit, if not a school, that paradoxically becomes the ephemeral tradition of those who recognize themselves in a small intellectual home, a broken fortress in the world's wasteland.

Baudelaire fully embodied the ambiguity of the modern. He enthusiastically greeted the future painter of modern life 'who can snatch its epic quality from the life of today', and hoped to celebrate 'the advent of the new', as he wrote at the end of his *Salon de 1845*.[35] But he also thought that any worthwhile modernity must inevitably become ancient, as he wrote in *Le Peintre de la vie moderne*.[36]

The new is tantalizing: the poet thought of inventing a new form, or giving it a new impulse. In 1864, the ideal that haunted Baudelaire became true: *Le Figaro, La Vie parisienne, L'Artiste, La Revue de Paris*, published several of his prose poems under the title of *Le Spleen de Paris*. The prose poem is the new musical form with no rhymes 'supple enough and rugged enough to adapt itself to the lyrical impulses of the soul, the undulations of reverie, the jibes of conscience'. Baudelaire knew where this nervous form came from: 'It was, above all, out of my exploration of huge cities, out of the medley of their innumerable interrelations, that this haunting ideal was born.'[37]

The ancient has to be well known: the historian tries to understand it beyond the deformations of the present. In 1864, Numa-Denys Fustel de Coulanges published *La Cité antique*. A historian can indeed choose to focus on the past in order to escape or to clarify the present. In any case, every historian would claim that history is dealing with what happened, with reality, or to use a phrase from the critical terminology, history legitimizes itself as the writing of the real. The most famous statement establishing history as the narration of the real is Leopold von Ranke's definition of history as aiming 'to show what actually happened' (*wie es eigentlich gewesen*), a dictum that, rightly or wrongly, embodied the conception of positivist historiography, its concern for the real.[38] The thirst for reality repeatedly acts as the impetus for any intellectual activity, in the realist novel, in Baudelairean allegory, or in historical research. Fustel de Coulanges took the proper positivist position, as he wrote in 1875:

> History is a pure science, a science like physics and geology. It aims solely to find some facts, to discover some truths. History studies the human being in its innumerable diversity, incessant modifications, as physiology studies the human body, or as geology observes and counts the globe's revolutions.[39]

This vision of history as the science of facts perfectly corresponds to the obsession of the second half of the century. Haussmann, too, in his contrast with the old generation at the Hôtel de Ville, spoke of 'the beautiful language that is the language of facts'.[40] The Baron was undoubtedly convinced that his figures, so dry and clean, had the same persuasive power as a scientific experiment, or a mathematical truth. Fustel de Coulanges was convinced that his thorough verification of ancient documents was capable of bringing back the language of facts as they really happened; only by the precise reading of the documents could history be rendered scientific. Nevertheless, in spite of the emphasis on facts and the enthusiasm for science that sum up the epistemology of the century, the historian represents a core of resistance to Haussmann's urban dream. If Baudelaire perceived the metropolis as the very place of the defeat of reason, Fustel de Coulanges's reading of the ancient city stands as a mental construction contradicting all the physical and spiritual features of Haussmann's Capital. Fustel never mentioned the Baron, but the main thesis of his *La Cité antique* is an implicit critique of the modern city, in spite of Fustel's good relationship with the Empire. The Haussmannization of Paris was such a gigantic phenomenon that any cultural aspect of the period is bound to be related to it. Haussmann's state capital meant: money, market, inclusion of the suburbs into Paris, transformation of places, values, desires. The most spectacular episode concentrating all the new endeavours was the Exposition Universelle of 1855. Even if Haussmann served only as consultant in its preparation, the exhibition embodied his ideology of the new and was conceived on the large scale he envisioned for the imperial capital.

Fustel's interpretation of ancient life was, on the contrary, conservative and religious. This entitled him to privileges under the Empire. As an ex-student of the École Normale, he was asked to teach there a few years after the publication of *La Cité antique*, in 1870. He became the special lecturer of the Empress Eugénie and her circle, to whom he taught the origins of French civilization. After the Franco-Prussian War and the fall of the Empire with the German victory, he became fully committed to the cause of a French Alsace, defining the principle of nationalities on continuity with the past.[41]

The first modern idea that is explicitly attacked in *La Cité antique* is the vision of antiquity as it was imagined by the thinkers of the French Revolution:

> The idea that we had of Greece and Rome has often clouded our generation. As we poorly observed the ancient city's institutions, we imagined that they could live again among us. We were deluding ourselves about liberty among the ancients, and simply because of that, liberty among the moderns was in danger.[42]

By insisting on the difference between the ancients and the moderns Fustel suggested a criticism of revolutionary intoxication. The main target was obviously Rousseau, who considered that the Romans were the 'model of all free Peoples' and Greece the place where 'the love of liberty' flourished.[43] Fustel suggested studying the ancients 'without thinking of ourselves, for they were total strangers'.[44] Nothing in the moderns resembles the ancients. Fustel is convinced that, even if they are studied in schools, and a cultivated Frenchman is exposed from a very early age to classical culture and becomes acquainted with the Parthenon before the Louvre, antiquity is far away from us. The historian thought that one should study the Greeks and the Romans seriously and comparatively, in order to understand what they meant by their term 'liberty'. As Benjamin Constant had already objected to Rousseau in his famous 1819 speech at the Athénée, *De la liberté des anciens comparée à celle des modernes*, their liberty was not our liberty; their institutions were not our institutions.

Against Rousseau's dichotomy between state of nature and society, Fustel wanted to prove that neither the individual nor the state but the family, was the foundation of Western civilization. Therefore, there was no state of nature. The family is both nature, the blood, the *genus*, and culture, a societal organization. Nature and culture were one and the same; the symbolic activity of religious cults could not be separated from concrete sacrifice – the food and beverage offered to the dead – nor from the territory where the living and the dead lived together. The family was characterized by the 'ritual' it performed in the home or, better, on the nearby land, the space where the family settled and continued to settle for generations.

The ancient city was constituted on the model of the family: it was defined by a common religion and a spatial enclosure. The city was based on the juridical notion of family property. Later, the city included more and more citizens – clients and plebeians. In Rome, for example, at the time of Servius Tullius, plebeians became part of the city and could perform their religious rituals. For both Greece and Rome, wars changed the social balance between the aristocracy and the plebs. This change caused a discrepancy between political constitutions and social status, which inevitably led to democracy. Against all democratic illusions, Fustel liked to stress that 'democracy did not suppress poverty; on the contrary, it made it even more visible. The equality of political rights increased the inequality of conditions.'[45] Then Christianity introduced new elements. As Momigliano remarked, Fustel thought that 'Christianity therefore made possible the transformation in the right of property, based no longer on religion but on labour'.[46] Ancient society was ruled by institutions, which are the network of beliefs instituted by a community, while modern society, after the advent of Christianity, is ruled by associations of individuals.

The two main theses of *La Cité antique* are that the state was more recent than the family, and that the first cult was the cult of the ancestors. Fustel went very far back in time, to the beginning of civilization among Aryan people, to make his point. He studied the very heart of tradition, tradition as the foundation of that 'far away and obscure time when there were neither Greeks, nor Latins, nor Hindus, but only Aryans'. All these people 'belong to the same race; their ancestors, in an extremely distant epoch, had lived together in central Asia'.[47] If the ideological implications of the whole concept of the Aryan Western tradition are nationalistic and inevitably racist, the intellectual implications are such that Fustel is one of the forefathers of sociology. He believed that history is the science of social facts, sociology itself. The most innovative feature of Fustel's thought is the important role he gives to belief, and the link he establishes between beliefs and institutions. A little later Durkheim, who dedicated to Fustel his thesis on Montesquieu,[48] would define sociology as the science of institutions, their genesis and their functioning. Durkheim's work, and especially *Les Formes élémentaires de la vie religieuse* (1912), is founded on the idea central to Fustel's *Cité antique*, that religion creates the social system. That same idea is seminal in Max Weber's reading of Protestantism as the religious foundation of the capitalist spirit. Questions of property and economy are to be read as deriving from the symbolic activity of religion.

The idea that religion is the beginning of social life created misunderstanding about Fustel's religious beliefs.[49] He actually did not believe in God. His respect for religion was the effect of his love for tradition: *la patrie*, the homeland, was not a piece of land, but a network of traditions.[50] Stressing the value of religion as the beginning of the social contract is not necessarily a profession of faith, but a point of resistance against the overwhelming power of money and interest as social motors. Haussmann's dream figured a total *homo oeconomicus*. The sharpness of figures, the economic plan of productive expenses would mould urban planning; the clarity of the city would make life easier. Good estimates would guarantee order on every level – political, social, psychological. Money is worshipped in its most abstract essence, in its financial logic. Haussmann's finances are closer to software than to money as it appears in Balzac's novels – heavy and full like matter, as concrete as land or gold. Financial logic would triumph, grasping present and future, sweeping the darkness of the past, as so many old buildings and old streets had been swept from the heart of the old Paris. Therefore, the state had to carry on this financial logic, with technological coldness, like a machine, as coordinated and effective as the sewer system Haussmann conceived and put into practice. The British theorists of interest, the champions of utilitarianism, always perceived the individual as the principal agent. Money, wealth, is a kind of prolongation of individuals pushing for their needs and desires. But, on the contrary, for state capitalism the individual does not really count. Central power has to proceed pitilessly.

Against the economic rationale stands the religious impulse; against the timeless purity of figures, the temporal richness of beliefs; against the abstractness of modern man, the concreteness of the ancients. Fustel insisted on the importance of the ancient cult which prescribed that the dead of the family should enjoy the light and warmth of fire, and be nourished every day. The terror of death for the ancient was not the loss of life, but the fear of remaining unburied and not receiving the honour of the ritual of fire and food. Ancient poems talk about wandering souls, and Fustel suggests that Virgil should be understood literally when he wrote, about Polydorus's burial: 'We lock the soul into the grave.'[51] Being dead without burial: that is the most horrible kind of homelessness in ancient times, times the historian cannot even date when he finds in the well-known texts of Greek and Latin poets and historians the traces of an earlier civilization, told as old stories, legends and beliefs, or curled up in a stereotyped formula, a verbal root, a word, a phrase, an inflection. Then, in order to avoid the misery of an unhappy death, a sacred fire was always burning and food was constantly brought by the family to the ancestors in the grave, which was in the house. Indeed, the home represented the physical centre in which religious belief, family, and private property were one and the same. No foreign person could be admitted, and men continued the family tradition, since women, at marriage, had to leave their family's cult and embrace that of the new family. According to Fustel, the family is composed of all the descendants from a common ancestor following the male branch. The Greeks called it *genos*, and the Romans *gens*. Momigliano comments: 'the *gens*, for Fustel, was not submitted to any superior authority: it was a State governed by the *pater* … each *gens* had its own cult, territory and selfish morality.'[52]

Fustel's ancient city proposed a world in which the values were totally opposite not only from the revolutionary vision of antiquity, but also from the contemporary world as one could see it around 1860. Life and death formed a continuity inconceivable for the scattered condition of the moderns. 'Any Where Out of the World', one of the prose poems by Baudelaire, starts with the sketch of the modern condition of interior exile: 'Life is a hospital where every patient is obsessed by the desire to change beds.'[53]

In 1864, the year of the publication of Fustel's *Cité antique* and of several prose poems by Baudelaire, Haussmann appointed a commission to solve the problem of Paris's cemeteries – Montmartre, Montparnasse, Père-Lachaise – which had been established by Napoleon I just outside Paris and, by 1860, were within the limits of the city. The Baron's idea, which met strong opposition and remained unrealized, was to build a huge cemetery at Méry-sur-Oise, a few miles north-west of Paris. It was a sort of supersonic project conceived by the most audacious of engineers: the cemetery would be connected to the city by a special funeral railway. Even death had to become part of calculation and technology. Cult and piety were reduced to a question of hygiene and efficiency.

But death, as envisioned by the poet, broke through the positivistic reconstruction of the historian and the triumphant figuring of the urban planner. Beyond any rational utopia, beyond the solid soil where traditions hold, without roots, without projects, Baudelaire's poetic creations incessantly move through life, in perennial exile:

> But the real travellers are those alone who leave
> For leaving's sake; hearts as light as balloons
> They never step back from their destiny,
> And, without knowing why, always say: Let's go![54]

'Le Voyage', the last of the death poems in *Les Fleurs du Mal*, carries on the allegory of a trip, perverting classical memories, figuring pieces of a new Odyssey, since here the travellers, intoxicated with space and light, escape from being transformed into animals by Circe. The poem ends with the personification of death:

> O Death, old captain, it's time! Let's weigh anchor!
> This country bores us, O Death! Let us get ready!
> ...
> Since this fire consumes our brains, we want
> To plunge to the bottom of the abyss, whatever it is, Hell or Heaven!
> Plunge to the bottom of the Unknown, to find something *new*![55]

In this poem, as in several poems, in 'Le Cygne', which begins 'Andromache, I am thinking of you!', fragments of classical images are juxtaposed with the new, as in the modern metropolis where bits of the past live together with novelty, as in Paris, capital of the nineteenth century, where everything becomes allegory ('tout pour moi devient allégorie').

An enigmatical being with no father, mother, friends, or country, the inhabitant of the modern metropolis is restless, similar to the lost, unburied soul of the ancient city, always rushing, running, roving, fretting, on a perpetual voyage.

4
Trieste as Frontier: From Slataper to Bazlen and Del Giudice

People think it is a matter of eternal truths when it is merely a matter of adjectives.

Roberto Bazlen

Scipio Slataper described himself as Slav, and wished to be Slav and a barbarian.[1] In 1912, when he was only 24 years old, he published *Il mio carso*, a novel which, despite being subtitled 'lyrical autobiography', begins with a dramatic movement in three parts, in which 'I' is opposed to 'you', 'savagery' to 'Italianità', and the 'fatherland' to 'here':

> I would like to tell you: I was born in the Carso, in a hut with a thatched roof, blackened by rain and smoke ... I would like to tell you: I was born in Croatia, in the great oak forest ...
> I would like to tell you: I was born on the Moravian plain and I used to run like the hare ... Then I came here, I tried to tame myself, I learned Italian, I chose my friends from among the most educated youth; but soon I must return to my fatherland, for here I don't feel too good.[2]

Slataper thus defines himself as Slav, barbarian and poor, by contrast with the Italians, who are 'here', that is, in Florence, where he had gone to study at the University. These friends of his were aligned with the Florentine review, *La Voce*,[3] with which he himself had been associated since he went to live in that city, where he published his *Lettere triestine*. Indeed, Slataper was in close touch with the writers Soffici, Papini and Prezzolini in 1912, when the review was passing through a critical period.

For a man from the North, Florence is the South. Thus, in *Nel paese degli aranci*, which appeared in *La Voce* in 1911, there is a reference to Goethe's 'Mignon', and to her famous song, 'Kennst du das Land wo die Zitronen blühn?' The Carso, on the other hand, stands for the North, or the symbolic meeting-point of North and South, as Slataper suggested in his study of Ibsen.

It would be tempting to lie, but the Florentines, being so cultivated and refined, are too intelligent and cunning for that. They would immediately grasp, thought Slataper, that 'I am a poor Italian trying to pass off his solitary preoccupations as barbarian. I would do better to confess that I am your brother'.[4] Slataper could not reject the values that he had in common with the *Voce* group, in spite of the critical period he went through. He had in fact hoped to become the editor of the review, but then he joined Salvemini and Amendola who had left. *La Voce*, according to Prezzolini, its founder, was a review that 'considered ethical and moral values to be of great importance in the lives of Italians'. The review was meant to represent the voice of Italian intellectuals, and to symbolize their moral commitment irrespective of political parties. *Il mio carso* therefore ended with a message of fraternity and a renewed commitment to work.

Trieste was the fatherland, Florence was 'here', and in Slataper's mind the two places were at once opposed and fused. Yet he wished to leave Florence, to regain Trieste and the Carso, which had been his past and would be his future. He wanted to return to Trieste, a city of three cultures, Slav, German and Italian. The 'Carso' is the name given to the mountains around Trieste, which are white and barren. Slataper wrote it as *carso*, with a small *c*, since for him it was an essential substance, the rock itself, as he wrote in his wartime notebook from 1915, a few months before dying on Mount Podgora. In Celtic, 'carso' means rock, or the life of rock, and one writes it much as one might write 'earth', 'sea' or 'wind'.

Savage and barbarous Slataper then was, though his Florentine friends were not. Savage and barbarous too are the sea, the mountains and the wind of Trieste, and likewise the narrator's soul and the language of *Il mio carso*. It was, declared Slataper, more a Nordic book than an Italian one. One can clearly hear how classical language is violated, how it is littered with items from the *triestino* dialect mixed with *toscano*. The syntax is mangled, with words twisted into audacious neologisms – sometimes harsh and rough words beginning with *s*, the quintessentially Nordic consonant according to Mallarmé: *squarciapancia* (bursting out), *strascinato* (dragged away), *sguazzacchiando* (splashing), *scricchia* (it creaks), etc. 'It is a new book,' said Slataper in 1911, 'a call to arms, a promise of salvation. Italian critics insist that, after Carducci and D'Annunzio, it is stupid to write barbaric[5] poetry. Therefore, I am stupid.' Slataper wanted to be obstinate, stubborn and hard as a rock.

Slataper is an author who identifies both his prose and his person with Trieste, where there is no separation between man and nature, or between memory and myth. The image of his grandmother and of his father's house belongs to the past, and to autobiographical memory, but the image of the child who swims in the Adriatic so far transcends memory as to be integrated into the eternal present of vital elements. Here the myth of strength and of youth emerges; the sea is simply at one with the muscles of the youthful body. The sea is the principle of true life, according to the Viennese writer Otto Weininger, an author dear to Slataper.

The mountain, the *carso*, is a life force too, so that the stones of Mt. Kâl (bald) near Trieste, and the bones of the young man share the same hardness. (When Benjamin Crémieux translated *Il mio carso* into French, in 1920, he called it *Mon frère le Carso*, thus underlining the kinship between Slataper and his mountains.)

Water and rock are part of the mythical body of the fatherland; they are primary elements, barbaric nature, so to speak without landscape, and therefore wholly different from the land of orange trees, of Papini's sweet and soft countryside. But one needs to add another primordial element, the wind of Trieste, its violent *bora*. Alboin, the barbarian king, descended upon the city in the Middle Age, fighting against this wind, against Trieste's hard nature.

The vital force, *élan vital*, rising up out of the primordial elements, was a constant motive in Henri Bergson, who had been launched in Italy by *La Voce*. Nature fuses with myth and history, constituting the force linking past to present, and gives notice of the age to come. Thus, like Alboin leading the Lombards into Italy, Slataper, the brother of the Carso, exhorts the other brothers of stone, the Slavs, poor peasants from the Carso, to go down to the sea.

Slataper is writing almost a song, and the singing resembles that of Walter Whitman; *Il mio carso* is a sort of *Song of Myself* in prose, in which the individual contains in himself the history of the past, a history of heroes and rebels, a history of work and of conquest. It is time for the Slavs to come into their own. They came from the North, had learned to fish in Venice. Trieste belongs to them, is to become their new Venice. The new race is barbarian, and must continue history, to forge the new age, and to reinvigorate the weak Italian blood, now 'sick with cerebral anaemia'. The prose too is barbarian, like that of the quintessential Italian poet, Gabriele D'Annunzio, whose images recur in Slataper's novel. One finds there D'Annunzio's favourite poetic clichés: the earth is bread on which we feed, the soul blooms like water in a bowl, and a nascent idea is the first flower of Spring. The reader is in no way surprised to find that the song ends, not unlike D'Annunzio's, with the announcement that 'Today a poet is born to the world.'[6]

Savage, barbarian Slataper. One can hear that the name does not sound Italian. His ancestors came down from the North, when Trieste was declared a free port by the Emperor Charles VI (at the beginning of the eighteenth century). *Slata* is Slovenian for 'golden', and *Pero* means 'Pen', so that the name Slataper may be rendered 'golden pen'; in Italian 'Pennadoro', which was what the writer liked to be called. It was as if destiny marked him out to be a poet, to write with a golden pen, like D'Annunzio, to write barbarously, like Carducci and D'Annunzio. Barbarism is an integral part of the Italian tradition, that of the great poets whom Slataper had studied so much.

His family had long been Italian; from Trieste, the city of three cultures. Their frontier identity made them at once more Italian and less Italian than the others, for instance, the Florentines. Slataper took pleasure in beginning a major article for *La Voce* on contemporary theatre by referring to Lessing, Goethe, Schiller, Wagner and Nietzsche as the 'writers who stand closest to my own culture'. Yet he ought not really to be taken at his word here, since, as he himself recounted in *Il mio carso*, he was turned down for a job at the Austrian Bank in Trieste on the grounds that his knowledge of German was limited (and on his journey to Vienna he himself would complain of this).

It was the custom in the early part of the century for people from Trieste to go to university at Vienna, Prague or Florence. The latter was the most obvious choice for Slataper, who had attended the Italian Liceo Dante Alighieri. Besides, his family was staunchly anti-Austrian and so, unlike Italo Svevo, he spoke the Triestino dialect, a form of Italian, at home. The Emperor's birthday was not celebrated in his family, and Slataper was encouraged to follow the reporting on the war in Ethiopia in a Trieste newspaper, *Il Piccolo*. The child exulted in Italian victories, and thought of his fatherland as being on the other side of the sea. The Italians of Trieste could cry 'Italia, Italia' as if they were still living out the drama of the Risorgimento, for they had not yet freed themselves from the grip of the Hapsburg Empire. 'Viva l'Italia!' was the refrain of Slataper's uncle, whom he loved so much as

a child. Slataper's grand-father was a follower of Garibaldi in his struggle for the unification of Italy. Later, as an adolescent, the young Scipio
was taken aback by the spineless patriotism of the group *La Giovane
Trieste*. To compensate for this lack of vigour, he dreamed of the heroes
of the fatherland, among them Garibaldi, and the Trieste irredentist,
Guglielmo Oberdan, who had been hung on the Emperor's orders, after
he attempted to kill him in 1898.

Slataper had been in the forefront of a demonstration in favour of an
Italian university for Trieste. Captured by an Imperial guard, he broke
free, cried 'Long live liberty, I am Italian', and ran towards the sea, so
as to wash in the Adriatic, *mare nostrum*: 'I washed my hands and my
face in the see. I drank the salty water of the Adriatic.'[7]

Yet no sooner had Scipio regained his freedom than his sense of
happiness drained away and, with salt still on his face, he felt the
blight of difference. Dirty and savage as he felt himself to be, he could
not identify with the city of Trieste, with the elegant Italians, with the
perfectly turned-out people who promenaded on the *lungomare*, on the
sea-front. He had nothing in common with the young men dressed in
long, swirling cloaks, or with the beautiful, bourgeois girls. For he was
a brother to stone, to the *carso*.

One can now understand better Slataper's initial yearning to declare
himself a Slav. It aimed to mark both origin and political alignment, for
the Slavs were not only the fathers, but also the oppressed, exploited
brothers. If only they could rebel and unite with the Italians! What was
needed was a genuine Adriatic irredentism, like that foreseen by Angelo
Vivante, a friend whom Slataper has met at the Trieste Circolo
Socialista. Vivante played an important role in the cause of Adriatic
irredentism. The cause of national liberty was also a social cause.

So it was that Slataper, before plunging into the most sordid taverns
in the old town, would turn his back on the *lungomare* and gaze at
Mt. Kâl. The 'carso', the mountain, once again took on all its symbolic
value as a place of origin. The 'carso' is pure, perfect and barbarous.
Slataper dreamt of a complete retreat to its stones such as that suggested
by Ibsen in *The Mountain*, a text that Slataper greatly admired. But this
could just be an aesthetic choice. Slataper felt compelled to lose himself
in the city. Zarathustra-Pennadoro would not stay on the mountain, for
the city, tiresome though it might be, was beautiful, rich and active.
City and mountain were not opposed one to the other, but in a crucial
relation of recognition, both being indispensable to all who aspired to
live morally. Thus, even Florence had its 'carso', Mt. Secchieta, where
the young man would go from time to time, when he could no longer

bear Florence, his books, his work for *La Voce* and his work on *Il mio carso*, which had originally borne the title *Sviluppo d'un'anima a Trieste* (*The Development of a Soul in Trieste*). Once on the mountain, he could find nature again; and yet, on the snow, he wrote the name of what took so much of his energy, namely, *La Voce*. For Slataper believed that one must keep one's commitments. He did not share the longing to retreat, the rustic pessimism of Giovanni Papini, nor the annihilatory violence of his compatriot from Trieste, Carlo Michelstaedter, who committed suicide at the age of 22.

Slataper himself, like so many readers of Weininger, was tempted by suicide. In 1910, his friend Gioietta, to whom *Il mio carso* is dedicated, had killed herself with a gun in Trieste, leaving nothing but assurances of her everlasting love for him. When Slataper heard of her death, he wanted to let himself die, to stop everything, just as he had wished to do some years before, when his mother was ill. Gioietta's death is the theme of the third part of the book, which talks about the author's youth. Yet, out of this tragic experience, Slataper acquired a renewed awareness of the value of life and of love. One has to go on living in order to love. A welling up of religious feeling overwhelms the writer: 'Nature, I thank you. You have set me free, and I thank you. I was full of law and of duty. I knew what goodness and what evil was ... in your goodness I obey you, divine nature.'[8]

Other writers in the group around *La Voce* had sought for a new religiosity of very much the same kind, involving faith in humanity and an aspiration towards fraternity and social commitment. One had to suffer and to work, to leave the forest and the wilderness behind, and become aware of the world, be in history, in all humility. The man who lives and obeys his conscience is a hero or a God.

Scipio's plan was both grand and simple. Once he had finished his studies, he declared that he would return to Trieste, become a school-teacher and live modestly with his sisters and a small circle of friends. Slataper could not accept the death that he had desired, for that would be a cowardly path to take. He is the very picture of a lofty idealist, and liked to refer to himself as the brother of Hebbel, the German writer whose journal and plays he had translated. For Slataper, literature culminates in a plenitude of awareness, in life, and sounds as a message of love.

Il mio carso has a religious overtone and moralism has the last word. What did Slataper understand of Nietzsche, whom he both invoked and criticized for having 'stifled life with words'. Slataper's moralism was in fact anti-Nietzschean, consisting as it did of the moralism of *La Voce* plus the driven identity of Trieste. The train runs directly from

Trieste to Vienna, as *Il mio carso* stresses and Slataper went to Vienna (in pursuit of a pretty prostitute who could, he thought, resolve his sexual problems – as he confessed in his diary); though he was a writer from Trieste, he was not familiar with the great central European culture of the period. He knew only of Otto Weininger, and that thanks to *La Voce*. In addition, he was familiar with the German Romantics and post-Romantics, through his courses at Florence, but he knew neither Freud, nor Kraus, nor Hofmannsthal. Slataper believed in nature, in everything in fact that Hugo von Hofmannsthal's Lord Chandos could no longer believe in. He is wholly lost to the cause of modernity. He died young, terribly young, but young though he was he found Picasso's pictures horrible. Slataper is a poet and moralist, he is committed and at the same time mistrusts books and knowledge; he is the prototype of the Italian organic intellectual. (This is how Antonio Gramsci describes the committed and omnipresent intellectual, an ideal central to thirty years of Italian Marxism.) A populist and convinced of the shortcomings of any purely aesthetic choice, he sought organic form and Goethean integrity.

Slataper has become a sort of document in the history of Italian literature, and in that of Trieste also, his provincialism and his passage through Florence earning him a national reputation. Paradoxically, what survives of his oeuvre are only fragments and scattered songs. There are also some passages on cities, on the traffic of ports, on the teeming mass of workers and prostitutes, which have led some contemporary Italian critics to compare him to Walter Benjamin although one cannot really credit Slataper with important insights of modern art and consciousness. (The comparison seems to be part of an effort to see Slataper as part of modernity after all.)

I cannot resist slipping in a personal memory here which dates from a period when Slataper was all but unknown except in Friuli and Venezia-Giulia, where he was, if anything, perhaps too celebrated. I entered a regional competition for young school children sponsored by Coca-Cola, the theme being the passage from *Il mio carso* on Mt. Kâl. Empires change their names and forms. Austria, a bureaucratic empire, belonged to the past, while the United States, a military and industrial Empire, belonged to the present. Besides, the American Consulate for the Venetian area was in Trieste until the 1980s, in one of the loveliest apartments on the Via Roma, a far-flung stronghold of the West, from the windows of which one could glimpse Yugoslavia. I did not write of Slataper as the great national hero who died in the war, nor of the Carso that is so precious to the fatherland. For I was much taken by his sentences and by his harsh prose. I won the prize: a bag full of bottles of Coca-Cola and a visit to the factory which had just been set up in the region on the road from Udine to Trieste. (A diabolic complicity between 'formalism' and American capital?) A Coca-Cola salesman drove me to the factory. He spoke with a strong American accent, like that of the soldiers at the base in Aviano, not far away from Udine. Since Slataper seemed not to interest him, I quizzed him about Kennedy, the White House and the skyscrapers of New York, which used to feature so often on television, until the Coca-Cola factory appeared on the road, built on a bigger scale than any other. I toured the factory and, when I saw the bottles dancing in a line, filling up with brown liquid and being capped in the twinkling of an eye, I forgot Slataper and all the rest of it, my soul gripped by advanced capitalist technology. Not long afterwards I would immerse myself in the gloomy annals of *Buddenbrooks* and of *Felix Krull*.

The values of Slataper were rooted in the tradition, in spite or perhaps because of his frontier identity. They were mother, fatherland and nature – all of those plain, homely things to which it is good to return. Trieste, said Roberto Bazlen, is 'a province because [it is] a root'.[9] Slataper, full of provincial moralizing, is not a free spirit (Piero Gobetti, an internationalist and a modernist, had savaged him in print). Slataper exemplifies the perennial backwardness, in relation to Europe, of modern Italian literature, which smacks of the provinces, of the limited horizons of provincial pedagogy and of provincial intellectuals. Thus, in an interview from *Note senza testo*, Roberto Bazlen allowed that Trieste was 'so very far from being culturally homogeneous that it has been a perfect echo-chamber', but observed that it had produced no new element in European culture. Svevo was an exception, being 'one of the rare contributions that literature in the Italian language has made to fin-de-siècle Europe', and besides Italy had failed to accord him proper recognition. One should not forget that 'Trieste, in spite of certain cosmopolitan features which, after all, are only such when considered within the non-European level of the Italian petite bourgeoisie – is a small city of 250,000 inhabitants'.[10]

It was Bazlen's misfortune that the cosmos itself made him claustrophobic. Bobi Bazlen, a Jew from Trieste, born in 1902, spent 16 years in Austria and in German schools, and, after the war and 16 years of Italy, left Trieste in 1934, and virtually never set foot there again. He lived in Milan, Rome and London; he worked in publishing and did not write.

There is a gulf between Bazlen and Slataper, which is why they cannot be read together, but only against each other. This gulf, which has its origin in what Slataper termed Trieste's double soul, Austrian and Italian, is of greater significance than was the difference between the generation before the First World War and the generation immediately after the Second World War. What divides Slataper and Bazlen is the awareness of modernity, of the crisis of the old order and of the necessity of silence.

Bazlen, who was an Italian irredentist because 'one had to' be on the side of the oppressed, did not really have too much to reproach the Austrians for. 'Austria, a wealthy country, with a ponderous and precise bureaucratic machinery that could obviously appear ridiculous and pedantic ... but it worked perfectly.'[11]

Bazlen was a genuine Central European, who understood Robert Musil's greatness. In 1951, after reading all three volumes of *The Man without Qualities*, he wrote an enthusiastic letter to the publisher Einaudi, declaring that, notwithstanding problems regarding its translation and its great length, the book should be published 'blind', since it indubitably represented one of the greatest experiments in the 'non-conformist novel' in the aftermath of the First World War.

A passionate reader, with boundless curiosity, Bazlen is a Lord Chandos, who knows the impossibility of writing. As far as he is concerned, no language and no literature will do. His refuge, in the crisis of the West and its values, would be Taoism, the wisdom of the East: 'I believe that one can no longer write books. So I do not write books. Almost all books are merely notes, written at the foot of pages, that have swelled to the size of volumes (*volumina*). I merely write notes at the foot of pages.'[12] His *Note senza testo*, assembled in his notebooks, were published by Adelphi in 1970, five years after his death (while his *Lettere editoriali* were published in 1968).

Bazlen was highly sensitive to historical ruptures, to those moments at which an epoch faces its own crisis: 'Up to Goethe, biography was subsumed by the oeuvre. Since Rilke, life did not correspond to the oeuvre.'[13] Yet the opposition between life and works is an old story. The quasi-aphorisms of the *Note* betoken the disaster of modernity, or its shipwreck, to use a term cherished by Bazlen, to whom the present day seemed rather gloomy: 'The world now is a world of death – formerly one was born alive and gradually one would die. Nowadays one is born dead – and some manage to come gradually to life.'[14] What Bazlen left us was a writing of disaster, which sometimes calls to mind Maurice Blanchot and his *Ecriture du désastre*, since the native of Trieste knew full well that the idea of an end is simply a prejudice, that end and beginning endlessly coincide, and that the oeuvre is absent, or can never be finished. But what was only a metaphor for Blanchot was a literal fact for Bazlen, since the former has always written about the impossibility of writing, while the latter did not really write. His notes and his unfinished novel, *Il capitano di lungo corso*, left in the drawer of his desk, were taken in hand by posterity. Publishers made him an author, but he was simply a reader, for Einaudi between 1951 and 1962, and then for Adelphi, a publishing house whose policies he did much to shape.

In his introduction to the *Note*, published by Adelphi, Roberto Calasso observes that the fact of Bazlen did not produce an oeuvre forms part of his oeuvre. The last of the Hapsburgs obeyed Wittgenstein and, having nothing to say, managed to keep silent: 'I have no ear for music I only manage to decipher the silences.'[15]

Whether we judge Roberto Bazlen to be one of the precious stones of modernism, or the black sun of the West in crisis, his very existence embodies the truth of some of the most repeated contemporary nihilist clichés: the end of literature, the absence of the work, the death of the author. Here we have to do with a writer without books and, subsequently, posthumously, with books without a writer. However, Bazlen did not write his own Lord Chandos letter, nor aphorisms in the style of Cioran. No matter how much we speak of the fragment as the literary form of modernity, here the fragments are crumbs.

Why, then, did Roberto Bazlen of Trieste not write and publish?

Daniele Del Giudice's novel, *Lo stadio di Wimbledon* (1983), is woven around the selfsame question, which determines the quest, or enquiry, of the first-person narrator. If it can be called an enquiry this is because the method employed in the narrative at first seems to resemble that used by the police. However, the method is really the professional interview. The protagonist starts his search with preliminary written information, then follows the live trail, going to all the right places, calling by phone, arranging an appointment, meeting up with people who are in the know, who ought to know a great deal about Bazlen. So the protagonist-narrator gets in touch with Bazlen's old friends from Trieste and with Ljuba Blumenthal, with whom he lived in London. The narrator seeks an answer that, as the novel goes on, is less and less concerned with Bazlen and more and more with himself and with his own longing to write. The narrator, for his part, has no name, while the name of Roberto Bazlen appears from the very first page as the object of highly detailed dialogues, and these take up a large part of the novel. Italo Calvino, in his note, says that the fact that the novel has to do with Bazlen is actually of no importance,[16] since the whole search is simply the story of a decision, namely, the decision to write.

But this is surely wrong. The references to Bazlen persist right up to the end of the novel, as if to signify that the narrator's decision belongs to a highly specific debate in contemporary Italy, a debate about the myths of Trieste and of Bazlen that Daniele Del Giudice accepts and rejects at one and the same time.

Trieste gives Italy a real link with European culture; Bazlen, together with Michelstaedter, are conscious about of the European crisis. What troubled them was the cult of authority with which, later, in the seventies, Italy in crisis surrounded them. Bazlen and Michelstaedter are, it is suggested, genuinely 'great', the former because he did not write and the latter because he committed suicide when very young, like Otto Weininger. Wholly bereft of hope, lacking in illusions and brooking no compromise, they showed modern man his true face, much as Gustav Klimt and Otto Wagner had aspired to do at the turn of the century. But that was long past, and 'crisis' would perhaps be the word that Lord Chandos could not bring himself to utter now, because it is so worn out that it no longer means anything. Bazlen, who understood *The Man without Qualities*, was in any event well aware of this. He wrote in his notes: 'the next culture would already exist if one could eliminate the residues of the past.'[17]

Instead of just regarding Bazlen's silence and lack of an accomplished work as a justification for considering him a great thinker, might we not say that he experienced some difficulty in writing? Thus, the narrator of *Lo stadio di Wimbledon*, feeling faintly vexed, put this point to one of Bazlen's friends, who seemed to accept it: 'Yes, he had some difficulty in holding things together, in organizing.'[18] Daniele del Giudice, on the other hand, seems to have had no such difficulties, for the novel is perfectly organized: everything in it coheres. Thus, the two halves of the novel are set in the two different cities, Trieste and London; there is a series of journeys to Trieste, all by train, without the narrator ever spending a single night there, and yet all the journeys are framed by brief naps taken to the rhythm of the train – a sleep as allegorical as is the flight by airplane from Rome Fiumicino to London Heathrow. Whereas London is presented as a great cosmopolitan city, Trieste seems a sluggish place, removed from the modern world, turned in upon itself and afflicted by 'a sort of precariousness, an atmosphere of war'. In Trieste, the antiquarian bookshop is hostile, while the one covering 'current affairs' offers only remainders, and the passers-by are Africans, Slavs or old Triestini who mistrusted foreigners. Trieste seems to sink irremediably into the past. The eighteenth-century book that attracts the narrator's attention in the local library is entitled *How an Old Place Ages the Writer*.

Bobi Bazlen is quite a mystery, then, as is Trieste, his birthplace, located between Italy and Yugoslavia, with a town hall square that is perfectly Nordic, says the narrator, 'as in Salzburg'. Was Bazlen a great man, whose life had been his work? Yet what if he had been an unpleasant character, as it had been hinted by one, just one of his friends, a woman, the famous Gerti who features in the poem by Montale? He was a baleful influence, she claimed, who had taken an excessive interest in other people and in their liaisons. He was merely a failure who had lived his life by proxy.

And what if to write is also to devour things and people? The narrator of *Lo stadio di Wimbledon*, seeming to be pro-Bazlen and anti-Bazlen at one and the same time, both discreet and self-effacing and yet capable of making decisions, has to go to Trieste several times. He has to cross all that silence in order to overcome it, and he has to see the place that had been Bazlen's primal scene, and which for that reason had been repressed. The narrator is an 'anti-Ulysses'. His conduct is informed by Bazlen's words as delineated in a sequence from the *Note*, itself entitled 'anti-Ulysses', designed to undermine the myth of Ulysses who, in Bazlen's opinion, is the epitome of the petit-bourgeois intellectual: 'until the end every path is but a false path – deceiving oneself means not accepting the path chosen.' Bazlen was caught in the snare of his own aphorism, whereas the narrator of Daniele Del Giudice's novel deviates from the chosen path, that of solving the Bazlen enigma, in order to pursue a personal decision, 'the path beyond death'. He wants to write in order that he himself should not remain stuck forever in death. The Bazlen thread, in the novel, is sustained right up to the very end of the plot, in spite of the narrator's wish to let it drop. If in London he sets off in pursuit of Bazlen, he gets tired of that, and finally he wants to rid himself from the weight of Bazlen's mystery. Discreetly, the narrator has thus devoured the other person. That is the cruel law of writing, and it would be cheating to fall back here upon the slogan of the perfect coincidence between reading and writing, for the work of the reader, which was Bazlen's work, is not that of the writer. Before the two activities can be merged, there is a need for the whole difficult process of wishing-to-write, the complex business of arriving at a decision.

'Writing is not important, but one cannot do anything else', so the protagonist of *Lo stadio di Wimbledon* proclaims to Ljuba Blumenthal, thus drawing a conclusion that is precisely the reverse of that drawn by Bazlen. The narrator of the novel considers that no moralism whatsoever is justifiable, whether it be the organic humanism that Slataper had espoused, and which is now so outdated, or critical nihilism in the style of Bazlen and Michelstaedter, which has become the contemporary obsession. The only possible morality is indeed that of form, or of literature as form. Such, then, is the process by which a writer commits himself, as a professional of writing, just as one might be a professional of some other thing, without there being any further mention of intellectuals, either for or against (Bazlen could never resist sounding off about intellectuals, who were to him quintessentially petit-bourgeois). Existentialism is long dead. Nihilism is something from the past, and so pretentious. Daniele Del Giudice belongs to the new, objective generation. He has understood the evidence, namely, that *Lord Chandos's Letter* does indeed mark a crisis, the impossibility of writing and of order, but that it also implies the possibility of a new look at new objects, which could only be achieved by adopting a beautiful form that rehearsed the classical styles. Daniele Del Giudice's writing is thus in a classical vein, his use of simple sentences imbued with a sort of tension resulting in a 'rhythmical balance between clarity and madness', to borrow Bazlen's observations on Goethe.[19] For example, we can read in the novel sentences like this: 'Who knows when, I am a ghost and must terrorize visitors. A horrible, heart-rending cry would be needed. I concentrate, I draw breath; I am awake, I cry. At first I am glad to have succeeded, then I resign myself to the raucous, bestial sound to which I belong.'[20]

It is perhaps a quality peculiar to Italian that can realize an ideal of simplicity in language, a sort of power inherent in vowels. There is a dance of form and chaos, a vocalic geometry that does not span the sounds but alternates vowels and consonants. Language is then like a well-turned, well-made object; in a sentence, the words follow each other as objects follow each other in space. Daniel Del Giudice's novel is as perfect as a designer object, and it does indeed contain precise, technical descriptions of several objects. By contrast with Bazlen, the young Italian author of the eighties is not afraid of banality. What could be more banal than the world of the things we live among, the trains, cars, furniture and clothes? What could be more banal than the small everyday acts – making a cup of coffee, having a bath, dialling a telephone number or going to a restaurant? Yet it is solely through such actions and objects that our life is constituted; there is no privilege accorded to man allowing him to eliminate the importance of objects. The captain in Bazlen's unfinished novel brought order to his cabin by getting rid of objects, or at least this is what the narrator of *Lo stadio di Wimbledon* thinks. Poor little objects, dealing with them is not easy, 'their presence is ineffaceable. Yet it is easy to be rid of them, they are terrible and defenceless.'[21]

Existentialism was the affair of the World War II generation, and existentialism does not interest the narrator, 'even if it was moving to think that all this was truly felt'. For it is only when he sets eyes on a military cemetery that he grasps that 'the Germans did not only exist in films'.[22] He belongs to a different generation, one familiar with advanced technology, with technical languages, with televised images and science fiction. This is a generation that has Walter Benjamin's aesthetic in its blood and therefore does not even need to invoke him – as people often do; it may be that Benjamin himself will no longer serve, his aesthetic having been superseded by the present state of technology, for it is the reproduction of the artistic object that nowadays preserves a kind of aura, that of the uniqueness of the series. But the unique series is being replaced by simultaneous series, as when we watch television using the remote control switch. Between Calvino and the *nouveau roman*, and notwithstanding Bazlen, who, in an editorial letter, violently attacked Robbe-Grillet, Daniele Del Giudice puts into effect 'the simultaneity of times and places', as it happens in the network of air-traffic. The airplane features on the cover of the novel – the cover being what makes a book a finished object, and here it is a reproduction of a hyperrealist picture by Elsie Driggs. The plane is central to the novel, because it represents the passage from Trieste to London, and the passage from the enquiry into why Bazlen did not write to the decision to write.

The plane is itself an enormous designer object, an achievement of perfect form and precise technology, and a realization of spatial and temporal simultaneity – on land and in the air, in the captain's cabin and in the control tower. As such, the plane eliminates provinces and links up the metropolis. And nobody today is impressed by the technological miracle.

The map regulating airborne navigation is called Mercator's Map; it is also called Representation. By means of this detail, the author suggests that literature, like this map, can be invented 'by means of a precise calculation, an almost perfect mathematics'. It is beside the point to object that literature is not a representation of the real. For it is the real as mathematically conceived through figures, or else it is the meeting-point of the possible and the real, in the same way as photography is the image that has grasped the real.

The allusion to photography brings us to one of the most important scenes in the novel, the one that frames and renders objective the narrator's long-delayed decision to write. There had been intimations of such a decision ever since his final journey to Trieste, but it was the first conversation with Ljuba that precipitated it. Words or sentences would not do, for the decision had to be wholly concrete, taking the form of a blindingly obvious image, an object or a *thing*. There was indeed an only too real thing, sitting there, forgotten, on a bench in Wimbledon stadium. It was a camera. The narrator had always been reluctant to look at the photos of Bobi Bazlen that his women friends had wished to show him, but now, when his moment of decision had come, he would have liked to fix his overall vision of Wimbledon Park, since it is the place where he made this resolution.

Being timid, phlegmatic and unsure of himself, the narrator fails to lay hands on the camera, which is grabbed by someone else. This was because, in the last analysis, he was in the process of committing himself to a different art of images, not photography but literature. The only possible answer to the Bazlen enigma lay in the thing itself, in writing a book, and not a book of critical essays but a story. There are really not many other instances in Italian literature of the process, much commented upon by Roland Barthes and already announced by Oscar Wilde, that Daniele Del Giudice's novel exemplifies, and that involves a fusion of critical with poetic or fictional writing. Here the fusion is achieved in the form of the novel, in opposition to all myths of criticism at any price, and above all to the Marxian critique of ideology, such as has characterized interesting intellectual experiments in Italy over the last twenty years. In fact, a sort of critical excess, even if not Marxist but rather nihilist – a perpetual wariness about the snares of illusion, of historical illusions – was precisely the sickness of Roberto Bazlen, which led him to view the work as itself a crime. Almost timidly, *Lo stadio di Wimbledon* is pitted against all those who would impute guilt to production, whether literary, architectural or of any other kind, and thus against all those who revere Bazlen for his silence. Between the inanity of pure artistic creativity and the terrorism of negativity, there is perhaps room for something else, the ethics of form, the pleasure taken in an object that is well made, the pleasure taken in making an object.

Conversely, Bazlen may himself already have recommended the novel form, and, in Ljuba's presence, he in fact gave the following advice to a young woman who wished to write an essay on a German writer: 'But why do you want to write essays? Tell these things as you imagine them, or as you have just told them to us.'[23]

Being anti-Bazlen and pro-Bazlen at one and the same time, the narrator of *Lo stadio di Wimbledon* does not dare to refuse the pullover that used to belong to Bazlen and that Ljuba Blumenthal insists upon giving him. He does not wish to wear it either and, once he has left her house, takes it off in an obsessively ritualistic fashion. For, at the moment of decision, with the date of his journey confirmed and his ticket already bought, when he feels himself to be on the brink of his venture, 'uncertain and determined', the risk of identification is still there, and the power of objects could still be unleashed, just as Bazlen conceived of it in 'The mechanics of the Tao': '(where man does not disappear) in the middle: a psychology of the inanimate (flats, bed-spreads ...).'[24] So the narrator does not throw away the pullover but holds it in his hand, tenderly, 'as one would hold a child'.[25] This, the last sentence in the novel, while the narrator is in London, gets back to its starting-point in Trieste: the psychology of the inanimate featured in the opening scene, in which the train broke down before reaching Trieste station, as if to signify the difficulty of arriving in that town. The psychology of the inanimate begins and ends the cycle of the novel, in its 'alternations of movement and rest'.

Thanks to Trieste, and the aura with which that city surrounds objects and places, the author manages to speak, in terms of 'objective' literature, of what represents the most subjective of choices, the 'fun-damental', and therefore crucial, decision of a subject. Nevertheless no indulgence is shown to the psychology of the character; the psychol-ogy is wholly in the objects. Moreover, like the whole city of Trieste, the objects in the novel are profoundly allusive (and it is this that rules out any direct comparison with Robbe-Grillet).

Just as Scipio Slataper addressed himself to the Italian intellectuals of the day, to the Florentines with whom he was connected, so too today's young writers have quite specific interlocutors in mind, namely, all those who, in the 1960s and 1970s, deployed the Marxist critique of ideology, read Hegel, Schopenhauer, Nietzsche, Heidegger, Benjamin and Adorno, imagined the contradictions of the modern and of the big city, and discovered Bazlen and Michelstaedter. The parti-cular decisions taken by the narrator, and so by the author, can only be understood in terms of such an intellectual context. To the mystical answer implicit in negative philosophy, Daniele Del Giudice opposes the choice of writing and the form of the novel. Furthermore, his is a novel of Trieste, not only because more than half of it is set there, but because, although deserted and strange, the frontier city serves as a point of departure for a new endeavour, one related to the great Italian experiments of Italo Svevo, and also to other European experiments. If Trieste is so alluring, it is because it lives inside the myth of fin-de-siècle Vienna, and because it represents a bridge to Europe.

5
Aldo Rossi: The White Walls of the City

For Aldo Rossi, every architectural project is 'an unfinished love affair: it is most beautiful before it ends'.[1] In architecture, as in love, it is when happiness reaches its height that we would like to withdraw, regain our freedom, since 'every moment that we become aware of things is coloured by the longing to be able to give them up'. *Forgetting Architecture* is the title that Aldo Rossi would have liked to give to his *Scientific Autobiography* (1981), a work published in English, in the United States, as if it were necessary to get away from Italy in order to be an Italian architect. The forgetting of architecture could be taken literally: Aldo Rossi does not just build but, to an ever greater extent, he draws, as is shown by *Il libro azzurro*, an exquisite sketch-book comprising a set of 48 drawings accompanied by notes, which encompass the habitual forms of his architecture: lighthouses (how can one help being reminded of those by Giorgio de Chirico?), cabins and the primary elements of architecture such as cylinders, columns, pillars, walls. But forgetting architecture also means breaking up its outlines, integrating architecture into a broader comprehension of the discipline, where the written page, the sketch, the plan and the construction are not too different from each other, since each repeats the same idea by different means. Above all, the forgetting of architecture implies the weight of time, the history of nature, of the human kind and the personal history that unfolds in buildings and cities. Speaking about his interest in art since his childhood, Aldo Rossi almost confesses:

> I knew that architecture was made possible by the confrontation of a precise form with time and the elements, a confrontation which lasted until the form was destroyed in the process of this combat. Architecture was one of the ways that humanity had sought to

survive; it was a way of expressing the fundamental search for happiness.[2]

Rossi's poetic, almost intimate vision – architecture is like a love story, architecture should be forgotten – seems to be very much at odds with the positive tone of *L'architettura della città*, a fundamental text in the contemporary debate, which first came out in 1966 and has been republished several times in various languages: it suffices to look at the table of contents to see the crucial role played by architectural facts, and urban structures and elements: *Fatti urbani e teoria della città*, *Struttura dei fatti urbani*, *Gli elementi primari e l'area*, etc. Aldo Rossi often remembers with tender irony his sound convictions at the time he wrote that book. There he declared:

> I understand architecture in the positive sense, as a creation insepa-rable from civil life and from the society in which it is made mani-fest ... thus architecture is consubstantial with the formation of civilization, being a permanent, universal and necessary fact.[3]

But actually for him there has never been any discontinuity between theory, project, construction and the artist's own life.

The work of Aldo Rossi lends itself to various kinds of interpretation: the architect sees in him the rationalist legacy of the Viennese Adolf Loos[4] or of Italian classicism; the art historian sees in him the metro-politan atmosphere of Giorgio de Chirico and of Mario Sironi; the historian of ideas might perceive, in the differences between the text of 1966 and the *Autobiography* of 1981, the transition from public to private man, from commitment to history to absorption in the self, typical of periods of crisis; the critic of ideology will see in Aldo Rossi's repetitions of form the ambiguity of the poetic, the nostalgia for art and order; those who love literature will be touched by Rossi's sense of responsibility in a personal choice, the identification of the self with the totality of a work. Poetry is so important for Rossi himself, who quotes several poets as having influenced his wish to be an architect, and reports his answer to the persistent questions he is asked about some features in his architecture: 'I have translated the last lines of a Hölderlin poem ("Halfte des Lebens") into my architecture: "*Die Maurern stehn / Sprachlos und kalt, im Winde / Klirren die Fahnen*" [The walls stand / mute and cold, in the wind / the banners creak].'[5]

The political optimism of the sixties obviously cannot return, but Rossi's fundamental ideas about architecture which first appear in his early theoretical text are still present in his 1981 autobiography: the rejection of any functionalist conception of architecture, which cannot be reduced to functions, despite the efforts of many modern schools to do so; the idea that city and architecture coincide, one being inconceivable without the other, and that the city (or architecture) lives through time. This means that the city has a history in which memory and forgetting are intertwined, for cities change through time but still keep their identity. Because of this vision of the city across time, functionalism is ineffectual, as Rossi says in his autobiography, at one point where he is referring to his own book, *L'architettura della città*. In fact places that have been built for one purpose can subsequently be put to a different use: 'I have seen old palaces now inhabited by many families, convents transformed into schools, amphitheatres transformed into football fields; and such transformations have always come about most effectively where neither an architect nor some shrewd administrator have intervened.'[6] This typological freedom fascinates the architect, who loves unexpected events that jeopardize function, such as the taverns under the arches of the Schnell-Bahn in Berlin, or the two-storey kiosks behind the cathedral of Ferrara. His motto will never be 'form and function', but is rather form and memory.

In cities, different historical periods accumulate, within the buildings different functions follow one another, making room for people's lives. Of all the photographs of the Gallaratese (the housing estate in Milan built by Carlo Aymonino and Aldo Rossi in 1969–74), Rossi says he likes best the ones where children are playing under the arcades of the building near the pilasters: he likes this proximity of human beings and stone, of biography and construction; he likes the interplay of the stable and the transitory, of the scientific and the existential, or the dream of an architecture seen through a child's eyes.

Lombardy

Indeed what has been seen through a child's eyes lasts forever. The images of childhood, the buildings of one's childhood, 'in the flux of the city' are fundamental; they form the core of a constant quest, creating an expectation, that of an event which, as in Giorgio de Chirico's pictures, may never materialize: 'I am more interested in preparations, in what *might* happen on a midsummer night. In this way, architecture can be beautiful before it is used; there is beauty in the wait, in the room prepared for the wedding, in the flowers and silver before High Mass.'[7]

Aldo Rossi feels he has never lost his ties with Lombardy: the beloved Sacri Monti,[8] the statue of San Carlone in Arona (Lake Maggiore between Piedmont and Lombardy), the lakeside Hotel Sirena (a building of bad taste with its acid green walls, but promising happiness, holidays, meetings with young girls), the Galleria in Milan, where the fog penetrates on winter days, and the horrible piazza Leonardo da Vinci, also in Milan, where Rossi, with other students of the Politecnico, spent long hours taking measurements.

Take, for example, that architectural structure typical of Lombardy and which can be found in Milan, in the working-class quarter of porta Ticinese dating from the end of the nineteenth century: houses with balconies. This Milanese typology is a concrete image of the city where Aldo Rossi was born, and fully inspired his Gallaratese project, where the whole construction extends along a gallery or passage with balconies. Thus time and geography, the past and the local style combine to provide the model for a piece of modern architecture, for the gallery is also 'an internal raised street'.

The places of childhood and of youth also include those experienced on journeys and long visits: Lombardy and its images blend with Belo Horizonte in Brazil, and with Seville. They can also stretch as far as Modena and Parma, as far as the image of the Tempio Malatestiano in Rimini or of Leon Battista Alberti's Sant'Andrea church in Mantua, which Rossi loved so much. The natural and urban landscape of the Po valley prompted the construction of his cemetery in Modena (1971 competition), whose conception is influenced by the 'world' of the Po and by what Rossi felt in the public gardens at Ferrara or Seville: 'a mixture of real experience, image, and afternoons wasted in Ferrara or along the river itself.'[9] Architecture is time and place: stones and buildings, chronological time, existential time, and weather merge in a strange feeling where movement and stillness are not contradictory:

> Between the houses of childhood and death, between those of play and work, stands the house of everyday life, which architects have called many things – residence, habitation, dwelling, etc. – as if life could develop in one place only. Through my own life and craft I have partly lost the concept of a fixed place, and at times I superimpose different situations and different times, as my reader has already seen.[10]

Aldo Rossi's Italy is that of Milan and 'need not contradict the notion of the citizen of the world';[11] his Italy it is the Italy of certain interiorized post-war images; of the Renaissance; of the Po valley. One can find the atmosphere of some of Rossellini, Fellini, Bertolucci or Visconti's films. Rossi's Italy is also international Italy, brimming over with different cultures. It is above all the Italy of the Hapsburgs, imbued with modern German and Viennese culture: Aldo Rossi's influences include Adolf Loos, Georg Trakl, Walter Benjamin, Mies van der Rohe (the modern architect who, along with Loos, he admires the most), and even Raymond Roussel, Melville and Conrad. An image, a sentence, a city, a building recalls others, beyond any frontier, in an endless flow of connections.

The analogous city

Rossi has often spoken of the analogous city – he refers to it in his *Autobiography* – suggesting that it is not a concept or a stable definition but an image, the very possibility of joining images, 'a circle' of relationships 'that is never closed', 'the unlimited *contaminatio* of things, of correspondences'.[12] The analogous city is very close to Baudelaire's 'Correspondances': an urban image can be associated to another urban image, but also to an atmosphere, a mood, a feeling. Rossi's style in the *Autobiography* is very different from the assertive tone of *The Architecture of the City*; it is elliptical, not conforming to an idea of treatise or system, nor to that of a continuous narrative. His mode of writing is that of fragmentation in the modern style, it belongs to the tradition of Italian hermeticism, proceeding by brief statements which, in their apparent simplicity, refer to suggestions in which theoretical intent and personal experience are inseparable, just as in his architecture the rational approach is combined with a violent and chilling effort striving to recapture an emotion, an event reconsidered and reviewed at a distance. There is no impressionism in Rossi's work, either in his writing or in his architecture, since his respect for the subjectivity of the artist is not sentimental but intellectual. Rossi's work eschews all irrationalism, aiming to integrate modern rationalism with that complex thing that is the human person with his feelings, obsessions, contradictions, memories. While organizing the international architecture section at the fifteenth Triennale exhibition in Milan, Rossi wrote the introduction to the joint work *Architettura razionale*[13] and made the film – called, after Adolf Loos's essay, *Ornament and Crime* – which was 'a collage of architectural works and pieces of different films which tried to introduce the discourse of architecture into life and at the same time view it as a background for human events'.[14]

For the Milanese architect, his discipline is a sort of science of the subject, where the universal and the general of known and recognizable forms would not annihilate the peculiarity, the uniqueness of a personal experience. Rossi's concept of the analogous city should not be interpreted in the abstract, Platonic sense, for it is the idea that comes after the event, after individual experiences, and it is presented in a realistic manner. The analogous city is the image of a place, of an architectural pattern, of an existing town, which might be composed by elements of different existing cities, and one that persists in the memory. Rossi's analogy is produced by an accumulation of objects, in a richness of references that, paradoxically, results in simplicity – the purism of the primordial elements or elementary forms that have often been discussed in connection with him. Memory can superimpose various elements or recognize similarity within difference: recollection and analogical association produce changes and metamorphosis in the same way as the altered usage of buildings transforms functions: 'Ever since my first projects, where I was interested in purism, I have loved contaminations, slight changes, self-commentaries, and repetitions.'[15] Taking the example of the Milan Galleria or Alberti's Sant'Andrea, Rossi proposes an analogy between architectural structures and mist. Constructed forms and geography merge together – contaminate, to use the term cherished by Rossi: 'If one enters Sant'Andrea in Mantua on those days when the fog has penetrated the interior, one sees that no space so resembles the countryside, the Po lowland, as the measured and controlled space of this building.'[16]

The 'contamination' produced by analogy is the principle itself of collage – and one of Rossi's 1977 collages was called 'Analogous city'. Nevertheless analogy consists in the detachment, in the rational division among elements, without any fusion or confusion. Aldo Rossi's analogy belongs to the type of the catalogue, where hierarchies are expunged and flattened out (mist, a meteorological element, is on the same level as a building), but order is indispensable (the mist is a different thing from the building, it is the feature of the Po landscape that inspires the re-examination of this landscape in terms of Alberti's rational forms). Aldo Rossi finds an analogy to his art in the work of Raymond Roussel, where a decision orders the composition: 'I detested the arbitrary disorder that is indifference to order, a kind of moral obtuseness, complacent well-being, forgetfulness.'[17]

Nostalgia

The architecture of Aldo Rossi, in the projects that have never been carried out as well as those that have, is born out of the tension between mathematical, scientific order and the relative disorder of personal, subjective life. Yet although a building, a town, is always in a profound relationship with the memory of the artist, Rossi does not mean to propose any myth of the artist, of art: a passionate reader of Adolf Loos and Walter Benjamin, he claims that the only people he admires in the contemporary world are the engineers (this is why his autobiography is labelled as scientific). The architect does not pursue the ideal of aesthetic purity. In fact, he entitled one of his 1975 engravings, where a series of architectural objects is assembled as if in a catalogue, *Diese ist lange her* (Now all that is lost).

Rossi is not nostalgic for a past, bygone world, where architecture was beautiful and triumphant; like Baudelaire, or Benjamin, he is aware of the need for the modern; that is, in the manner of Loos, he is so uncompromisingly rational that he is forced to accept all the aspects of the contemporary metropolis, even the ones he finds ugly. The city, that mixture of past and present, is alive in all its parts: how can one deny, for example, the existence of suburbs? To this reality of the present day Rossi responded with his projects for working-class housing and with his 1965 project in Segrate, where one sees, on the outskirts of Milan, the nudity of absolute, almost atemporal, architectural forms (such as the hollow trapezoidal triangle of the fountain in the piazza del Municipio). A similar atemporality is expressed by the suspension between two cultural identities, that of an agrarian society and that of an industrial society, which is precisely the condition in which Milanese immigrants from the south of Italy live every day, passing from one type of society to another.

Aldo Rossi's nostalgia is not nostalgia for the past, for an heroic past. He is aware that is no longer possible to give expression to the hopes of the seventies when, for instance, he wrote in the review *Casabella-Continuità* that 'traffic, today the chaotic symptom of congestion, will become the regular pulse of a dynamic and ordered society'.[18] The utopia of 1968 is far off, even if Aldo Rossi shows – briefly, swiftly, as if it were the recollection of a dream – a glimpse of the celebration of the Revolution. In the critical end of the twentieth century, in 'the poverty of modern culture' which makes necessary 'a popular movement', one must be content with 'small things, having seen that the possibility of great ones was historically precluded'.[19]

Aldo Rossi feels a strange nostalgia for the moment in which the event takes place, whether in life or in the theatre. The aim of the artist is to represent and fix the present, while it flickers:

> Every midsummer evening has its companionship and its solitude, and the architect or the playwright must grasp the broad outlines of

a scene quickly because he knows that the character and even their feelings may change, or that in any case the representation will be different in time.[20]

The architect writing his autobiography feels a nostalgia for life, for youth, that inescapable law of time that erodes human lives far more than it does buildings, that requires the repairing of forms, gestures, thoughts, making every change imperceptible and derisory: 'As I have said, *Forgetting architecture* comes to mind as a more appropriate title for this book, since while I may talk about a school, a cemetery, a theatre, it is more correct to say that I talk about life, death, imagination.'[21] Rossi feels nostalgia not only for the purism of his early style, but also for the end of architecture, that moment when time is stronger than any matter: 'Thus the temporal aspect of architecture no longer resided in its dual nature of light and shadow or in the ageing of things: it rather presented itself as a catastrophic moment at which time takes things back.'[22]

Time swallows our desires and indicates that an event is over, and that it can never be repeated, even if one repeats the scenario. Roland Barthes saw photography as the crystallizing of what has been lived and the harrowing ambiguity set up by the presence of an image that tells us: never again. Aldo Rossi sees the same thing in architecture, in the city, in the beautiful illusion of the Modern movement destroyed by the bombs of the Second World War. Nevertheless, for him the project is only possible when destruction has taken place, when the emotive appearance of the event is over: 'everything becomes representable once desire is dead ... Almost paradoxically, whenever there is a loss of desire, the form, the project, the relation, love itself are cut from us and so can be represented.'[23]

Wanting pre-exists, but cannot coexist with 'the drawing, the project or the ritual'. And architecture is more a ritual than a creation, at once exorcism trying to conjure up the end and an image of the end; it is made up, like nostalgia, of this alarming dual aspect of the loss of any wish and the necessity of this loss for representation in order to make possible the representation: 'I do not know how much of this is joy or is in fact melancholy.'[24]

A sense of ending overtakes us when we look at one of the drawings from *Il libro azzurro*, where, in the very persistence of stones, the oblivion or destruction of architecture takes place through a collage of various urban images and objects: a large blue coffee-pot is on the same scale as the buildings, the factory chimney, the telescopic tower, the house recalling the buildings of New York with fire escapes made of black iron on their façades. And, to increase this disconcerting equation of man, stone and objects, the profile of the statue of San Carlone, which belongs to the landscape of Rossi's childhood, stands between the New York-style building and the tower, on the same scale as the house and the objects: the head of the statue cannot be seen but its hand extends upwards like a mute cry at the centre of the drawing, bigger than the roofs and chimneys. The whole drawing is a disquieting collage of more or less familiar images and gives them an atmosphere of death. This sort of spectral classicism of urban landscape can be found in the verses of the poet Rossi likes so much, Georg Trakl, such as 'Immer klingen die weissen Mauern der Stadt' ('Always the white walls of the city resound'). This is in fact Rossi's commentary, traced in that other kind of drawing which is handwriting: 'The urban landscape seems to me more and more characterized by those features that arise from abandoned constructions, collapsed buildings or sundry sedimentation ... '[25]

There has been a great deal of talk about monumentality in Rossi's designs and, especially in the United States, he has also been seen in the tradition of Italian Fascist architecture.[26] But Rossi's forms, even when they are monumental (as in the cemetery in Modena), never testify to the power of the monument; rather they are the archaeological relics of an abandoned, lost or remote city, or one that has been destroyed by war: far from the glamorous din of history, or of heroic grandeur, they absorb the silence that history or time itself, imposes on them, and which was always there: 'I love the beginning and end of things; but perhaps above all I love things which are broken and then reassembled, as in archaeological and surgical operations.'[27] Mythically, the moment of ending is Lorca's 'Cinco de la tarde', the time of great equality that is death; it is the time always shown by the clocks in Rossi's drawings.

Aldo Rossi often puts together elements of the ancient city and features of contemporary reality – like Giorgio de Chirico in the series of paintings called *Piazze d'Italia* – while his pencil line or the sombre atmosphere of several of his urban landscapes recalls the painting of Mario Sironi – as in the black and white drawing of the project for the theatre in Parma. But the reference to Sironi or to de Chirico[28] (of which Aldo Rossi hardly ever speaks) is echoed by self-reference because every building is now just a citation of Rossi himself: one can see again the passage with columns of the Gallaratese building, the triangular prism of the fountain in Segrate, the round shape of the school of Fagnano Olona; and, maybe, the three people in the square on the right are not raising their arms towards the end of architecture.

At times, for example in the middle of the campus of Princeton University, in those suburban places where nature and architectural objects do not make up a town – missing that coincidence of Rossi's between town and architecture – I feel the lack of the skyscrapers and subway of New York, of urban space and life (one feels so much in the *Autobiography* the presence of friends, the intellectual excitement at an evening get-together in a Milan bar): then I know what it means to be European. It just means having in one's head, in one's very being, images of towns, and the atmosphere of a street or a square, that combination of stone and sky that de Chirico could only find in Italian cities. Nothing is simpler than a *piazza*, the culminating point of the fusion between architecture and city, centre and suspension of the town. And out of this simplicity arises a multitude of things, memories, allusions and dreams as in Rossi's drawings and as in this passage by de Chirico:

> I find myself in a square of great metaphysical beauty; perhaps it is the piazza Cavour in Florence; or perhaps one of those very fine squares in Turin, or perhaps neither the one nor the other; to one side can be seen porticoes surmounted by apartments with closed shutters and solemn balconies. On the horizon can be seen hills dotted with villas; over the square the sky is very clear, washed clean by the storm.[29]

But cities, images of cities, pile up in our memory, through analogy, 'through a kind of cross-referencing',[30] and one can find the city of stone and of monuments not just in European cities but anywhere and also in the United States, that place where 'modern architecture failed so badly'.[31] Stating the importance of the United States for the autobiography of his projects, Rossi admits: 'New York is a city of stone and monuments such as I never believed could exist.'[32] It is actually the city which made Rossi understand the truth of his arguments in *L'architettura della città*, since, as in Loos's design for the Chicago Tribune, it is 'a synthesis of the distortions created in America by an extensive application of a style in a new context'.[33] And if one walks around the Wall Street district on a Sunday morning, one gets the impression of walking 'through a realized perspective by Serlio or some other Renaissance treatise-writer'. And Rossi continues: 'I have had a similar experience in the villages of New England, where a single building seems to constitute the city or the village, independent of its size.' From town to town, from analogy to analogy, one can compare, as Aldo Rossi does, Trieste – white and desperate as in Italo Svevo's novel

Senilità (Senility) – to New York, the city-monument[34]: 'The comparison of these cities is not so unusual, not only because in both there is the presence of the sea, but also because both are related to that primordial city built on the sea, Venice.'[35]

Theatrum mundi

Venice is a city, an experience, essential to Aldo Rossi. Not only because he has taught there but also because this city is the site of one his most extraordinary projects: the floating theatre designed and built for the Biennale of 1979–80.

Several features of Rossi's art are concentrated in this construction which, unfortunately, was demolished after the Biennale 'with an efficiency rare in this country'[36], Rossi says in his 1982 book *Teatro del mondo*: in the first place the floating theatre revives a traditional structure, for its model belongs to the history of the Venetian Renaissance; secondly, its relationship with the city is simultaneously one of discontinuity and continuity, since the simple, naked and unornamented forms of the theatre are in contrast with the Venetian palaces, but they are nonetheless wholly bound up with the wooden architecture and the landscape of the Venetian lagoon, the neighbouring islands and the Po delta. The floating theatre also reproduces a pre-monumental Venice that 'is not yet white with the stone of Sansovino and Palladio. It is the Venice of Carpaccio, and I see it in the internal light, in the wood, and it reminds me of certain Dutch interiors which call to mind boats and are near the sea.'[37]

Against the backdrop of this analogous city par excellence, Venice, the floating theatre may offer an unlimited number of analogies: its tower, for instance, could be a minaret, or one of the spires of the Kremlin. Moreover, the form of the theatre is one that has cropped up on several occasions in the career of Aldo Rossi. The primitive stage of the theatre is based on a memory from his childhood: the puppet theatre in Bergamo, in the summer. Rossi's passion for the theatre is rooted in his fascination with time and its mystery: 'For certainly the time in the theatre does not coincide with time measured by clocks; nor are emotions bound to chronological time; they are repeated on stage every evening with impressive punctuality and exactitude.'[38] Theatres induce the charm of repetition of identical movements broken by an unexpected action. The theatre is the structure that best expresses the link between architecture and human events.

Aldo Rossi often speaks of Raymond Roussel, of his *Théâtre des incom-parables*, where 'the theatre is surrounded by an imposing capital city formed of innumerable huts'.[39] The hut is a simple, primordial and essential model in Rossi's imagery, imbued with the memory of holidays, like the cabins on the island of Elba, which turn up several times in his drawings. On the outside the floating theatre of Venice resembles them. But it also resembles another model dear to the Italian architect, the lighthouses of New England and Maine in particular, the land of Melville – pensive forms, between land and sea, between sky and rock, between beginning and end. The exterior of the Biennale theatre derives from the contamination of all these forms, while the interior derives from the study of the Anatomical Theatre in Padua (1594), which had already provided the inspiration for a drawing crammed with self-citation, the *Teatrino scientifico*.

The interior and the exterior 'are also part of the meaning of the theatre' and 'the beauty resides in the place where the subject encoun-ters different meanings'. Nothing can be beautiful 'if it only signifies itself, only signifies its use'. What is beautiful today is the 'contamina-tion' of various elements, the superimposition of different images and impression imprinted in the artist's memory, since, as Rossi writes: 'The emergence of relations among things, more than the things them-selves, always give raise to new meanings.'[40] And so, in connection with his Venetian theatre, Aldo Rossi returns to his rejection of the idea of function and use: architecture is symbolic and profoundly poetic. Thus Venice, city of stone, and the floating theatre, immense ephemeral form, invite one to forget architecture, to grasp the beauty of the Adriatic sea that Rossi loves so much, of the 'seashell, daughter of stone and the whitening sea', as the poet Alcaeus wrote, quoted by Rossi.[41] Venice with its Rossian theatre invites us to rediscover, by for-getting, the wonder of architecture, its astonishment, as if seen through a child's eyes: 'Astonishment has a hard crust made of stone and shaped by the sea, like the crust of the great constructions of steel, stone, and cement which form the city.'[42]

6
Massimo Cacciari and the Philosophy of the City

> Ne suis-je pas un faux accord
> Dans la divine symphonie,
> Grâce à la vorace Ironie
> Qui me secoue et qui me mord?
>
> (Am I not a discordant note
> In the divine symphony,
> Thanks to the voracious Irony
> Which shakes me up and bites into me?)
>   Baudelaire, 'L'Héautontimorouménos',
>   from *Les Fleurs du Mal*

Venice's spleen

Venice, June 1973: the city was overrun by the national Festival dell'Unità, the yearly festivities of the PCI, the Italian Communist Party.[1] Venice itself was transformed: in every *campo* (square) there were red flags, bookstalls, public speeches, food, wine, music, songs, *compagni* (comrades) from everywhere, Italy and abroad, of every age, every social class. One could hear a lot of discussion, a mixture of voices and accents from various regions of Italy, with different local political experiences and also different political lines, following the tendency of a given Federazione, or even Sezione (the hierarchical organizations of the Communist Party, active at the level of the nation, region, city, town, suburb). In the city there was a sense of feast, the pleasure of the crowd, of community life, of the *polis*, of political debates. Venice was ours; it was the 'red city' for a few days, in spite of the Christian Democratic tradition of the Veneto, the most 'white' region of Italy. Maybe the

Revolution – a word used in those years, not yet bereft of its sound and meaning – is like a great Festival dell'Unità in an unreal city like Venice, a huge coming together, a vast Communist International, workers and intellectuals together, as if there were no gap. We were all there at the culminating moment of the Festival, when the General Secretary of the Communist Party, Enrico Berlinguer, spoke. It was impossible not to be moved by the city, the sense of a large community of people from everywhere with a similar political vision, the buildings, the sky, the water, the noise, and then that silence when Berlinguer, who died 11 years later addressing the crowd in a square in Padua, started his speech:

It is the first time that a national festival of the *Unità* takes place in Venice and in the Veneto region. The choice of Venice is a good one, because in this city – unique in the world – the activity and initiative of comrades, friends, workers made the festival a mass event. It represented a new and unusual experience for the city, for all Venetians, as well as for our Party. The Venetian people responded enthusiastically to the Party's initiative proving how fake is the conception of those who believe that only a small elite can enjoy culture, art and science, and would like to give to the people nothing but a vulgar and commercialized under-culture.

It is not by chance that the will to make culture belong to all people is coming from a Party like ours. We want the working class to inherit the entire progressive, beautiful, true things that mankind created in its secular path. We want the working class to embody the new universal values that will renovate social and economic life, the relation between people and classes, as well as the science, art and culture of the whole world.[2]

We students and intellectuals of Venice's Sezione Universitaria, listening to that redemptive, humanistic language, felt as Stendhal did in a church, not believing but being deeply moved by the ritual of the Mass. We were thrilled by the crowd, the city and the event, but, obviously, could not believe in those sentimental words about progress, universal new values, new relations among classes. We knew Massimo Cacciari's lesson, as he writes it in 'The Dialectics of the Negative and the Metropolis',[3] the first essay in *Architecture and Nihilism: On the Philosophy of Modern Architecture*: 'In a Metropolitan situation, the revolutionary process itself is totally intellectual... The geometric clarity with which, in the final analysis, class interest is posited, eliminates all possible teleological or ethico-sentimental synthesis.'[4]

To deny the metropolitan situation – we knew it by heart – means to believe in the conservative nostalgia of a better, more natural human life, or in the progressive utopia of a realized good society. To eschew the Metropolis, as Cacciari says, inevitably means to propose a backward attitude: 'And therefore any discourse of the city in itself necessarily becomes at this point reactionary.'[5] We were nevertheless aware that the public square where Berlinguer spoke to the masses was not our group at the Sezione universitaria nor Tafuri's seminar at the Istituto di storia dell'architettura. But we were especially aware that behind Berlinguer's celebration of Venice and the Party there was a political project that would eliminate any Stalinist mentality: he had been secretary since 1972 and, when he was vice-secretary, at the 24th Congress of the Soviet Communist Party in Moscow, he had already stated that every communist party had the right to follow an autonomous line dictated by the specific conditions of every country. He was opening the way within the left to a different understanding of politics and alliances.

A few months after Venice's Festival dell'Unità, Berlinguer proposed to the country the *compromesso storico* (historical compromise) – a new relation of collaboration between the Italian left and centre, and a Communist Party for all of Europe. Berlinguer obviously disturbed many of the old generation in the PCI who were attached to a centralized party structure; at the same time he disgusted the revolutionary purists so typical of the extreme left in those years after 1968, who so virulently opposed any institutional structure. But, together with the clear tendency towards social-democratic positions, a new wind was blowing within the Italian Communist Party, an organization that traditionally represented the working-class voice, constituted a large opposition presence within the Italian Parliament, and was always much more that a simple electoral machine: an institution really connected to the mass movement of workers. This made possible for Cacciari to join the Party. He was coming from an extreme left *operaista* experience (*operaista* meaning supporter of the doctrine that power should be given to the workers), and his collaboration with the review *Contropiano* marked his move in the direction of the party. *Contropiano* was started in 1968; its title was clearly indicative of its stand against capitalist planning (from economic to urban planning), and opened with Antonio Negri's article on Keynes and capitalist state theory in 1929, followed by Mario Tronti's study on the changes in the content of working-class struggles at the international level from the thirties to the sixties.[6] The first issue of *Contropiano* listed three editors:

Antonio Negri, from Padua, who was the leader of the group *Potere Operaio*, Alberto Asor Rosa, from Rome, who was a member of the PCI and had always been committed to an *operaista* direction within the party,[7] and Cacciari, from Venice. Cacciari had been active in the factory agitations and other working-class fights since 1968, during important years in Italian politics when new working contracts were negotiated among trade unions, government, and the employers of the largest Italian factories and corporations. Fiat in Turin and Pirelli near Milan, as well as the huge industrial area next to Venice, Mestre and Porto Marghera (with its chemical plants of Montedison and thousands of workers),[8] had been one of the centres of the fight between the working class and capital – as one said at that time in 'straightforward' Marxist language.

Cacciari's theory of the metropolis reflects on problems of organization, from work and revolution to services and industrial growth, to state and institutions. The militant practice in the factory necessarily confronts questions of organization. Cacciari, together with others writing in *Contropiano*, had given much thought to the question of the relationship between the workers' struggles and an institution like the PCI, even when he was politically active outside the party and sometimes strongly critical. The debate over the PCI and the *entrista* position (which favoured joining the party in spite of disagreements with its main tenet) brought about the schism with Negri, who reinforced the *operaista*, interventionist and anti-state position. Negri's article on Marx, in the second issue of *Contropiano*, was his last as he left the helm of the journal, which continued under Asor Rosa and Cacciari through 1971. That crucial second issue of 1968 began with an eloquent editorial stressing the complex class situation and the necessity 'to get rid of an excessively unilateral vision of theoretical and political work'.[9] This editorial insisted on the balance between theory and action, but nevertheless considered the reflexive component as indispensable 'before' experience or political action: 'We will continue to think that the working-class slant on capitalist society implies, if correctly formulated, a clear and totally demystified description of the object to be known and a similarly clear indication to transform that knowledge into action.'[10] Knowledge and action – or theory and practice – were perceived as equally important, but the stress on the priority of knowledge, description and analysis of phenomena implied the criticism of an agitation for its own sake. This criticism, particularly important coming from *operaisti* activists, shows a certain faith in institutional forms and implies the recognition that the modern and contemporary world is made of abstraction: the process of intellectualization, under-standing and rationalization presides over all activities from economics to politics to law to everyday life, as in the metropolitan situation where institutions, the circulation of money, and the transformation of any material reality into figures shape experience itself.

The question of how to relate mass movements to institutions and institutions to mass movements was important to *Contropiano*'s political exploration, at a time in Italy when the line between action and terror-ism was to become tragically blurred. Nevertheless, Cacciari did not romanticize the Party and its role, as he had clearly pinpointed in public speeches, meetings and writings that there are phases and crises in the relation between party and class movements. In *Ciclo capitalistico e lotte operaie: Montedison Pirelli Fiat 1968*, he saw a radical change since 1960: the workers began to form an essential avant-garde who contested the traditional role of the party at the moment it was losing control of the class movement and seemed incapable of organizing the workers' struggles.[11] Cacciari wrote extensively on the workers' movement in the sixties, and, already in that second 1968 issue of *Contropiano*, previously mentioned, in a review article on May 1968 in France, he spoke of the difference between the situation in Italy and that in France, where the students' movement had been attacked by the official communist news-paper, *L'Humanité*, and by the communist trade union, the CGT. Both were stuck in an old position, a frozen institution, incapable of making the vital link between movements and party. Cacciari focused on the strength of the Italian workers' movements as indispensable in deter-mining the interactions among the working class, Party, and trade unions. He also stressed the role of the 'political mediation that the party expresses at the institutional level'.[12] Cacciari voiced his suspicion for immediacy of any spontaneous agitation without organized struc-tures, and his belief that the intervention of the party can be larger and stronger than that of any group. The overture toward the Italian Communist Party was clear; at the same time, within the Party, there was openness to social forces and people capable of renewing the Party itself.[13] After the first issues of *Contropiano* appeared, Cacciari joined the PCI, where the Berlinguer's line would blow the dust off an old way of understanding politics.

As we stood there, at the Festival dell'Unità, we had neither populist dreams of an idyllic society nor any illusion about a subversive culture, or a subversive use of culture. We were convinced that art and culture have 'an inevitable bourgeois nature', as Alberto Asor Rosa writes in a 1968 article on Trockij and Majakovskij, where he attacked the literary

Stalinism of the first Congress of Soviet Writers (1934) as founded on the utopia of the coincidence between the intellectual and the revolutionary. He was aiming at that whole myth constantly present in the avant-garde attitude:

> In our opinion, the use of art and literature as instruments to communicate the political discourse should be completely rejected ... Socialism has never been necessary to make good literature. Writers will not be necessary to make revolution. Class struggle, if it is real class struggle and not just populist protest, peasant agitation, sentimental admiration for masses' virgin strength, does not need to take the road of this illusion. Class struggle has other voices to express itself, to make itself be understood. And poetry cannot keep track of it, because poetry, great poetry speaks a language where *things* – the hard things of everyday strife and fatigue – have already taken the value of a symbol, of a gigantic metaphor of the world. The often tragic price of poetry, the price of its greatness is that what it says is not practice, nor will ever get back to it.[14]

We were suspended between the heart and the brain, feeling and intellect, the inevitable emotion of the great ethico-sentimental synthesis sketched in Berlinguer's speech, and scorn for that community illusion, conscious as we were that there is no other reality than the tough, tragic 'geometrical clarity' of the metropolis, with its endless social and political tensions. We had no choice other than intellect, or *Verstand*: we had *negative thought* in our veins.

In order to understand the concept of negative thought, so essential to achieve the architecture of fulfilled nihilism Cacciari talks about in the epilogue of *Architecture and Nihilism*, it is necessary to keep in mind that the essays in this book offer an overall view of Cacciari's trajectory, from the late sixties to the beginning of the eighties, from his Marxian-oriented investigation on the German urban sociologists of the beginning of the twentieth century to his metaphysical inquiry into some aporias in the work of the Viennese architect Adolf Loos. It is necessary then to reconstruct Cacciari's network of references. I would say that this configuration operates in a whirling movement, where synchronic and diachronic elements of various order clash, in an disorderly order, as in a theatre, where the actor's voice, the physical presence of people and objects, the setting of the scene, the visible and invisible work make everything come together. There is no linear history; and, probably, intellectual history should be conceived like a choreography constructed by the intellectual historian who makes practical choices to sketch the puzzle that is historical analysis.

Cacciari's choreography is formed by the political experience of the working-class movements and the Communist Party; by the passage from an avant-garde position to militancy in a large party institution; by the four years of intense work for *Contropiano*, equally devoted to class analysis and what would today be called cultural criticism or cultural studies; by the interdisciplinary and radical setting of Venice's Istituto di Storia, directed by Manfredo Tafuri since 1968 and committed to a Marxian critique of ideology and of the ideology of architecture. In this complex choreography made of various people and institutions – a party, a school, a journal – at least two names are indispensable: Alberto Asor Rosa, whom I have already cited, and Manfredo Tafuri, whose importance will be stressed below. Then, of course, there is Venice, the city and its inland, with its Porto Marghera, whose chimneys one can see from the Giudecca Canal, as in a De Chirico painting where the desolate and dark towers of a warehouse or a factory are juxtaposed with the ancient columns of a white, classical square. One can also think of that beautiful photograph of Aldo Rossi's floating theatre built for the 1979–80 Venice Biennale: the theatre seems almost attached to the Punta della Dogana, to the Salute Church, moving in the water between the Giudecca and the Grand Canal; its roof points to the line of ancient palaces followed by one row of wrecking cranes and then another of industrial chimneys fading away in the sky.[15]

This juxtaposition of Palladio's churches and Marghera's factories suggests why one of the most sophisticated and difficult theories of the metropolis came from the city that seems most untouched by the contemporary world. It is as if in Venice one finds the reaction against its mellow and touristic image, an elaboration of a philosophy that fuses together political militancy, Adolf Loos's hatred for ornament, Baudelaire's vision of Paris, George Simmel's 'nervous life', and Walter Benjamin's understanding of anguish and shock as the basis of modern experience. Maybe the contrast between the city in the Adriatic lagoon and the industrial setting is so visible, so violent in the Venetian skyline that the philosopher or the cultural critic can forge exactly from this contrast the difference between city and metropolis, together with the ideological construction that hides, in the very heart of the modern mode of production and life, the metropolitan reality, while fabricating the illusion of a city with human relationships. Venice, small and ancient as it is, with no cars, apparently so ideal a refuge from the hustle and bustle of today's world, allows a powerful intuition of modernity. Venice overcomes its physical dimension and becomes larger than Paris, London, or New York; it becomes an allegory, as the buildings of Paris did for Baudelaire in 'Le Cygne', the famous metropolitan poem which I have already referred to, that is a splendid commentary on the great works of urban renovation in the second half of the nineteenth century:

> Paris changes! but nothing changed in my melancholy!
> New buildings, scaffoldings, blocks,
> Old suburbs, everything to me becomes allegory.[16]

Real allegory

The term 'Metropolis' is an abstraction, an allegory, as Cacciari suggests by using the capital letter. Today, we would say that the metropolis is an impersonal agent. Negative thought, or the negative or negativity, should be synonymous with metropolis, if the metropolis is correctly understood in its total impersonal reality and in its power of abstraction. Cacciari's philosophy of the metropolis should not be interpreted in simple realistic terms. Of course, behind it there is the concrete experience of Porto Marghera's fights in the late sixties and early seventies, but in the texts collected in *Architecture and Nihilism*, Cacciari is not speaking of a specific city with precise chronology and statistical data, even if Paris, the capital of the nineteenth century, and the German *Werkbund* and Vienna at the beginning of the twentieth century constitute clear references. Cacciari grasps, through the concept of the metropolis, the German urban sociology of Weber, Simmel and Benjamin, the nihilistic architecture of Adolf Loos, the real allegory of the modern (as in *L'Atelier du peintre: Allégorie réelle*, the title of Courbet's famous painting that questions the status of pictorial representation itself). Cacciari stresses the modern condition of a crisis that is and should be completely assumed as the inevitable foundation of life, experience, subjectivity itself. His work is not historical research. His work is strictly interpretative: interpretation of interpretations, illuminations and sparks that provoke a sort of general understanding of abstractions or give keys to further readings of important moments in the making of our modernity.

The metropolis is the reality and the metaphor of the modern world, and also our contemporary world as Cacciari defines it: 'the general form assumed by the process of the rationalization of social relations', following the 'rationalization of the relations of production'.[17] The metropolis implies traffic, factories, services, commercial life, market economy, offices, administrative institutions, the state, political organization, crowds, social tensions, the constant law of the circulation of money. The metropolis in a nineteenth-century world constitutes the opposite of nature, the country, the village, the suburb. But some metropolitan features were already typical of the European Medieval city, studied by Max Weber, at the moment it forsook tribal life. The metropolis shows the impossibility of synthesis, of the city as synthesis where conflicts disappear or are hidden or preventively repressed, as Cacciari states in 'Loos and His Contemporaries' (the second part of *Architecture and Nihilism*). The metropolis defeats any community mentality: the conservative or regressive attitudes, from family life to the image of people coming back from work to 'cultivate their kitchen-gardens', as well as the progressive ones, from the image of technological comfort and individual freedom to the dream of mass liberation and to the vision of Venice as unique city in the world. Any progressive attitude becomes backward because, in spite of its futuristic glamour, it dreams of old types of relationships among people.

Cacciari's militant experience in the factory could not but help his formulation of the political problem of the metropolis as capitalistic system and site of social conflict. The factory experience would offer ground for reflection within a review whose aim was to present 'Marxist materials'. *Contropiano* was committed to political and theoretical rigor in 'an epoch of deep change', as the political situation of western Europe's working class was transformed by 'the breaking off of the Soviet system and the global return of the European working class to the revolutionary front'.[18] (This was written more than 30 years ago.) In that rich, exalting, 'multiple and contradictory class situation' that 'manifested itself at several levels', the review stressed its working-class point of view, while 'facing an extremely vast gamut of interests',[19] providing therefore a thorough critique of ideology from economics, to working-class history, architecture, urban planning, literature, film and philosophy. *Contropiano* insisted on its negative role, centred on the destruction of bourgeois culture yet refusing the illusion of constructing a working-class culture; in the political language of the time, when we spoke of the 'bourgeoisie' and 'working class', the editors of the review refused to be hampered by 'any exclusive discourse' and planned to offer various hypotheses and themes of research.[20]

In those exhilarating years of political confrontation and intellectual creativity, there was no fundamental discrepancy then between Cacciari's article 'Porto Marghera's Montecatini-Edison' and an essay on 'The Genesis of Negative Thought'[21] (whose Nietzschean insight is close to 'The Dialectics of the Negative and the Metropolis'). There was no contradiction between Asor Rosa's readings of Lukács or of Thomas Mann, and the militant political and economical articles on the trade union, the Party, the salary contracts, and the class composition. One could continue the list, showing that it was part of the same intellectual battle to publish Mario Tronti's essays on the working class, on extremism and reformism, Antonio Negri's study on John M. Keynes, and Manfredo Tafuri's reading of Weimar and of Vienna socialist urban planning from 1920 to 1933.

Cacciari's philosophy of the city – or of the metropolis – was the logical continuation of his political activity, in the double practice of militancy and intellectual research. Asor Rosa had put it in his cutting *operaista* tone, which would be a perfect antidote against what I would call the *campus* illusion of cultural studies in the United States: the idea that an academic community is politically radical because leftists fight to introduce new fields of study and new contents in the curriculum. In the 1966 preface to the second edition of *Scrittori e popolo*, Asor Rosa clarified his position:

> We were saying that the elimination of cultural battle meant for us the full assumption of the political discourse of class ... To practice cultural analysis ... is impossible – *doesn't have any sense* – if one is not capable of fully carrying on the political work that the situation demands. We do not simply allude to the plurality of levels that a serious movement must keep present all at once: but, in a very direct and elementary way, we speak even of the physical simultaneity of the two levels [of political work and cultural analysis] in the persons themselves of the comrades-researchers.[22]

The plurality of levels or doubleness in physical terms, even beyond the level of political militancy, is an almost necessary condition of modern life, of modern subjectivity. Cacciari suggests in the epilogue of *Architecture and Nihilism* that the 'inconsistencies and conflicts' between the seventies essays and his later work on Loos (1981) are not as strong as they might seem at first and represent a development into his inquiry of nihilism. I would say that they are coherent parts of an intellectual movement centred on a plurality of levels and on a continuous acknowledgement of contradiction or breaking off. Cacciari is even more double or multiple or inhabited by differences than any of the well-known gurus of the late twentieth century: for almost three

decades he has been a professor in Tafuri's Department of Historical
and Critical Analysis (previously the Istituto di Storia dell'Architettura),
an intellectual and a public political figure, back and forth from the
local to the national levels.

First, as said before, an activist in the factory at the time of the
operaisti movements, later a well-known Communist deputy in the
Italian Parliament (from 1979 to 1984), then briefly within the PDS
(Democratic Party of the Left), after the secretary, Ochetto, gave a new
direction of what was the PCI until a few years ago, Cacciari was in
1992 an independent on the left (he created the group 'Il Ponte', the
bridge) and is essential to the political life of Venice: he nearly become
mayor in 1990 and is a member of the City Council. Further, he has
been major of Venice from 1993 until 1998. But in order to grasp the
multifaceted mind of Cacciari, it would be enough to focus on the different layers of his writings. Beside the richness of his references coming
from various disciplines – from literature to economics – the most
evident scandal is his move from his early works to his later ones. Up to
Krisis (1976) his research can be defined in the terms of his commitment to Marxist analysis. From *Icone della Legge* (1985) to his third
revised edition (1992) of *L'Angelo necessario*,[23] Cacciari pursues a theological investigation, studying ancient Greek, Christian and Jewish texts
as well as the mystical component of Benjamin, Rilke and Heidegger.
But if one considers how important Benjamin has always been for
Cacciari, there is no scandal then, not even a conversion, because mysticism and Marxism are the two halves of Benjamin's work. There is
rather what might be called a conversation, the constant dialogue that
one work has with another, regardless of time and location.

Conversations

To insist on the theory of the metropolis is for Cacciari the full, almost
physical awareness of the fact that cultural analysis cannot eschew political work. To insist on the metropolis means to grasp, via the urban theme
so important in Benjamin, the most basic Marxist touchstones: the
factory, capital, the cycle of money and goods, state organization as the
foundation of political economy. As Benjamin understands it, there is
continuity from factory work to metropolitan life. He compares the uniformity Edgar Allan Poe saw in the attire, behaviour and facial expressions of the metropolitan crowd in 'The Man of the Crowd' to the
uniformity Marx saw in industrial labour, where in the assembly line the
workers have to move like automatons.[24] The metropolis, Cacciari insists,

is a system: 'a multi-articulated urban type – a comprehensive service … a qualified organization of the labor force, a scientific reserve-supply for industrial growth, a financial structure, a market, and the all-inclusive center of political power.'[25] The metropolis implies the physical space of the big city as well as the network of ideological constructions of different kinds around it, embodies both the awareness of urban proletariat and the abstract dimension of work: the reality of the factory and the sophisticated cycle of the circulation of money.

The theory of the metropolis, combined with the militant practice in the factory at the time when Italy encountered its own industrial revolution through workers' struggles, confronts the devouring strength of advanced capital that is capable of restructuring itself on its own crisis, the conflicts antagonizing it. The Cacciarian theory perceives crisis as fundamental to capitalist development; then the point becomes, in strictly militant terms, how to use it, how to make the crisis functional to the working class and not to the capital. For the sake of cultural analysis it is worthwhile identifying tendencies and formulating, as suggested by *Contropiano*'s editorial in 1968, 'a clear and totally demystified description of the object to be known'. In this way Cacciari perceived negative thought and its dialectics, or a negative thought in motion.

In his 1969 essay 'On the Genesis of Negative Thought', Cacciari analysed Schopenhauer, Kirkegaard and Nietzsche as the thinkers of negative thought. Their critical reading of Hegel marked the beginning 'of a rigorous systematization of an anti-dialectical thought'.[26] Cacciari opposes dialectics and negative thought. Dialectics are historically positive, operate in a logical and temporal order, synthesize everything, even what appears as 'eccentric', unfamiliar 'to the structure, needs and purposes of that order'.[27] Cacciari states that, in contrast to this positive side of dialectics, he calls 'negative' that mode of thought that rejects the dialectical synthesis and tries to determine as central what is eccentric, what is crisis. The philosophical analysis encompasses ideological awareness, as Cacciari continues: 'There is no doubt that the opposition [of what he defines, that is, negative thought] to dialectics *means* the criticism of the ideological and social structure of the bourgeois system, as well as the refusal to be integrated positively and actively in its process of rationalization.'[28] At this point there is a switch that is not a reversal but what can be called a leap, or better a trembling. The trembling of negative thought makes it the most refined engine of the development of the system it wants to reject. Negative thought becomes functional in the system exactly because it is capable of interrogating all the non-functional – today we would say 'marginal' – elements that cannot be synthetically absorbed into the system itself. Cacciari leaps to the extreme consequence: 'Precisely because of its negativity, of its obstinate radical refusal of bourgeois system and ideology, the anti-dialectic thought can present itself as ideological *function* of this same system.'[29]

Cacciari, in his philosophical investigation, was echoing Antonio Negri's inquiry on economy and law. In the first issue of *Contropiano*, Negri launched his reading of 1929 and Keynes:

> [The year] 1929 represents a moment of exceptional importance ... 1929 sweeps away even the nostalgia for those values that 1917 destroyed. In the black Thursday of Wall Street, in the catastrophic falling down of the Stock Exchange, are rightly falling the state myths, the political myths of a century of renewed bourgeois hegemony on the working class ... It is the end of *laissez-faire* ... The beginning of a new period in the history of the contemporary state is marked by the fact that, in this already socialized world, the recognition of the emergency of the working class – and of the ineliminable character of this antagonism – can no longer be denied... . The capitalist reconstruction of the state is conceived on the discovery of the radical antagonism of the working class.[30]

But in addition to this conversation with Negri's analysis, Cacciari was actually pinpointing, in what I called the trembling of negative thought, the tragedy of any radical thought, from the political radicals like Marx, obsessed by the fact that he had to use the language of capitalism, to the poetic or aesthetic radicals like Baudelaire who knew the devouring shocks of irony.

Cacciari's interpretation of the German urban sociologists in *Architecture and Nihilismus* continues that of Schopenhauer, Kirkegaard and Nietzsche in his early essay on negative thought. Both Simmel and Benjamin reached the negativity of the metropolis, but at a different level and with different implications.

According to Cacciari, Simmel grasped the metropolitan 'nervous life', that disagregation of subjectivity typical of the modern. He pictured the violence of the process of intellectualization that determines every gesture in the metropolitan reality. But Simmel could not stand up to the most radical consequences of what he himself perceived: at the very limit of modern tragedy he found signs of the freedom and development of humankind. He found the individual, and not the capitalist machine that grinds away all possible human conditions, all possible synthesis.

Therefore Simmel operated an ideological construction, where the metropolis ended up being human, like the community, the city, as in the past. Close to Simmel is Lukács, reader of Simmel. Lukács perceived the impressionistic character of the German sociologist, but missed his negative thought on the question of tragedy. Lukács understood tragedy as the full form of essence. But there is no essence in the negative thought, only leaps and points of breaking off. Benjamin extends this insight, to reveal the radical negativity of the metropolis. Together with Benjamin, Nietzsche appears as the one who did not return to nostalgic positions of synthesis and fully understood the inevitability of tragedy with no hope of consolation.

Cacciari is actually interested by two positions that can be called the almost negative one and the fully negative; or the utopian and the tragic; or the synthetic and the radical; or one oriented toward historical continuity and one embracing crisis as the engine of changes that defy programmatic prediction. Nevertheless, the failure of prediction should not be interpreted as the praise of irrational forces. Cacciari is suspicious of immediacy even in political fights, and, as a thinker interested in a critique of ideology, he rejects as ideological construction any irrationalist interpretation even of the Romantic period – of Novalis and Schlegel – that precedes what he calls negative thought.[31] No rhyzomes, no philosophy of *imagination au pouvoir* (imagination in power) in the Italian theory of the metropolis.[32]

The reader should then be aware that there are two types of rationality or rationalizations: one positive, hopeful, sunny, even if in contact with modern negativity, and the other one dark, with no hopes, no nostalgia, no projects, but endlessly at work as a process of rationalization, integrating the failure of reason into its total rationalization. As Cacciari will phrase it in his 1980 *Opposition* article, 'Eupalinos or Architecture': 'The uprooted spirit of the Metropolis is not "sterile" but productive par excellence.'[33]

Many *rapprochements* are possible, connecting the theory of the metropolis to other important European trends of the sixties and the seventies, fashionable in the US since the eighties. One could disregard what I would call more internal discrepancies, and, in a sort of quick survey of the most important theories of the second half of the twentieth century, see the proximity of Cacciari's philosophy with Jacques Derrida's, as if Cacciari constructed a deconstructionist thought not on language but on the allegory of the metropolis. The Derridian input is justified both by the emphasis given by Cacciari to difference, and by the fact that Cacciari was introduced to Derrida's work by his aesthetics professor at the University of Padua, Dino Formaggio. One could also see, in spite of the Cacciari's short critical note against Jacques Lacan, some affinity with the Lacanian psychoanalytical nihilism, since his unconscious is at work exactly where the *cogito* fails. All these are theories of reason below degree zero, where the old reassuring rationality is broken, and negativity colours everything with its dark hue. But there is no alternative, no hymn towards irrational forces finally liberated after the oppression. Such is the harsh law of negative thought.

The various authors mentioned by Cacciari would finally enter either in the position of the quasi-negative or in that of the fully negative thought. But Cacciari's ability – and sophistic touch – relies in that he is constantly juggling with that unbalanced point where one position drastically changes into the other. The readers follow for several pages Simmel as an example of negative thought, while Cacciari gives a voice to his negative thought; at the same time they hear another voice combined with Simmel's – Cacciari's voice – and they are already warned by a few sentences here and there that the German sociologist will not finally get to the fullness of the negative. When the reader finally gets to Benjamin and Nietzsche, he or she is brought back to the almost negative position by the rich debate within the *Werkbund*, by the reading of Goethe, by the critique of Lukács, reader of Simmel.

Cacciari's philosophy of the metropolis offers an insight to all those who believe that architecture is more than constructing a building, a complex act condensing visible and invisible political and ideological implications, aesthetic and moral choices. Cacciari does not help those who want to get more detailed information about Vienna or the German *Werkbund* or Loos or Benjamin, although he offers a daring interpretation of all these figures and movements, sketching what Pierre Bourdieu would call an intellectual field where various agents take up various positions.[34] In Cacciari's lectures and essays there always resounds a tone that does not come from the quiet of the classroom nor the peace of the library. Sure, one can find the obscurantism and the love for abstract terms typical of the philosophy of the Kantian and Hegelian tradition (of Continental philosophy), but this style shows also the power of a cutting word or a condensed sentence that needs to reach a conclusion when agreement is urgent to come to a decision, to conclude a final negotiation.

Cacciari's style does not have the political illusion of the avant-garde: changing the world through language, or feeling different, radical because a few oppositional stereotypes are combined with an approved set of references and quotations. His language is broken by the practice of political activism in the real world, and shows the existence of an untenable contradiction: the fact that there is a cultivated, preposterous language for professors and that there are words burning with action, loaded with work and rage, and nevertheless controlled, intellectual in their formulation. Cacciari's words aim at a political effect, a cold reason overcoming the simplistic opposition of victory and defeat, while continuing a precarious balance, veering to identify the right targets. Cacciari's rhetoric, perhaps even more brutal in English, does not obey to the rules of radiant clarity and soft persuasion of the ancient *polis*. His style recaptures the spoken word in the metropolis where there is no warmth for passions nor peace for reflection, but the anxiety to master reality, failing which one is overwhelmed by the traffic, the crowd, the unexpected event. In the metropolis, unlike the *polis*, meetings do not take place in a reassuring public space, but in a hall next to the noise of the assembly line, to the acid smell of chemical products. The rhythm of metropolitan life and metropolitan relations is embodied in Cacciari's language, in the spasms of allusions, ellipses, endless inverted commas and italics, harsh German philosophical terms thrown every two lines without translation as if they were provocatorily breaking the classical musicality of Italian vowels. This language, continuously chopped in short sentences obsessively constructed on the third person singular of the verb *to be*, is disturbing, non-harmonious, violent; it carries the trace of the harshness of metropolitan life, what Baudelaire called:

> ... the hour when, under the cold and clear skies,
> Work is waking up, when works in the streets
> Scream like a dark tornado in the silent atmosphere.[35]

The reader should hear in Cacciari's difficult, nervous, broken, repetitive style the echo of discussions in moments of struggle, the raising of the voice when the contractual tension comes to a crucial point; the sharpness of a political assurance that corners those who think differently and are not as quick as the speaker; the pauses to let other people talk, while the speaker is nevertheless thinking about his next intervention in that effort of listening and at the same time mentally organizing his own reply; the hammering of a conviction that must become evident and effective in lobbying. In the fights in factories, where a minute is money for both workers and capitalists, there is no time for demagogic effects nor for the seduction of great humanitarian visions. Even political rage has to be controlled, intellectual: it aims for the metallic clarity of figures. Everything has the dryness of a contract, the cruel logic of a negotiation under pressure, in a confrontational peak, where no passion is allowed because it would create confusion. The Italian *autunno caldo* (warm fall) of 1969, the period of violent strikes that led to new agreements between workers and capital, left its indelible imprint in Cacciari's style. That imprint will stay forever, also in his later books, even if they seem so far away from the preoccupations of the sixties and the seventies.

Architectural theory against the historiographical tradition

Cacciari devoted a section of 'The Dialectics of the Negative and the Metropolis' to artistic representation, clearly leading to Loos's architecture of nihilism. Against any irrationalist illusion of redemption by art,[36] of an art that would finally save the world by proposing a different use of itself or new content, Cacciari identifies the tragic dimension of some artistic languages that do not try to eschew the negativity of the metropolis. Poe, Baudelaire, Kafka and Nietzsche speak the language of contradiction, displaying all the signs of alienation, dismissing any hope in any possible alternative. This is the true nihilistic position, that also frames Loos's architecture, as Cacciari writes in 'Loos and His Contemporaries' (the second essay in *Architecture and Nihilism*): 'All anti-expressive, anti-synthetical, anti-natural composition is nihilistic.'[37] The repetition and calculation of Poe's short stories recalls that of Loos's architectural exteriors: they mimic the standardized production of the metropolis and are 'pure use value – as in the "rail-car" of the Stein house (1910) and the house at Northartgasse (1913)'.[38] That artistic choice is searching for neither salvation nor consolation nor escape: the great, tragic forms of the artists mentioned by Cacciari can do nothing but be analogous with the negativity of the metropolis. They obsessively describe, present the hard lines of alienation, in the most literal sense of the term, *alius*, other, always different, never coincident with anything, never reconciled with a supposed origin or nature.[39]

Poe, Baudelaire and Kafka are also some of the writers on whom Benjamin concentrated in constructing his reading of the effects of metropolitan life on human perception and everyday life.[40] The line from Poe to Benjamin constitutes a crucial trajectory for any radical thought. All the texts by Cacciari collected here are contained within a reading of Benjamin; it could be said, using a term so important in 'Loos and his Angel' (the third essay in *Architecture and Nihilism*), that they are commentaries on various passages from Benjamin. They are comment and not criticism, since the aim is not to explain Benjamin but to follow the associations inspired by his texts, or fragments and images coming from his texts.

There is a modern Italian trend in the twentieth century that caught and even enhanced the European dimension of urbanization and metropolitan life: Giorgio De Chirico's metaphysical cities and squares; Mario Sironi's urban industrial landscape; Alberto Savinio's enigmatic irony; the architect Sant'Elia's buildings that seem to belong to a science-fiction film; Italo Svevo's novels where the tormented inhabitant of Trieste lives all the contradictions of the modern. The list could continue, stressing Italo Calvino's mathematical literature, forged by the logic of metropolitan life. It would impossible to leave aside the feeling of harsh metropolitan emptiness and uprootedness that derives from Aldo Rossi's Fontana di Segrate, or from many of his sketches where all natural dimensions are perverted, where a coffee-pot is as big as a building. Or one can think of the totally unnatural, stony scenarios of Massimo Scolari's paintings.

This important Italian anti-organic, metropolitan tendency fiercely opposes the construction of a little Italy(!), a *Strapaese*[41] totally immersed in village life, peasant, petit-bourgeois reality, pathological provincialism. The peasant type of Italy is imbued with a populist ethos that has a nineteenth-century origin, when Italy had a huge historical delay in its economic and political development compared to England and France. The peasant type is also the image of an agrarian Italy that corresponded to the fascist economic plan, the populist vein of fascism as well as a left-wing populism attached to the image of the national-popular. In his complex reading of Antonio Gramsci in *Scrittori e popolo*, Asor Rosa pin-pointed the paternalistic position of Gramsci, who himself insisted that the new literature cannot but be historical, political and popular:

> It must tend to elaborate what is already existing, polemically or in whatever other way; what really matters is that it should be rooted in the *humus* (earth) of popular culture, as it is, with its taste and inclinations, etc., with its moral and intellectual world, even if it is backward and conventional.[42]

The debate on Italian populism, on its conservative and progressive forms, is extremely complicated, and offers an interesting case for some crucial questions in cultural analysis, such as national identity, canon, popular culture. Asor Rosa often suggests venturing 'in a very delicate but tantalizing area of experimentation', that would question the substance itself of the Gramscian vision.[43] Any Italian radical enterprise cannot but oppose the myth of origins, roots, countryside, nature. It must reject the motif of the organic, wherever it comes from, even the leftist thought of Gramsci, whose most simplistic slogan is that the intellectual must be organic.

The theory of the metropolis, its non-nostalgic negativity, its favourite references from Paris, capital of the nineteenth century, to Vienna, capital of the beginning of the twentieth century, express very well the multicultural frame of mind of a technological age; at the same time they reject the sentimentalism, the tears, the countryside and the rural dream of two or three centuries of Italian literature. This ideology seems to go on and to please the most conventional, folklore image of Italy: Giuseppe Tornatore's film *Cinema Paradiso*, cited at the Cannes Festival in 1989, is one example. This sentimental and successful film reinforces a nostalgic view of simple, pre-industrial community life in a Sicilian Village, while some Italian metropolitan films are completely unknown outside Italy, such as Ricky Tognazzi's *Ultrà*, or Marco Risi's *Meri per sempre* (1989) and *Ragazzi fuori* (1991). Tognazzi presents a metropolitan and violent Italy in his story of young hooligans going from Rome to Turin; Risi depicts a desperate Palermo. For the two directors the metropolitan dimension does not simply rely in the story about urban realities, but also in the formal rhythm of the film itself, mimetic of the nervous, fragmented life of the metropolitan experience.[44]

Fredric Jameson, in his 1985 article on Manfredo Tafuri, entitled 'Architecture and the Critique of Ideology', pin-pointed the peculiar blend of the Italian weariness with the Gramscian vision: 'There are, of course many reasons why radical Italian intellectuals today should have become fatigued with the Gramscian vision, paradoxically at the very moment when it has come to seem reinvigorating for the Left in other national situations in Europe and elsewhere.' Jameson, who criticized Tafuri for his 'stark and absolute position', proposed a position that 'may be called neo-Gramscian', recalling 'the "organic" formulations' of the classical Marxian text.[45] Jameson is fully aware of the Italian reaction against the 'institutionalization of Gramsci's thought within the Italian Communist party', and suggests that Gramsci is assimilated, 'in the Italian context, to that classical form of dialectic thought which is everywhere repudiated by a Nietzschean post-Marxism'.[46] But Jameson prefers to read Tafuri within the frame of mind of what I would call a general history of Marxist thought, not within the frame of mind of a theory of the metropolis, which I consider the indispensable perspective to approach both Tafuri and Cacciari.

The theory of the metropolis uproots any organic nature, any *humus*, any belonging, just as architectural theory, as developed at the Venice Department of Critical and Historical Analysis, breaks through comfortable divisions of disciplines and through habits of thought. In this perspective it has its historical reasons within Italian culture; it cannot be locked into a deterministic pattern and should be seen as a conceptual device that allows one to rewrite history – or the history of architecture, or the analysis of the work of a single architect, such as Adolf Loos.

The notion of the metropolis is not static like a thematic category, but rather has the dynamic movement, the nervous life of a work-in-progress. Lewis Mumford, for example, collected examples of cities, but he did not construct a theory of the metropolis.[47] Or, to cite another example, Raymond Williams uses the theme of the country and the city to explain different phenomena: this opposition identifies a tension present in many cultural attitudes of the West.[48] The opposition of country and city has an almost positivistic calm, it serves the purpose of ideological analysis, always present in Williams's enterprise. Nevertheless, Williams's opposition does not get to that trembling contradiction undermining any statement in the whirlpool of positions continually on the verge of turning upside-down.

The notion of metropolis is neither thematic nor historiographic. It belongs to the anti-historiographic mode of Cacciari, a chapter of what I call a conversation with Tafuri, since conversations can be ideal, but also part of an institutional enterprise.

Any serious evaluation of cultural studies and its institutionalization today in many universities in Great Britain and in the United States should consider not only the famous experience of the Birmingham Centre for Cultural Studies,[49] but also the Venetian experience of Tafuri's department at the School of Architecture, and the interplay between political and cultural struggles suggested above.

I emphasize Cacciari's collaboration with *Contropiano*, where Tafuri published articles that later became well-known books, like his *Progetto e Utopia* (1973) which constitutes a whole rewriting of his 1969 *Contropiano*'s article, 'For a Criticism of the Ideology of Architecture'.[50] Cacciari started to teach at Tafuri's Department in the early 1970s, and the interwoven activity of politics and culture is quite clear in the Venetian experience. It should now be stressed how it challenged the typical historiographic tradition of more than a century of Italian education and academic production, founded on a linear development: history, or the history of given discipline, understood a series of authors and movements to be orderly and categorized according to a seemingly linear definition of the various disciplines.

The anti-historicist stand was also taken by Asor Rosa – the editor of *Contropiano* who was teaching at the University of Rome, not at the Venice School of Architecture – in his *Scrittori e popolo*, which is organized around clusters of investigation: the nineteenth century, the period between the two wars, the Italian Resistance to Fascism, and then specific writers such as Carlo Cassola and Pier Paolo Pasolini. In his 1988 preface, he writes that *Scrittori e popolo* 'wanted to be a decisively anti-evolutionist, therefore anti-historicist, and therefore anti-progressist book.' He then identified the link between the nihilist attitude and the opposition to the historical mode of thinking: 'The criticism of History was then parallel to the criticism of bourgeois culture, while representing its secret justification: and we cannot hide that already at that time a substantial nihilistic attraction nourished our anti-historical position.'[51] Asor Rosa stressed his intention of 'doing intellectual work', and not of continuing 'a cultural tradition', and even less that 'particularly absurd form of cultural tradition, that is the national cultural tradition, with which, hopefully, we always succeeded in never identifying.'[52]

Tafuri suggests a similar anti-historical position – in the sense of opposing linear history. His 1971 *Contropiano* article, 'Austrian Marxism and City: *das Rote Wien*', starts with a complaint about the textbooks of history of modern architecture: Hitchcock, Zevi and Benevolo ignored the 'historically exceptional episode of Vienna's social-democratic administration, between 1920 and 1933'.[53] Tafuri notes that only in political history, or in specific works on that Viennese period, can one find documentation on that event, forgotten by the history of the discipline. In his seminal 1968 book *Teorie e storia dell'architettura*,[54] Tafuri makes a clear stand on the question of modern architecture and the 'eclipses of history' – such is the title of the first long chapter. He criticizes much of the historiographical tradition, what he called, in a preface to the second edition, the 'worn out idealist historicism', and even the 'watered-down official Marxism', of Lucien Goldmann and Galvano Della Volpe. Here he aims, as in *Progetto e utopia* (published in English as *Architecture and Utopia: Design and Capitalist Development*), to question the idea of architecture itself, always presented as if it were an untouchable reality, an eternal value and not an ideological construction, an institution, a contingent reality. He specified that the term 'ideology' meant structure 'of the false consciousness that intellectuals offer to the ruling classes'.[55] Later, moving towards a more Foucaultian understanding of history, he modifies this straightforward Marxist definition, and reads architecture and its languages as discursive practices that forge reality. But, beyond the Marxist tone or within it, Tafuri already indicates in *Theories and History of Architecture* a different way of writing history, that rejects the paradoxically non-historical mode of linear history.[56]

In the above-mentioned article on Tafuri, Jameson stresses the three different perspectives in which he thinks Tafuri's work should be examined: the Marxist context in which it was produced, the context of a contemporary event at a global scale, and the discursive form in which Tafuri works. The Marxist context is that trend of contemporary Marxism that repudiated 'what the Athusserians called Marxist "humanism"', in which Jameson includes 'very specifically its "Utopian" component as symbolically represented by Marcuse and by Henri Lefebvre.'[57] Jameson calls this trend post-Marxism and places within it the French *nouveaux philosophes* and 'Tafuri's collaborator, Massimo Cacciari'. Jameson also perceives 'some kinship with T. W. Adorno's late and desperate concept of a purely "negative dialectics"'.[58] The vaster contemporary event, which has American equivalents, is 'the critique of high modernism, the increasingly omnipresent feeling that the modern movement itself is henceforth extinguished.' Finally, the perspective of Tafuri's form – that is, historiography (or better: narrative history) – confronts Tafuri himself 'with the problem of writing history, and in this case of writing the history of a discipline, an art, a medium.'[59]

Jameson understands the dilemma that the writing of history poses to anyone who wants to do more than 'small-scale semiotic analyses of discrete or individual text or buildings', referring to the well-known 'crisis in narrative or story-telling history since the end of the nineteenth century'.[60] At the same time, he aims at the description of the postmodern condition as the determining feature of the Tafurian dilemmas, all the more so since Tafuri himself did not even mention postmodernism. Jameson does not miss the formal quality of Tafuri's work, and, in a cogent analysis, compares Tafuri's *Architecture and Utopia*, Adorno's *Philosophy of Modern Music* and Barthes's *Writing Degree Zero*:

What the three books I have mentioned have in common is not merely a new set of dialectical insight into literature, but the practice of a peculiar, condensed, allusive discursive form, a kind of textual *genre*, still exceedingly rare, which I will call dialectical history.[61]

Nevertheless, Jameson's wish to give the correct ideological formulation of Tafuri's work, pushed him to rush to the labels post-Marxism, postmodernism. These terms can categorize an episode and indeed can be clarifying, but they imprison an intellectual effort in definitions that paradoxically reinforce the linear, historicist approach of what Jameson himself could not help calling 'the history of contemporary Marxism', even if he grasped the rare achievement of what he calls 'dialectical history'.[62] In other words, I think that rather than emphasizing the Adornian kinship, Tafuri and Cacciari are to be placed into the Benjaminian project, or in the conceptual tension of the metropolis.

The stand against linear histories implies another historical choice: rereading the past with a clear concern for the present situation – the present from which we are looking at the past – and trying to read the past in that dramatic moment in which events produce the ephemeral spark of their own brief present. But these events are intense and complicated by a network of personal intentions, failures of those same intentions, institutional struggles, historical memory and oblivion, and conscious and unconscious factors at the collective and individual levels. How could this complexity be contained in the simple sequence of events told by linear history, in the notion of an authorial chronology of works and places, or in the notion of an intellectual movement with a series of names? To give a sense of the type of history that rejects historicist flatness, one could quote Benjamin's 'Thesis on the Philosophy of History', where he discusses the French historian Fustel de Coulanges as the prototype of nineteenth-century positivistic history, what in France is called *histoire historisante*. Benjamin criticized this approach:

> To historians who wish to relive an era, Fustel de Coulanges recommends that they blot out everything they know about the later course of history. There is no better way of characterizing the method with which historical materialism has broken. It is a process of empathy whose origin is the indolence of the heart, *acedia*, which despairs of grasping and holding the genuine historical image as it flares up briefly.[63]

Benjamin defined historicism as being without theoretical armature and culminating in universal history: 'Its method is additive: it musters a mass of data to fill the homogeneous, empty time.'[64] Tafuri rejects this homogeneous time, and conceives his history and theories of architecture on what Benjamin called 'a constructive principle', typical of materialistic history.

Only an understanding of intellectual work as ornamental limits the role of technique to that of mere embellishment. Only 'the indolence of the heart' leads to the belief that history is an accumulation of data. The way in which the object of investigation is chosen, composed, presented, even mistreated, makes a difference. Benjamin, in his 'Thesis on the Philosophy of History', phrased this other type of investigation with the words that can sum up a whole direction of research typical of the second half of the twentieth century, where history and theory are interwoven:

> Thinking involves not only the flows of thoughts, but their arrest as well. Where thinking suddenly stops in a configuration pregnant with tensions, it gives that configuration a shock, by which it crystallizes into a monad. A historical materialist approaches a historical subject only when he encounters it as a monad.[65]

It is in this anti-historicist mode of understanding history that I propose to read Cacciari and Tafuri. In the first section I presented an epoch, an endeavour, and a place that, in my opinion, are indispensable background for reading Cacciari's *Architecture and Nihilism*, and in the next section I shall examine the intellectual presence of an institution, the University of Venice's Department of Historical and Critical Analysis.

The shock of history

In 1975, when Cacciari published in Italy the essay 'Loos and his Contemporaries', the Department of Historical and Critical Analysis was in what I would call its golden age: it had a definite profile and a publisher, Officina in Rome, where Cacciari published both *Metropolis* and his study on Loos.[66] The Department played a clear role within Venice's School of Architecture, representing an interrogation on the architectural profession itself, an end to the illusion of producing thousands of architects who would have the opportunity to build. The *Contropiano* ethos left its mark in academic research, in the work oriented towards the critique of architectural ideology, such as *The American City: From the Civil War to the New Deal* (*La città americana: dalla guerra civile al New Deal*, 1973), which brought together four essays by Giorgio Ciucci, Francesco Dal Co, Mario Manieri Elia and Tafuri, all of whom taught in the department. The preface of the *American City* shows both the type of non-historicist historical commitment as well as the work of the critique of ideology (which obviously challenges historicism):

> What, in effect, we have discovered with our research, is not a differing history but certainly another history [of the New World] ...
> Our efforts have been directed at demonstrating how the levels of integration of cultural products and ideologies are based not only on an implicit vocation but also on a well defined complex of techniques, which, in its turn, is even partly shaped by the intellectual production as a whole. The direct transformation and utilization of ideology and culture as a technique – even where the ideology is the most regressive, the culture weakest, and the technique least evident – appears to us the most important fact to emerge from our studies.[67]

Against the additive method of historicism, this book also concentrates on blocks and clusters, as in Tafuri's *History and Theories*. For example, in the first chapter, 'Modern Architecture and the Eclipse of History', Tafuri identifies a crystallized moment, a moment of shock where the problem of history and the negation of history emerges well before twentieth-century artistic avant-gardes with their typical rejection of history. The moment chosen by Tafuri is the Tuscan fifteenth century. A new image of Brunelleschi emerges: far from rooting him in the architectural tradition of an unbroken classical antiquity, Tafuri shows how the architect dehistoricizes the language of the past by translating historical values into the present, founding a new language on fragments of the classical world. The quotations and allusions of Brunelleschi were aiming at constructing a new reality, and therefore burnt away their historical value. The churches of San Lorenzo and Santo Spirito and the dome of Santa Maria del Fiore are 'autonomous and absolute'[68] architectural objects that break the order of the medieval city.

But the shock is not simply provided by Brunelleschi, as if Tafuri were moving from a historicistic analysis to a formalist-linguistic approach. The shock is produced by the double movement of dehistoricization offered by Brunelleschi's symbolic system as well as by what Tafuri calls 'the philological rehabilitation' of Alberti's *De re aedificatoria*. Brunelleschi and Alberti faced each other as two poles of historiography: the first represents a conception of the past as usable for the present and disembodied from its connection with antiquity, whereas the second represents a heroic vision of the past as evasion of the dullness of the present.

Similarly, Cacciari's essay 'Loos and His Contemporaries' in *Architecture and Nihilism* culminates in the two poles of Loos's 'Roman' period and the seminal house attributed to Wittgenstein. The reading of Loos and his contemporaries is a monad, a crystallized moment where Cacciari performs his critical construction. Cacciari's essay is not a monograph, neither historical nor philosophical, but what Benjamin calls 'a configuration pregnant with tensions'. The first tension is the notion of the metropolis as seen in the first essay 'The Dialectics of the Negative and the Metropolis', which gives the constructive principle where tensions are incessantly at work. Cacciari couples Loos's essays of the early twentieth century with the journalism of his friend Karl Kraus: together they constitute a thorough criticism of the German Werkbund and the Viennese Werkstätte. Cacciari focuses on that period at the beginning of the twentieth century where two avant-gardes – the Vienna Secession and the 'negative' group of Kraus and Loos – seem to represent two poles: the community utopia and the full consciousness of metropolitan alienation. The community utopia, represented by two architects of the Secession, Joseph Hoffmann and especially Josef Olbrich, is based on the illusion of recuperating a use-value of work: handicraft labour appears as a pure quality escaping the alienation of exchange-value. The reader will find in 'Loos and His Contemporaries' arguments that continue to draw on the basic features of utopias, like the idea that the artist is a free creator and can be emancipated from the horror of money's circulation and the loss of human quality that it implies. Loos's attack on ornamentalism has nothing to do with a stylistic attack, Cacciari insists, but rather emanates from the metropolitan awareness, the metropolitan logic, his refusal to look for a lost world of use-value.

As usual, Cacciari is interested in the point of instability where intellectual positions shift or are ambiguous, what he sometimes calls 'unresolved dialectics' – as when he discusses the architect Otto Wagner, who insists on the importance of the functional aspect of architecture and opposes the art of building to style. 'Wagner's critique of the idea of the garden city' is a critique 'of the city as an image of community'.[69] But the metropolitan ideal of Wagner is to liberate the metropolis from the vampire of speculation through artistic form; in this way he can be reintegrated in the ideology of the Werkbund, the Werkstätte and the Viennese Secession.

In his reading of the Ringstrasse, Carl Schorske offers a similar interpretation of Wagner and of what Cacciari calls his unresolved dialectics, 'from the "tattooed" house, the Majolikahaus of 1898–1899, to the building of the Neustiftgasse; from the autumnal, floral, almost

Olbrichian interiors of the first Wagner villa, to the perfectly apparent, comprehensible space of the Postspaarkasse.'[70] Schorske stresses the link between Klimt and Wagner, who called the painter 'the greatest artist who ever walked the earth'.[71] If Klimt's search for the modern man 'was essentially Orphic and internal, a quest for that *homo psychologicus* who had already emerged in the literature of the early 1890s', Wagner's search presented a different type of modern man:

> An active, efficient, rational, modish bourgeois – an urban man with little time, lots of money, and a taste for the monumental. Wagner's metropolitan man suffered from only one pathological lack: the need for direction. In his fast-moving world of time and motion, what Wagner called 'painful uncertainty' was all too easily felt. The architect must help to overcome it by providing defined lines of movement. The style of Klimt and the Secession helped Wagner in this efforts.[72]

Whereas Schorske follows Wagner's movements from the primacy of function to his commitment to the symbolic language of the Secession, Cacciari sees in Wagner the discrepancy between his understanding of functional architecture and his Secessionist tendency to worship art. The difference between Schorske and Cacciari lies in the form of their research. Schorske confronts the dehistoricization of modern man in historical terms: his analysis of Klimt, or Wagner or Freud is concerned with a chronological accuracy and situated in the most precisely reconstructed network of cultural exchanges, friendships and beliefs. Here one can find not the flatness of historicism, but a genre of comprehensive research where personal, institutional and political histories are fused within a closely argued textual analysis of written as well as visual and musical materials that always shows the contradictions of intellectual programmes, intentions and realizations. I would say that the actors of the Viennese Secession are present, as present as concrete realities: the Ringstrasse becomes the physical centre of the confrontation between two artistic generations, and the tension culminates in the figures of Camillo Sitte and Otto Wagner, 'the romantic archaist and the rational functionalist' who 'divided between them the unreconciled elements of the Ringstrasse legacy'.[73]

Cacciari, on the other hand, obsessively moves all the characters of his early twentieth-century Vienna on the conceptual grid of the metropolis. This grid twists any biographical continuity and narrative structure towards the impossible, unreachable, devouring point that would be the achievement of the metropolis – or the completion of nihilism. Cacciari couples Wagner with Loos in a comparison where Loos appears as the one who grasped the multiplicity of languages of the metropolis and its necessary distortions, from which it will never be liberated because these distortions are 'inherent in the language of the Metropolis'.[74] But Loos is not the last term of the metropolitan tension, as Wittgenstein constitutes the other extreme of the response to Wagner's unresolved dialectic.

Cacciari's thesis rejects the historiographic tradition that simplifies Loos as a rationalist or proto-rationalist architect.[75] Cacciari is aware of Loos's unresolved dimension, of his ideological switch after the First World War that might have increased the tendency to include his work in the category of rationalism. Up to a certain point the discrepancy between the exterior and the interior of a building parallels the multiplicity of languages of the metropolis. But after the war, the conflict between outside and inside becomes more and more directed to the recuperation of the 'artistic nature of the interior'.[76] At this point another monad comes onto the scene, the way already prepared by glimpses and allusions, when Cacciari speaks about Loos's logico-philosophical attack on the Werkbund. Wittgenstein, one of Loos's contemporaries, is already present, in the words and production of the architect – as Kraus is part of the same struggle against ornament fought by Loos. But toward the end of Cacciari's essay, Wittgenstein returns as an architect, as if philosophy materialized into architectural forms. How could a historicist history of architecture pay attention to this episode, so small – one house built by a philosopher, a *capriccio* that does not fit with the orderly sequence of buildings, architects, movements and styles which fill the homogeneous time of historicism?

But within the structuring notion of the metropolis, in a history concentrated on tensions, the Wittgenstein house, *Oikos*, constitutes a culminating moment. The terrible silence of *Oikos* – a theorem in 'its impenetrability and anti-expressivity'[77] – is coupled to Loos's notion of Roman architecture as similar and yet opposite. In spite of his lucidity in understanding the metropolitan condition and criticizing his contemporaries at the beginning of the century, in spite of the blunt difference between the exterior and the interior of his buildings, the later Loos, in his reading of Roman architecture, according to Cacciari, brought a dimension of sociality: 'From the Romans, says Loos, we have derived the *technique* of thought, our power to transform it into a process of rationalization.'[78] Technique and time are values: technique is transmitted and confirms the temporal trajectory expressed by 'from'. Architecture has a value within public life. At the other extreme, Wittgenstein's house never looses its quality of being a theorem, 'infinitely repeatable, infinitely extraneous to all value – but also infinitely unicum'.[79]

The city of scrambled alphabets

In 'The Dialectics of the Negative and the Metropolis' the concept of the metropolis culminates in a totally assumed negativity – such as that of Benjamin or writers like Poe, Baudelaire and Kafka. In 'Loos and His Contemporaries' the concept of the metropolis reaches its highest point with the multiplicity of languages – an argument Loos fully grasped. Cacciari writes that Loos does not see art as transcending handicraft and industry; his emphasis is 'on the mutual "transcendence" of all these terms: that is, on the functional multiplicity of the languages.'[80] Cacciari continues: 'To separate means to set in conflict; not to establish abstract hierarchies of value but to measure-calculate specific differences, on the basis of specific functions as well as specific histories and traditions. Where the Werkbund imagines bridges, Loos posits differences.'

Cacciari warns against what could be called the postmodern temptation, even if he never uses this term, either in the 1970s or in the 1980s. He suggests that it would be completely wrong to interpret Loos's multiplicity as compositional eclecticism:

> What is most important here is not the variety of languages but their common logical reference: the need for every element and function to formulate its own language and speak it coherently and comprehensibly, to test its limits and preserve them in every form – to remain faithful to them, not wanting idealistically or romantically to negate them.[81]

Exactly because of this, 'in the regressive atmosphere of the post-war period',[82] Loos's *Chicago Tribune* project can be seen as Tafuri (quoted by Cacciari) describes it: as 'a polemical declaration against the Metropolis seen as the universe of change', 'a paradoxical phantom of an ordering outside time', and at the same time an incredible attempt of control, a 'total possession of the compositional elements'.[83] Loos is testing the limits of languages and functions. The *Chicago Tribune* project is not a *divertissement*, which would be an eclectic explosion, a game, a fantasy. What Tafuri calls its gigantic and pathetic will to exist 'in the face of the Metropolis' represents the awareness of what happens to languages when they are not preserved, when one does not remain faithful to them. In his *Scientific Autobiography* (1981), Aldo Rossi, another reader of Loos, could not help thinking of Loos in New York, at the very moment he grasped the truth of the equivalence he had posited between city and architecture ever since his *Architecture of the City*:

> New York is a city of stone and monuments such as I never believed could exist, and on seeing it, I realized how Adolf Loos's project for the *Chicago Tribune* was his interpretation of America, and not of course, as one might have thought, a Viennese *divertissement*: it was the synthesis of the distortions created in America by an extensive application of a style in a new context.[84]

Rossi insists on the importance of the Chicago Tribune project in his preface to Loos's essays, and considers Loos's piece on that competition together with *Ornament and Crime* essential to the understanding of architecture in general:

> This latter piece is to my mind particularly pertinent today, at a time when 'postmodernism' is being praised with the same superficiality and the same arguments as modernism was: with everything packaged into a discussion of form – forms which 'change as quickly as a lady's hats'. For Loos the experience with the *Chicago Tribune* competition is a decisive one. In this experience he measures himself against the classical world, the great architectural works, and the American city, which made such a deep impression on him ... While European modernists were getting excited about the constructions of Wright, dreaming about who knows what sort of exotic democracy, Loos was resolutely exploring the streets of downtown New York, amazed at the dark, immense buildings of Broadway and the perspective offered by the buildings of Wall Street. The beauty of this nucleus of American business struck him in much the same way that the beauty of aristocratic and capitalist London had once struck Engels.[85]

For Cacciari, the multiplicity of languages is an important motif in 'Loos and His Contemporaries', the second part of *Architecture and Nihilism*, but it does not become a practice until the third part, 'Loos and His Angel'. Here Cacciari doesn't just announce the multiplicity of languages, his own text *is* this multiplicity. One may think of his references not as simple notes but as conversations with Benjamin, Scholem,

Kraus, Loos, Rilke, Heidegger, Derrida, Levinas, Canetti, Agamben, Severino, Savinio, Tafuri, Schmitt, Lou-Andreas Salomé and others; or, in other terms, most of the mental adventures that made the twentieth century. Cacciari uses all the languages of the twentieth century, from political and legal thought to mysticism and religion, from the investigation of the foundations of Western metaphysics to the practices that resist the aporias of thought, from the persistence of a long rationalist tradition to its fragmentation, its feminization. Because the metropolis is finally all this: the immense effort to rationalize and the defeat of reason; the place of exchange-value, of the circulation of money, and of their opposite, the intimacy, the non-circulation of Lou's buttons, which she collected as a child, or the patient artisanal work of Joseph Veillich, Loos's friend, on whom the architect wrote what Cacciari calls some of his 'most beautiful' pages.[86]

Surprisingly, after the insistence on Loos's criticism of the Werkstätte's nostalgic attitude, of their handicraft ideal of quality objects in the epoch of exchange-value, Cacciari discovers another Loos who 'tells us with what patience and endless care Veillich worked at his furniture'.[87] Should one see in Cacciari's interpretation a conversion from the hardness of the theory of the metropolis to vernacular and to tradition, as if an organicistic faith had corrected his previous position? Should one see in Cacciari's essay a move similar to the one that took place in architecture, going from what Robert Venturi has called the moral rigour of the Modern Movement[88] to that eclectic, pluralistic, quotational mood of so-called postmodern architecture? Did negative thought become postmodern, did it become a written *divertissement*, after so much political and theoretical commitment?

It would be misleading to suggest that there is a contradiction between Cacciari's two texts of the early 1970s and 'Loos and His Angel' (1981). One should be patient and reread this text – patient like Loos's Viellich, or like the reader Nietzsche longs for at the beginning of the *Genealogy of Morals*, a reader who would have 'the skill to ruminate'. There is a strict logical movement that leads from Wittgenstein's *Oikos* to a further reading of the Viennese philosopher and the entire beginning of the century in Vienna: between 'Loos and His Contemporaries' and 'Loos and His Angel' Cacciari wrote his crucial work on Vienna, *Dallo Steinhof* (1980). Or one should proceed with Cacciari's texts as we are supposed to with Loos's buildings, going from an exterior to an interior that does not try to accommodate the exterior, but is different, and different at every moment. That Loosian gap, with no hierarchy between the exterior and the interior, already participates in the multiplicity of languages. One should always keep in mind the passage cited above about the Loosian multiplicity of languages, the need that every element has to formulate its own language, 'to test its limits and preserve them in every form – to remain faithful to them'.[89]

The multiplicity of languages inevitably poses the problem of tradition, and of 'being loyal' to it. In the section of 'Loos and His Angel' called 'Being Loyal', Cacciari stresses Loos's insistence on tradition. The Michaelerplatz is an attempt to solve compositional questions, as Loos said, 'in terms of our old Viennese masters'.[90] Loos's view of tradition stood as a criticism of the creativity of the architect, 'the architect as dominator'[91] wanting to establish the hegemony of one meaning over the others. Wittgenstein talked about the absurdity of a single language that pretends to represent the world, and Loos's craftsman does not impose the unicity of a language; he does not create but rather interrogates. He continuously questions 'language as a combination of linguistic games, a repetition of the assertion that to speak of one language (or of one game) is mere abstraction'.[92] And Cacciari continues: 'Language is tradition, use, praxis, comprehension, and the contradiction existing among the various openings onto the world.' All this means transformation.[93]

This logic of transformation – as Cacciari notes in his epilogue – rejects any idea of overcoming, or rearrangement of elements in hierarchical order. The thought of multiplicity, difference, and transformation had already appeared in a 1977 essay by Cacciari on Deleuze and Foucault. Here Cacciari criticizes a fundamental naturalism in the conception of desire as formulated by the two French philosophers,[94] and ends his discussion opposing another understanding of games to their conception of desire as game. A 'game' for Cacciari does not correspond to the liberation of desire, to its totalizing image. A game 'shows the new space of the multiplicity of languages' as well as 'the plurality of techniques and the conventional character of their names'. A game requires rules that were not invented but assumed, transmitted. Only by recognizing this cruel conventional – not natural – structure of a game is it 'possible to affirm its transformability'.[95] In order to transform, it is necessary to know the rules, not to have the 'indecent pretense' to create the game.

Cacciari indicates in 'Loos and His Angel' that Loos's craftsman represents exactly the link between game and habit, knowledge of the rules and new combinations:

The deeper one's participation in a game, the more these openings issue from practice itself, from habit. The truly present has deep roots – it needs the games of the old masters, the languages of posthumousness. This tradition therefore does not unfold from book to book, drawing to drawing, line to line, but follows the long detours, the waits, the labyrinths of the games among the languages, among linguistic *practices*.[96]

'Loos and His Angel' insists on the idea of the game, which was also important in Cacciari's investigation on Wittgenstein in *Dallo Steinhof*, the text that bears testimony to Cacciari's will to pursue research in manifold directions: 'The possibility of variants are immanent to the game – otherwise the rules of the game will be sublimated in new ideal forms, in new Invariants.'[97]

Nothing could be farther away from Cacciari's concept of games than postmodern free association and immediacy, that mode in which some architectural productions or critical productions freely quote, patching together pieces from here and there without listening to their specific languages, without being loyal to them.[98] Against any fanciful chattering stands the severity of a desperate transparency that does not communicate – such as the glass of Mies van der Rohe, or of Loos's American Bar, completely different from the glass Scheerbart talked about, enthusiastically foreseeing a new glass civilization.[99] In his reading of Mies van der Rohe, Cacciari wrote:

> The sign must remain a sign, must speak only of its renunciation of having value – and only by means of this renunciation will it be able to recognize its true functions and its own destiny: only a language illuminated by its own limits will be able to operate.[100]

Clearly the renunciation of the farce of value, great synthesis, and free fantasy go together with the consciousness that any construction – written or musical or visual or architectural – is an assemblage of parts. It is worthwhile to cite again, as Cacciari does, Mies van der Rohe's wish that building should 'signify truly and only building', and his conviction that 'the building is an assemblage of parts, each of which speaks a different language, specific to the material used'.[101] Tautology and vernacular are at the extreme limits of language.

The fleeting gaze of the angel

In that Nietzschean meditation on the writing of history that is 'The Historical Project', the preface to *The Sphere and the Labyrinth*, Tafuri also faces the question of the multiplicity of languages, and warns against the danger of *wirkliche Historie* (real history): to conceive history as recognition, that is to say on the presupposition that there is a unity of history, 'based on the unity of the structures on which it *rests*, on the unity, as well, of its single elements'.[102] Then Tafuri quotes Foucault and his cruel 'will to knowledge' that does not allow the consolation of universal truth. But Tafuri also warns against the other danger, undoubtedly very strong today, that the awareness of multiplicity again becomes the reconstitution of some unity:

> The danger that menaces the genealogies of Foucault – the genealogies of madness, of the clinic, of punishment, of sexuality – as well as the disseminations of Derrida, lies in the reconsecration of the microscopically analysed fragments as new unities autonomous and significant in themselves. What allows me to pass from a history written in the plural to a questioning of that plurality?[103]

Tafuri is the historian who knows what I would call, borrowing from the terminology of architecture, the historical material, the various historical materials, their nature, limits, characteristics, resistance, ability to endure time. Tafuri is aware of the importance of the historical project, the calculations that ensure its realization, and the artisanal work – the *giochi di pazienza*, game of patience, as the historian Carlo Ginzburg calls it – required to put together the historical puzzle. Tafuri explores the risks of every position, the questions one should ask of the material and the work – patiently, endlessly, sensitive to the necessity of adjustment, continuously adding nuance to the reciprocal input of theory and practice, of documents and concepts. What really matters is the ability to listen to the voice of transformation, to dare to change – that's the only way to be truly loyal. One should not be astonished therefore that Tafuri's research in the 1980s, such as his *Venice and the Renaissance*,[104] seems to have abandoned the cutting edge of Marxian analysis and adopted the mode of investigation typical of the Annales School. Moreover, an accurate understanding of the conceptual direction that the Annales School gave to historical analysis is inconceivable without that questioning of institutions – and the institution of history – coming from Marxism.[105] In a 1985 article Tafuri posed the terms of the problem:

> If one wants to grasp the complexity of the relational network of contemporary art, it is better to give up the simplistic mode of traditional classifications, or at least recompose in another way its divisions. A

history of architecture that would replace this same history in its social
and political context, will give little importance to purely linguistic
phenomena and will reread texts and documents in the light of
mentalités history.[106]

The point is not to be imprisoned in an orthodoxy that sticks to dog-
matic formulas that are reassuring in their fixity. This is the profound
lesson of Benjamin.[107] There is no abandonment of the initial positions
of *Theories and Histories* in Tafuri's research of the 1980s, which shows
the influence of *mentalités* history. On the contrary, there is the loyalty
of a transformation. One of the founding fathers of the *Annales*, Lucien
Febvre, rejects linear history as strongly as Benjamin does. It would be
enough to quote Febvre's paradoxical and emphatic exclamation
against what Benjamin would have called *acedia* and what Febvre
called the 'intellectual laziness' of the historicist mode:

> The Past does not exist, the Past is not a given data. The Past is not a
> collection of cadavers nor should the historian's function be that of
> finding all these cadavers, giving them a number, taking pictures of
> each one of them, and finally identifying them. The Past does not
> produce the historian. It is the historian who gives birth to
> history.[108]

Cacciari writes that, for Loos and Kraus, 'the past is transformed into
the vision and hearing of a living, incessant questioning – into a
problem par excellence',[109] but they never seek in it an 'eternal image'.
If Tafuri adopts the patience of the historical work, Cacciari follows the
Benjaminian investigation of history, as the entire third part of
Architecture and Nihilism is inspired by Benjamin's famous image of
'Angelus Novus':

> A Klee painting named 'Angelus Novus' shows an angel looking as
> though he is about to move away from something he is fixedly con-
> templating. His eyes are staring, his mouth is open, his wings are
> spread. This is how one pictures the angel of history. His face is turned
> towards the past. Where we perceive a chain of events, he sees one
> single catastrophe which keeps piling wreckage upon wreckage and
> hurls it in front of his feet. The angel would like to stay, awaken the
> dead, and make whole what has been smashed. But a storm is blowing
> from Paradise; it has got caught in his wings with such violence that
> the angel can no longer close them. This storm irresistibly propels him

into the future to which his back is turned, while the pile of debris before him grows skyward. This storm is what we call progress.[110]

This passage, never fully quoted by Cacciari, is a constant reference; it can be said, in the words of Nietzsche, to be an aphorism that 'stands at the head of that essay, and the body of the essay forms the commentary'.[111] Tafuri, the historian, firmly looks into the debris of history, into its blinding whirl; Cacciari, the philosopher who has been deeply touched by Heidegger's questions, traces the movements of the figure of the Angel. He follows its image, and writes an enigmatic commentary on it.

The passage from the first essays in *Architecture and Nihilism* to 'Loos and His Angel' is marked by the movement away from the language of critique of ideology – even if this language was never compact, unique, as in Cacciari's passages on Loos interiors and exteriors, that fully belong to the mode of art criticism; or by the last pages on *Oikos* that defy any definition of genre, and, like the best passages of 'The Dialectics of the Negative and the Metropolis', burst out in a sort of sharp poetic brevity. Cacciari does not reject or condemn the language of the critique of ideology but rather perceives its function, understands that it is a language among others. Studying Wittgenstein in *Dallo Steinhof*, Cacciari focuses on the crucial difference between philosophy and mysticism. Philosophy stumbles on the 'fetishism' of showing and describing the world as it is, while the mystical 'shows from inside the limits of possible propositions'.[112] Cacciari is fully aware of the dream 'of an immanent and forever alert "criticism of ideology"', as he calls it in his epilogue. He knows that it belongs to nihilism, to its opposition to synthesis as well as to mere games of fantasy. He also knows that this lucidity is part of the utopia of nihilism, of its will to rationally control everything, to reach a fully transparent, functional order. To recognize this extreme utopia means to test the boundaries of nihilism itself, the boundaries of language, the murmur of the multiplicity of languages.

The language of 'Loos and His Angel' is inhabited by multiple voices: it is commentary. In his essay *Das Andere*, 'Loos teaches by "strolling", by indicating, by hinting',[113] as Cacciari observes. Not unlike Loos, Cacciari has 'the melancholy rhythm of a stroll', rather 'than the insistent tempo of a critique'.[114] Strolling is that mode of seeing, thinking and writing that confronts the limits, not knowing what can be anticipated, not wanting to reach a conclusion. Strolling is a metaphor for the commentary; it can also indicate the practice of the one who looks into architectural forms, traditions and habits, wanders into space and meanings, and reads 'the difference existing between their present function and their previous significations'.[115]

Strolling also allows the opportunity of looking at the visible, but with an eye to the invisible, with no expectations nor solutions, as in the initial lines of *Dallo Steinhof*, that seem to describe a stroll to Wagner's Steinhof church:

> Two symmetrical rows of thoroughfares, at the foot of the Viennese forest, lead to Saint Leopold church ... Wagner's church, at the top of the buildings for the psychiatric hospital of the city of Vienna, comes out of the deep green wood with its shining copper dome. It is impossible to say what this work anticipates – it is impossible to say what reaches it.[116]

In the epilogue to *Architecture and Nihilism*, Cacciari points out the utopia of nihilism, the aporia of what he calls the architecture of fulfilled nihilism. In the Heideggerian vein, he tries to reach that uncanny point of thought where difference, flickering like a flame, can never be grasped but sheds light in perennial movement, and therefore no definition is ever possible as the final word, as the solution. Cacciari forces the limits of language, with notions like the completion of the architecture of fulfilled nihilism, that nevertheless can never be completed. Cacciari's style and comments emphasize the nihilistic elements of the architecture of nihilism, inaugurated by Loos's Café Nihilismus. The trajectory of the theory of the metropolis brings negative thought to the mode of commentary, mystically – not philosophically – conceived as a plunge into the limits of language.

In *Dallo Steinhof*, Cacciari quotes Kraus, who says that we are at war with language. Kraus stressed the continuous character of this fight: 'the limit of language is not providentially assigned to us so that we can simply put order inside it.'[117] And citing Wittgenstein, Cacciari suggested the necessity of immersion, of 'shipwrecking' on the limits of language. The Cacciarian determination to face the limits of language also means facing the limits of the architecture of nihilism. Cacciari's research is part of his Heideggerian reading of Wittgenstein's reflection on the expressible and the inexpressible, and the almost 'gravitational force that the inexpressible brings on scientific propositions'.[118]

But the Heideggerian investigation of language is very different from Wittgenstein's logic, even if it belongs to the same twentieth-century obsession with language; it pertains to the realm of words and their meanings. I would say that, beyond the vast literature and debates on his philosophy and his politics, Heidegger's influence in our time has been an obscurantist mode of thinking, writing, asking questions, making endless distinctions – in short, the practice of deconstruction. It is well known how important this style has been for Derrida, and it is clear how seminal it is for 'Loos and His Angel', for Cacciari in the 1980s. It would be enough to think of 'Eupalinos and Architecture', where Cacciari follows and interprets in the light of the theory of the metropolis the Heideggerian interrogation on dwelling and building.

In this Heideggerian sense, it would be logical to associate Cacciari and Derrida. But one should always keep in mind a major difference, not of philosophy, but of temperament (using Baudelaire's term for painters), which places Cacciari within a Catholic culture and the political militancy I discussed above. Derrida contemplates language as writing, and has a deep suspicion of the voice, whereas Cacciari is endlessly fascinated by the voice and oral language, precisely because of its instability, its precarious balance, its dazzling, fleeting, ephemeral character. In a passage from *Dallo Steinhof* on Schoenberg, Cacciari comments on the presence of the text as a structural element in musical composition, and on the emergence of the voice and song.[119] Also, at the very moment Cacciari unfolds the Wittgensteinian conception of games, his natural tendency is to refer to the spoken word: 'But such possibilities [of variants] cannot be described *a priori*: they proceed within the dynamics of language that is contingent on the intention of the speakers – intention that takes out of accumulated knowledge, testing, experimenting, transforming it, playing with it.'[120]

Not a home but an adventure

The question of the multiplicity of languages cannot but be present for someone who has studied so deeply the moment of *finis Austriae*,[121] the end of Austria, of the Hapsburgs' Empire (of which Venice was part until the unification of Italy). In an essay on Hugo von Hofmannsthal, 'Intransitabili Utopie', Cacciari points out that the world and the language of the Austrian writer did not correspond to the cosmopolitan vision of the Enlightenment, nor to a totalizing idea of Europe, but to 'the multiplicity of languages that turn around the great Hapsburg Reich'.[122] Against a conservative reading of Hofmannsthal, Cacciari insists on the importance of Hofmannsthal's vision of the poet as a seismograph, recording all the movements of the earth. This image shows that the poet does not invent a language but carefully listens to traditions, to their most imperceptible movements, without trying to fuse them in a mythical unity.

One of Hofmannsthal's themes as identified by Cacciari is that of things and time passing, which poses the problem of the past. How can one face this fading-away? How to look at it without falling into nostalgia?

Time goes by, ideologies and beliefs change; institutions, people, objects and fashions disappear, endlessly. The metropolis itself is an image of the slipping away of everything, as Baudelaire writes in 'Le Cygne': 'Paris changes!' A true theory of the metropolis ought to include the many voices of the passing away, and the only non-nostalgic way to look at it, which is to think of transformation. The response of intellectual searches to the slipping away of things and time is probably a whole history that it is yet to be written. A vast range of attitudes would come up, from the obstinate repetitions of the same themes, concepts and forms, to silence. One could look to Aldo Rossi's intimist attitude towards architecture, his melancholic nostalgia for youth and for the great hopes of the past, and, not unlike Loos's Veillich, his tenderness for small things; or Roland Barthes's bold statement that 'intellectual conversions are the very pulsion of the intelligence'.[123] In that history, one could see melancholia and will to change, fear and bluntness, oblivion and memory, hope and regret – all those disquieting elements at the source of a blurred line between the conservative impulse and the thirst for the new.

How should one face the changes in knowledge, institutions, parties, political lines? How can one resist the refusal to change of all those very things that are changing? Where do we place our loyalty? The difference between Cacciari's (and Tafuri's) position and Asor Rosa's on these issues should be stressed. As in a de Chirico painting, in Asor Rosa's 1988 preface of *Scrittori e popolo*, there is a chilling image of what I would call stubborn nostalgia for the past, the political life of an almost heroic past. He insists that the *operaista* position does not make any sense today, because there is 'simply' no class that would be able to assume that role – and that adverb, 'simply', is loaded with regret. Then, addressing the young generation, he speaks, almost in spite of himself, of the everlasting validity of those past values, because everything is still, 'as in a station where the train did not start moving'.[124] In that immobility everything is waiting for the signal – to start all over again, to go where it was thought the world would go, 30 years ago or more.

Cacciari, on the other side, is loyal to the theory of the metropolis – even to its extreme consequences, with no nostalgia for something which existed before and should be found again – because this nostalgia would be the ideology, not the theory of the metropolis. The constitutive vigour and nervous life of the metropolis implies continuous transformations. The are no motionless trains in stations waiting years and years for something that will never come back again. As suggested by Simmel, Cacciari notes that 'modern, metropolitan life is but the force that drives things forward toward those *transformations* due to which a problem can be solved only "by means of a new problem, and a conflict by means of a new conflict".'[125] And the metropolis becomes the metaphor for the contemporary world: or better, it is the letter, the concrete reality of the contemporary world, as Cacciari suggests in 'Eupalinos or Architecture':

> We are in an era, says Foucault, in which the world is perceived as a network that simultaneously joins juxtaposed and distant points. This space alienates the 'pious descendants of history', for whom the world was like a large street which developed different 'meanings' through different ages. Neither does this space resemble the hierarchical space of the medieval city, where the juxtaposition of places referred to the 'value' of their respective functions. The present-day space of the metropolis is made up of the non-hierarchical flow of information connecting disciplines and functions, of discrete aleatory currents, whose movements are not teleologically comprehensible but only stochastically analyzable.[126]

In the metropolis of the present the notion of the political itself is changing: in a 1982 essay on the concept of the left with the emblematic title of 'Sinisteritas', Cacciari indicated that in our era the traditional vision of political parties cannot represent the concrete forces of the political today. Cacciari started this investigation with the usual Heideggerian questioning of words, their meanings and their visible and invisible implications. A major influence in his rethinking of the political is the controversial figure of Carl Schmitt, who after March 1933 became the ideologue of the Nazis.[127] Schmitt is one of the most important political thinkers who studied the relationship between the concepts of the state and the political, and stressed, as noted by Leo Strauss, that 'all concepts in the mental sphere, including the concept of "mind", are in themselves pluralistic, and are to be understood only from concrete political existence'.[128]

Against any abstract vision of politics, Cacciari proposes an immersion into the concrete, open, clashing, disorderly, stochastic – in the

statistical and musical senses of this term – situations of the contemporary world, which, like the metropolis, is intrinsically unstable, continuously catastrophic. Neither the classic monolithic, substantialist
language of politics – in which a party corresponds to a precise, stable
ideology – nor the vision of a technocratic future based on a supposed
common scientific language can describe the continuous transformations of the contemporary world. In its open and competitive system,
there is an incessant 'rapidity of transformation of directions', and an
equally incessant 'experimental mobility of strategies'.[129] Even the
modes of political commitment are changing: no existential dramas of
the assumption of a belief, but an a-logical level of responsibility.
Without any political sentimentalism, the same thinker who gave
years of thought and struggle to the workers' movements, and had
been Communist Deputy and Mayor of Venice, dared to say that the
left could get rid of its foundational myths, such as the one of 'the
working class and its Promise'. Maybe what 'the left' means today,
Cacciari suggested at the end of 'Sinisteritas', is an acute sense of the
loss, the fading away of the very myths of the left. The pure political
does not exist any longer, nor the 'Great Political', but a 'Great
Opportunism' is possible. The political is limited by individual *loci*, the
contingent, the local, the plurality of the locals; the opportunist – in
the sense of grasping the opportunity – awareness of the changing of
situations and programmes.

The nervous logic of the unstable or transformable was obviously a very
important theme for Simmel, with whom Cacciari started his own theory
of the metropolis. In his preface to *The Sphere and the Labyrinth*, Tafuri
quoted Simmel's essay entitled 'Fashion': 'the way in which it is given to
us to comprehend the phenomena of life causes us to perceive a plurality
of forces at every point of existence.'[130] To perceive tensions, antago-
nisms, the plurality of forces, to feel the incessant transformation of directions, and to listen to the multiplicity of languages, ought to uproot the
idea of belonging to a home, of dwelling, in the physical and metaphorical sense. The architecture of the metropolis must be aware, beyond any
utopia of urban planning, beyond that utopia that is the idea itself of
urban planning,[131] that there are no more dwellers; the politics of the
metropolis must recognize the same condition of loss of place – since
the local is not the rediscovery of a small organic community but the
epiphany of the ephemeral, the contingent, the migrant.

Simmel, although he had grasped the metropolitan condition of life,
clearly showed in his short 1907 essay on Venice what Cacciari calls
his ideological vision of the community. He opposed Florence to

Venice and seemed frightened and at the same time fascinated by the impression of artifice he received from Venice:

> In Venice one can see realized the duplicity of life ... Double is the sense of these squares, that, because of the lack of vehicles and the narrowness of streets, look like rooms. Double is the sense of meeting, pushing, and touching of people in the *calli* ... Double is the sense of life in this city – now a crossing of streets, now a crossing of canals, so that it does not belong either to the earth or to the water: and we are always seduced by what appears behind the Protean shape of Venice, as if it were its real body ... Venice has the equivocal beauty of adventure which floats rootless into life, as a torn flower floats into the sea. That Venice has been and will be the *city of adventure* is just the most perceptible expression of the deepest destiny of its image: it cannot be a home for our soul, but nothing but adventure.[132]

7
Absence and Revelation: Photography as the Art of Nostalgia

The pleasure that kills

Any research on photography, cinema, video and television necessarily entails a reflection on technique.[1] This reflection is not merely technical in nature; it is also cultural since it explores the impact of such media on the ways in which we live, think and act. In making such an assertion one has to mention Raymond Williams, one of the most important critics of our time, who from the 1950s to his death in 1988 worked to redefine the meaning of culture in the post-war world. Against the conception of culture as a given and eternal set of universal references – epitomized by the canon of 'great works of art', the idea of high culture that informed British intellectual life for almost two centuries – Williams put forward a notion of culture which corresponded to the realities and tensions of Western liberal democracy. In *Culture and Society* (1958), he wrote: 'The history of the idea of culture is a record of our reactions, in thought and feeling, to the changed conditions of our common life.'[2]

These changed conditions of life are connected to technical advances and therefore include material shifts as well as shifts in feeling and thought. Any mutation is measured by our reactions to it, to its effects on our minds and gestures. Williams believes that 'particular changes will modify an habitual discipline, shift an habitual action'.[3] The term 'discipline' here can also be pushed to its academic sense, embracing the disciplinary struggle that Williams found himself caught up in during the 1950s and 1960s.[4]

What I want to argue is that one cannot trace a general history of the study of media without taking into account photography, the technique underpinning both film and television. There can be no cinema without photography, since, as Christian Metz notes,[5] film is comprised of immobile images which are projected on a screen at a regular pace and separated by black pauses resulting from the occultation of the camera by a rotating curtain. A discontinuous movement, passing from one photogram to another, creates the impression of continuity. Moreover, as Walter Benjamin suggested in a famous essay, photography is *the* technique that precipitated a radical change in the production of the artistic object but also in our perception of the world. For Benjamin the invention of photography marked a new configuration in the consumption and meaning of the work of art, since technical reproducibility ensured that art would loose its 'aura' of uniqueness. The birth of photography in the first half of the nineteenth century accompanies the beginning of industrial mass production and its also marks the starting-point of art itself as mass phenomenon bringing together both the artistic object and its reception – the response of men and women in front of that object. Therefore the spark of cultural analysis, as opposed to a supposedly pure art history or a total critique of ideology, relies on the attention given to the interaction between individuals and the artistic product.

Benjamin proceeds to suggest shifts in the nature of that interaction. One has to reconstruct the initial surprise – or rejection – provoked by the technical miracle of fixing transient images. Benjamin cites an article from the *Leipzig City Advertiser*, which regarded photography as scandalous on the grounds that only the artist who is 'divinely inspired' was allowed to produce images. The *Advertiser's* journalist wrote: 'To try to catch transient reflected images is not merely something that is impossible, but, as a thorough German investigation has shown, the very desire to do so is blasphemy.'[6] However, Benjamin continues, after they had recovered from this initial surprise or shock, people developed an indifference to the multiplication of images in much the same way as they did towards the proliferation of information through print – that other technique which did so much to change human perceptions of the world.

Benjamin and Williams share both a Marxist concern for the history of technique, and that other Marxist touchstone, a vision of the nineteenth century as the inauguration of our modernity, of our culture, which occurs at that point in history precisely because of the explosion of technique and, in particular, the beginning of the mass production of words and images. Such new techniques break with past habits and disciplines, forging new modes of perceiving and feeling.

However, there are slight differences in emphasis between the two commentators. Benjamin regarded journalism *and* photography as being at the root of the 'absent-minded attention' of modern men and women, and, in his *Short History* of *Photography* (1931), he sketches a brief comparison between the two. Williams, on the other hand, identifies printing as a 'major technical advance'[7] – one of the greatest technical developments in human history that created new means of communication – but photography which was so crucial for Benjamin is not central for him. Indeed, in Williams's list of the important technical advances, photography is not even mentioned:

> The major advances in transport, by road, rail, sea, and air, themselves greatly affected printing: at once in the collection of news and in the wide and quick distribution of the printed product. The development of the cable, telegraph, and telephone services even more remarkably facilitated the collection of news. Then, as new media, came sound broadcasting, the cinema and television.[8]

However, Williams does suggest that, similar to the recorded voice, photography implies the *absence* of people, which in turn suggests a possible major effect of the new means of communication: that of absence as an indispensable component of the audio-visual dimension of contemporary life. In the attempt to show how culture today indicates a process rather than a conclusion, he considered the 'neutral' or impersonal aspect of techniques:

> The only substantial objection that is made to them is that they are relatively impersonal, by comparison with older techniques serving the same ends. Where the theatre presented actors, the cinema presents the photographs of actors. Where the meeting presented a men speaking, the wireless presents a voice, or television a voice and a photograph... . The point about impersonality often carries a ludicrous rider. It is supposed, for instance, that it is an objection to listening to wireless talks or discussions that the listener cannot answer the speakers back. But the situation is that of almost any reader; printing, after all, was the first great impersonal medium ... Much of what we call communication is, necessarily, no more in itself than transmission: that is to say, a one-way-sending. Reception and response, which complete communication, depend on other factors than the techniques.[9]

Photography here appears as a substitute for human presence, as the reflected image that stands at the basis of contemporary communication. The impersonality of media, of one way-sending, voices without bodies, photographs of actors and people instead of their presence – all these are the elements which constitute our everyday life where we constantly face absence as the existential foundation of our experience, from politics to domesticity.

Indeed, today (much more than at the time Williams wrote *Culture and Society*), in what we call our postmodern world, we find ourselves constantly dealing with hundreds of absent bodies. We are bombarded by images, voices, computerized instructions, by technical glow and murmuring, and have become indifferent to the lack of human presence that the impersonal media carry within themselves. The reception of media is therefore founded on this almost automatic pact with absence: in the world of mass communication, in the glimmering metropolis of computers, TV screens, electronic devices, we act without surprise, without missing a type of exchange that implies the presence of interlocutors. Meanwhile the young generation has become as acquainted with the remote control as the inhabitant of the big city is used to traffic, automatic movements and anonymous passers-by.

The contemporary familiarity with absence is part of the process of alienation that nineteenth-century writers such as Poe and Baudelaire and of course later Benjamin (in the tracks of major German sociologists such as Max Weber and Georg Simmel writing at the turn of the century) identified as typical of the modern condition. Indeed, alienation was the founding experience of metropolitan life. Simmel called it the nervous life of the modern metropolis; Benjamin the interiorization of shocks – with shock and anguish becoming such a mental habit that they pre-ordain human perception. In his essay 'On Some Motifs in Baudelaire', Benjamin regards a poem from Baudelaire's *Les Fleurs du Mal*, 'A une passante', as exemplary of metropolitan alienation (I commented on this poem in Chapter 3). In the big city even eroticism is a solitary experience: the lyrical voice tells of a sudden street scene, where a man glimpses a beautiful woman quickly disappearing in the crowd and traffic. There is no conversation, no human contact, only one-way communication, con-veyed in broken sentences that cannot even hold together in the conti-nuity of syntax as the poet mentally addresses a few words to the woman, an anonymous 'you' who will never give an answer:

> .... Fugitive beauty
> Whose glance suddenly made me reborn,
> Will I ever see you again if not in eternity?
>
> Somewhere else, far from here! too late! probably *never*!
> Because I ignore where you flee, you do not know where I go
> You! whom I would have loved, oh, you who knew it![10]

This short and convulsive meditation on the ephemeral and the impossible derives from the power of a glimpsing vision, of two gazes that seem to cross briefly but fail to meet in any real encounter. The Baudelairean gaze at the passer-by, her sudden and inaccessible glance, epitomize a situation which is the opposite of any phenomenological continuity, of any intersubjective exchange. The broken desire reproduced in the fragmented rhythm of Baudelaire's poem, in the spasm of its lines, suggests the reaction to the purely visual as the act of gripping a person through the eyes, of reaching the most unconscious desire, the barest and bluntest demand of love, for another person who is constitutively absent. As vanishing image, unattainable body (as inconsistent as the photographs of actors which, in Williams's words, mark the shift from theatre to cinema and television) the Baudelairean passer-by is symptomatic of the metropolitan reality that brutally changed the culture of the nineteenth century, and quietly continues to change thoughts, feelings, desires and relationships in our contemporary audio-visual world.

While technological advance has enhanced the effects of the nineteenth-century metropolitan phenomenon, the alienation inherent in the reception of mass media stands as a reversal of what we can call the conditions of representation in the nineteenth century or in the first half of the twentieth century. Prior to the ascendancy of the techniques of mass communication the world was comprehended through direct experience more than through images whereas today one can argue, rather paradoxically, that there is more representation than material world. Nineteenth-century artists who have been labelled as 'realist' had to respond to the richness of reality and cope with the poverty of representational means caused by limitations in particular techniques, certainly when compared with our own technological power. Particular forms such as the novel or painting were slow, even if an individual artist, such as Balzac, tried to produce at a frantic pace – almost as if the human being could follow the machine rhythm of printing. And, even if printing in the nineteenth century did undergo major technical advances, those transformations seem almost irrelevant compared to the quickness of the media world.

The development of photography served to clarify the connection between the history of techniques and of ideas – particularly anthropological and sociological perspectives. However, the study of the new medium could not be comfortably integrated into the nineteenth-century disciplinary structures of universities. Photography might relate to concerns of fine art, history, communication studies or sociology, but yet cannot be subsumed under any of these categories. How can one really separate the concern for chemical elements reacting to the sun or the lights in the photographic studio from the surprise caused by the rapidity of technical reproduction, and the blasé attitude towards the very quickness with which representations and images can circulate? This quickness of reproduction increasingly obfuscates the beginnings of photography when the camera caught what was present in front of it – be it a person, an object, or an urban or natural landscape. Nevertheless, as always when our historical memory is blackened by technical ease, collective reminiscence is powerfully and unconsciously at work. Consequently, I would suggest, the indifference of our electronic age is actually built upon that inaugural surprise at the first mythical photographs, the astonishment in which, in the nineteenth century, humankind perceived its own image in the silver mirror of the camera and the black-and-white shades of the photograph.[11]

Probably one of the primary objectives of media studies should be to stress the transformation that took place with the global holding of the image. Such is the advent of photography, and its continuation in the film image.

The imprint of what Benjamin called photography's '*here and now*' (*hic et nunc*) is always there in the photographic print itself, which therefore accomplishes the miracle of a mirror marked for ever by the outlines of the reflected image, fixing for all time the transient reflected image. The real presence of the photographed person, place, object – vanishing in an inexhaustible absence, always lacking – lingers forever in the halo of photography, as the unconscious memory of its historical dimension, even in the most sophisticated contemporary montage and *truquage*, which do not need the presence of anything in the flesh. If it were not so why would we insist on photography's documentary value? We see, therefore how could we not believe what we witness as recorded in the very place (*hic*), at the very moment (*nunc*) it happened or is happening? The realist value of photography and televized images is exactly what embodies the possibility of information-disinformation, the more or less nuanced manipulation of the interplay between fiction and reality.

Michelangelo Antonioni's film *Blow-Up* (1966) offers an acute reflection on the intertwining of truth and *truquage* in photography. How could photographs be falsified if they did not carry within themselves the trace of photography's power, of its inaugural astonishment – that is, its possibility of grasping the ephemeral moment as it happens? If the reproduced image is hellish and dangerous for the correspondent of the *Leipzig City Advertiser*, that is because photography is a sort of *ménage à trois*. It is where the object (what is photographed) and the subject (the viewer) face themselves with a precise mental perception: the idea of a presence turned into absence. In other terms, the object appears to the subject as something absent (according to Sartre's definition of the image). The three terms, then, are: subject, object, absence. Simultaneously real and evasive, photography, like Baudelaire's passer-by, exists in the gap between what it is and its reception, in that discrepancy between the object and the subject.

The interplay between reality and absence constitutes the status of photography. Williams understands this when he speaks of the photograph of absent actors in cinema and television, while Benjamin analysed that absence as a new phenomenon – one which is, I insist, a variant of the situation of the Baudelairean passer-by. In his essay on the history of photography, Benjamin did not simply reflect on the technical aspect of photography – what could be called the photographic object – he also speculated on the reception of photography, on the way in which the subject feels and thinks in front of the photographic object, which in this way marks its difference from art:

> In photography ... one encounters a new and strange phenomenon: in that fishwife from New Haven [1843, by David Octavius Mill], who casts her eyes down with such casual, seductive shame, there remains something that does not merely testify to the art of Hill the photographer, but something that cannot be silenced, that impudently demands the name of the person who lived at the time and who remaining real even now, will never yield herself up entirely into art.[12]

Although written in an impersonal mode or in the passive form – 'something that cannot be silenced, something that impudently demands' – what is active in Benjamin's passage is the spectator, who, in the moment in which he or she receives the image, cannot but question its state of reality, and in doing so almost misses with nostalgia that piece of reality when the person in the portrait was there, alive, present in flesh. The spectator of photography holds the same position as Baudelaire looking at the passer-by in the street, being in that same situation of alienation and thirst for reality, imprisoned in that 'impudent demand' for the real person, that eventually splits up in the many questions of the Baudelairean voice. Benjamin continues:

> However skilful the photographer, however carefully he poses the model, the spectator feels an irresistible compulsion to look for the

tiny spark of chance, of the here and now, with which reality has, as it were, seared the character in the picture.[13]

That irresistible compulsion, that 'tiny spark' of time and reality, which the spectator is seeking is rather different from the famous situation of the *regard de l'autre* (the gaze of the other) in Sartre's *L'Être et le Néant*, when one person reaches consciousness of himself or herself through the gaze of another human being. In a public park, two people look at each other, they realize that they themselves are looking because of the other, and they realize that they exist in a perfect two-way balance. In what can be called the phenomenological stream, one person has the sense of his or her own identity thanks to the recognition implied by the other, mirroring with his or her own eyes the received gaze. The Sartrian scene implies the impact of physical presence, the consciousness of the self in an adult rather than infantile, intersubjective exchange where the subject obviously has full control of his/her own motion and language. The Sartrean action is a dual fulfilment of the Cartesian *cogito*[14]: I look at you looking at me; we both know that we are looking at each other. The action is slow. Time has, so to speak, a chronological dimension between the extremes of the ephemeral and the eternal which we are able to master.

But the passer-by episode, on the other hand, is constructed on the overlapping of the ephemeral and the eternal and takes place in a 'tiny spark of chance, of the here and now'. The two gazes are irredeemably discrepant; they never meet, their temporal dimension is, literally, that of the twinkling of an eye, and then comes the solitude of the meditation on eternity. One person watches the other; he looks with desire, and already violent nostalgia for what is taking place as something which will never happen. The other person is simply on the other side of the street – she is beautiful, desirable, impossible, real and unreal at the same time, as if her action were frozen in the intransitive verb to *look*, and not to *look at*, a verb suspended with no preposition and neither direct nor indirect object, or the object being so removed that it will never be reached. The woman is an image, an optical object, and the subject is left without one-to-one recognition, burning in the tension of a desire that, far from being fulfilled, stands as alienation, as an anguishing wish for the impossible. Desire is then flickering in a continuous questioning ('Will I ever see you again if not in eternity?'), to which absence inevitably gives rise, reiterating the quest with a powerful fantasmatic activity. The visual *per se* has an almost total power, and rejects the merely physical for an endless mental visualization or representation.[15]

Benjamin had a clear insight into this when he briefly suggested that photography 'makes aware for the first time the optical unconscious'. One can connect this with the theme of the cultural effects of technological changes indicated by Williams, and suggest that it is this very 'optical unconscious' which is at stake when we are the spectators of film and, especially, television – the fragmented, sparkling, interrupted production of images to the rhythm of the remote-control, the glimmering of clips. In the act of spectatorship there are subjects situated beyond the possibility of being recognized by the gaze of the other, anonymous viewers whose desire is enticed. We look, for example, at Madonna's body moving with music and song, ungraspable in the vertiginous spasms, the jumps and cuts of the convulsive editing of images. In this act we undoubtedly resemble the inhabitant of the metropolis perceiving the passer-by in the middle of traffic and noise, strained in erotic contraction: 'And I, tense like an eccentric / Drank in her eyes, sombre stormy sky, / The sweetness that enthrals, the pleasure that kills.'[16]

Images have an inevitable pornographic character. Fredric Jameson begins his book *Signatures of the Visible* (1990) by stressing the irony of our civilization, a civilization that has transformed human nature into just one sense, that of sight:

> The visual is *essentially* pornographic, which is to say that it has its end in rapt, mindless fascination; thinking about its attributes becomes an adjunct to that, if it is unwilling to betray its object; while the most austere films necessarily draw their energy from the attempt to repress their own excess (rather than from the more thankless effort to discipline the viewer). Pornographic films are thus only the potentiation of films in general, which asks us to stare at the world as though it were a naked body.[17]

The production of images is founded on both the provocation and the boredom of pornography – the indifference we can have towards it, even if we look for excitement. Our perception, our mind and our senses are so used to the excess of images and their enticement, to the naked body of the world, that there is no surprise, no possible shock, because, as Benjamin understood, the shock is already interiorized, is already part of our internal world, of our psychic predispositions. Our reactions to the overwhelming world of the audio-visual oscillate between indifference and appeal. We know that Madonna is absent, yet we are compelled to question her reality, to desire the fragments of her body so carefully constructed as sexual machine, as fetish. She, the image *par excellence*, wants to be wanted, she is the object of scopophilic pleasure (pleasure in looking) *par excellence*, shining on that spark of unfulfilled desire posed as the condition of desire itself. The scenario is inevitably, and abstractedly, sado-masochistic: we will never touch her, she can go on torturing the spectators, giving glimpses of the pleasure that kills.

It is possible to develop these thoughts into a feminist analysis of what is at stake in vision. In her famous article, 'Visual Pleasure and Narrative Cinema', Laura Mulvey argues that 'it is woman as representation that crystallizes'[18] the paradox or the tension between sexual instinct and narcissistic identification with the image seen. She also identified that these two crucial terms as used by Freud were 'formative structures, mechanisms without intrinsic meaning'.[19] They could only become meaningful thanks to a work of idealization, but their major feature is non-realistic: 'Both pursue aims in *indifference to perceptual reality*, and motivate *eroticized phantasmagoria* that affect the subject's perception of the world to make a mockery of empirical objectivity.'[20]

While a thorough theory of the image would necessarily have to take into account the question of gender (and is a type of analysis perfectly coherent with my reading of Baudelaire's female passer-by), this is not my objective here. Rather, in the reminder of this chapter I will consider some theoretical and historical issues in relation to photography, and, more specifically, attempt to construct a network of concerns around photography and image in general through the interplay of key texts by Williams, Benjamin, Bazin, Barthes and Jameson. My aim is not a critique of their various positions, either explicit or implicit, which in several cases obviously lacks an investigation of gender. Rather, I would like to highlight, within the puzzle offered by some texts by those writers, something essential to the understanding of photography, and therefore cinema: that is, the rapport between absence and reality. If photographs are different from filmic images and even more so, as Jameson suggests, from 'the glossy images of postmodern film', nevertheless one cannot forget that 'they are technically and historically related'.[21]

Black-and-white is blue

We might think that photography and cinema are a part (alongside painting) of the history or the anthropology of the idea of the real. Eric Auerbach, rejecting any narrow academic conception of realism as a school founded in the nineteenth century, identified realism as the major concern of Western art from Homer to modernity. The point, of course, is not that of identifying an eternal cultural value that would force any human experience into a Western mould, in a sort of teleological comparative history, but rather to examine the insistence of the notion of the real, and to ask certain questions of it. For example, what are the different values given to the real in various historical periods and in various geographical areas? When and how was it charged with a particular meaning, so that it became central to the way in which knowledge has been organized or epistemological problems posed? How have various techniques and optical means – perspective, photography, cinema – intersected to produce antagonistic significations? How mutually dependent are a positive (and positivistic) and a negative sense of the real?

I would argue that, from Balzac to the contemporary critics, the notion of the real has primary importance. Writing in the nineteenth century, Balzac drowned in the excess of the real world – where objects, matter, things, books, people, ideas, words piled up in an uncontrollable quantity. But the master of the French realist novel was already perceived by Baudelaire as a visionary. Forcing the limits of the realist experience culminating in Balzac's descriptions of the big monster, Paris, Baudelaire carved out another notion of reality: an allegorical one, where Paris became undescribable, but haunting as a spectral presence – which is absence. Consequently Paris can be totally identified with the mysterious woman, the ephemeral passer-by tinged with the colour of eternity. On the other hand, it is precisely because of the shifting meanings of the term 'realism' that Brecht could later talk about another realism which does not correspond to the great organic genealogies of the realist novel, but rather to the technical power of montage, like in Dos Passos's novels, or to the allegories of Shelley.[22] Neither did the thirst for the real escape the surrealistically conceived investigations of Lacanian psychoanalysis. The hard core, the impossible kernel of the real holds up, ineluctably tied to what is symbolic and to what is imaginary.[23]

Visible or invisible, easy or impossible to grasp, full or empty, concrete and abstract, opaque and virtual – reality has been a cultural obsession. In the modernist era a whole host of concepts move around the real, allowing all the paradigms from reification to de-reification, passing through the exaltation of the concrete, the nostalgia for the physical thing, the search for the truth, the belief in the document, the allegorical value of the fictional, the imprint of the symbolic. Behind all this an old dream is lurking – the desire to be reality, to be the thing itself, beyond the representational power of words and images. It is a dream of blind materialism to immediately turn into the idealism of the full thing, dispensing with the need for representation in the fullness of the presence of the present. God stands at the horizon, in the divine mystery of creation. Yet how is it possible even to conceive of such a desire for reality, without that gap that is our thinking and speaking about it? In the moment I see reality, I am marking the distance that makes reality problematic, tingeing with absence what is present. Such is the drama of representation. Any artistic theory – either holding onto representation or denying it – is part and parcel of the same drama. Hence the misery and splendour of the term 'realism'.

In 1945 André Bazin wrote one of the most important essays on photography, at a moment when the medium was already a century old, and cinema half a century. In this essay, 'The Ontology of the Photographic Image', Bazin established a link between cinema and photography within the perspective of the psychological history of plastic arts. Moreover, in his subsequent writings, including his seminal work on Italian neo-realist cinema, Bazin established himself as one of the great interpreters of realism. His modernist fight to endow cinema with artistic dignity is paradoxically constructed upon what I would call a non-modernist vision of the world. This is probably due to his Catholicism, inevitably infused with a conception of some essential human unity and the belief in some inner signification of things. If modernism is born with Baudelaire and his poetics of the 'modern' – of the modern metropolis as the only (completely alienating) reality – then any belief which is founded on unity, continuity, and the fullness of some spiritual experience through matter, is inevitably idealist and non-modernist.

As already suggested, *Les Fleurs du Mal* continually hints at the presence of Paris, not by describing it but by showing its effects on human perception. Baudelaire's poems subvert the poetic idealism of a world where nature, God and human life respond to each other in a perennial harmony. The lyric poems of Baudelaire are disharmonious, Satanic, cruel, innovative both at the stylistic level of a versification, which did not respect traditional metrics, and at the content level, which was striking in the scandalous choice of themes; they mark, as Benjamin has shown, the essential cultural switch in the nineteenth century which corresponded to the new forms of production, and to the market economy typical of the metropolitan reality. 'Modern' here means fragmentation, expressed in the very form of the other crucial work by Baudelaire, *Paris Spleen*, in which the intuition of montage is already present. The poet announces to his friend Arsène Houssaye that these poems were conceived as segments, as pieces whose order was irrelevant but whose rhythm corresponded to the 'abstract modern life', to the broken rhythm of the modern metropolis where the human subjects are constantly divided, constantly exposed to the nervous life of their inner perception moulded on the nervous reality surrounding all their gestures.

The reality of modernism is abstract where the Catholic vision of the world is spiritual, pointing to a mysterious correspondence between things and their meanings. However, I would argue that realism cannot exist without some degree of allegory, because even the most flat conception of it – namely, that realism is a copy of things – must refer to some organizing notion, such as the idea of the evidence of facts. Catholic realism is allegorical in the sense of it being a transfiguration of something concrete into its hidden meaning, while the modernist realism – that of Baudelaire – on the other hand, derives from an intellectual almost mathematical operation. It refuses both description and transfiguration but it believes in a process of idealization that turns reality into mockery; it has the power of abstraction and deformation. The famous poem 'Les Sept Vieillards' ('The Seven Old Men') recounts the hallucination of the poet-inhabitant of the metropolis, who is convinced he sees an old man multiplying in front of him. The poem begins with a powerful vision bordering on absurdity:

> Swarming city, filled with dreams,
> Where ghosts grab passers-by at full day!
> Mysteries rise all over like sap
> In the narrow channels of the mighty giant.
>
> One Morning, when, in the sad street,
> Buildings, whose height was increased by the mist,
> Were similar to the two embankments of a grown river,
> When, like a stage setting resembling the actor's mind
>
> A filthy and yellow fog flooded all the space around,
> My nerves stiffed like a hero's, I followed ...[24]

As in many of Baudelaire's poems, if we examine this work, if we catch its reel-movement when, in the following lines, the old man multiplies to the number of seven, we see hallucination implanted in the real, or one inextricably connected to the other. The modern resides in this realistic hallucination. In painting and cinema modernism moves towards expressionism – exactly that allegorical, disturbed and distorted technique which perverts 'realist' (in the simplistic sense) reproduction into symbolic colours and shapes, such as those deformed buildings and that yellow fog hitting the eyes and the ears of the reader in Baudelaire's poem, not unlike the violent images of Fritz Lang's *Metropolis* assaulting the viewer's perception.

Not surprisingly, expressionism was the type of cinema that Bazin could not stand, and against German expressionism, he fought for the virtues of Italian neo-realism. His enthusiasm for Rossellini and neo-realist cinema in general was founded on the awareness that the illusion of reality given to the spectator 'can only be achieved in one way – through artifice'.[25] But Bazin did not see a violent tension between the epistemological and the aesthetic senses of the phrase 'reproduction of reality'. On the contrary, for him:

> The 'art' of cinema lives off this contradiction. It gets the most out of the potential for abstraction and symbolism provided by the present limits of the screen, but this utilization of the residue conventions abandoned by technique can work either to the advantage or to the detriment of realism. It can magnify or neutralize the effectiveness of the elements of reality that the camera captures.[26]

Technique, so important for Bazin, is at the service of reality, of the world that cinema is supposed to represent according to the movement of our desires. Nothing in Bazin's writings, not even his most acute concerns for technical devices, such as in his famous analysis of *Citizen Kane*, leads to an identification of technique as that primary force within which human beings live and change, as that breaking-point from which a cultural jump is activated in spite of some delays in mentality and habits. Rather, for Bazin, technique is always an instrument; it is never above human spiritual life.

For the spiritualist, technique is often the tangible shape taken by human spirituality; for the materialist, technique dominates and shapes the human. The difference between Bazin's progressive Catholic approach[27] and the modernist-Marxist relies exactly in this value of technique. (We know, of course, that there is a militaristic and fascist conception of technique: it is the instrument a few people use to dominate and crush other people.) Jameson, who in 'The Existence of Italy' pinpointed the ontological-metaphysical Bazinian project, puts it clearly:

> I am tempted to say that all technological explanation has, as its strong function or 'proper use,' demystification, generally in the service of a materialist philosophical position: de-idealization, then, de-spiritualization in whatever sense or context, provided it is under-stood that is *not* a position but rather an operation, and *intervention*, whose aims and effects depend on what is being demystified, generally the innate tendency of literary or cultural critics to an idealism of meaning or interpretation.[28]

But arguably the main source of Bazin's enthusiasm for neo-realism is what might be called the passion for the peculiar melancholy of the black-and-white – the historical nostalgic essence of photography, that inescapable longing for reality imprinted in any photograph before the advent of colour. Jameson is again full of insight on this point. Quoting Kracauer on Benjamin, he stresses the 'global relationship between melancholy and the visual'.[29] In the essay 'In Defense of Rossellini', Bazin developed what Jameson sees as his 'ontological' nostalgia:

> Neo-realism … is always reality as it is visible through an artist, as refracted by his consciousness – but his consciousness as a whole and not by his reason alone or his emotions or his beliefs – and reassem-bled from its distinguishable elements. I would put it this way: the traditional realist artist – Zola, for example – analyses reality into parts which he then reassembles in a synthesis the final determinant of which is his moral conception of the world, whereas the consciousness of the neo-realist director *filters* reality. Undoubtedly, his conscious-ness, like that of everyone else, does not admit reality as a whole, but the selection that does occur is neither logical nor it is psychological; it is ontological, in the sense that the image of reality it restores to us is still a whole – just as a black-and-white photograph is not an image of reality broken down and put back together again 'without the colour' but rather *a true imprint of reality* [my emphasis], a kind of luminous mold in which colour simply does not figure. There is ontological identity between the object and its photographic image.[30]

Bazin, within the context of neo-realist cinema, once again stressed his thesis on photography, establishing a necessary link between neo-realism and black-and-white, which is the kind of *rapprochement* we cannot avoid now, in the era of the glamorous colour of the postmodern. What Bazin called the ontological identity between the object and its photographic image raises up in the consciousness of the spectator like a revelation.

The idea of revelation is crucial in 'On the Ontology of the Photographic Image', which begins with the precise intention to find a continuity in a human endeavour. Photography is part of the history of plastic arts, whose primordial human intention was the sacred battle against death. Embalming the dead as in Egyptian religion and painting the portrait of Louis XIV both demonstrate the same human impulse: the attempt to preserve life by a representation of life, the need to remember, to win time through the immortal character of form. Bazin described the tension implied in the history of the plastic arts by way of the concept that would become his favourite theme in film criticism: realism. The history of the plastic arts is the history itself of resemblance or realism. A double realism glimmers through Bazin's argument, articulating the aesthetic and the psychological as the two halves of the same question. Human beings are thirsty for reality and they move between the aspiration to spiritual reality and the replacement of the external world thanks to its duplication, what Bazin calls *eidolon*, or image of the external world.

Bazin reveals his idealistic-spiritual vision as fundamental for human experience. It is not that he does not see that human beings live in alienation, but rather that they are perceived as going beyond their alienation, exactly in those miraculous moments in which an ontological identity – a coincidence – is found between the thing and its image. The spiritual tension is a promise, a fulfilling synthesis, or a reassuring return to some previous golden age, before the split. The history of the visual arts, culminating in photography and cinema, leads humanity to that aim.

Unlike the Marxist-modernist oriented idea of periodization which emphasizes the new conditions of life in the nineteenth century, Bazin's periodization endows photography and cinema with the power of the happy rediscovery of a more spiritual age. For him they echo back to some miraculous balance that existed before the invention of perspective, what Bazin calls 'the original sin of Western painting'. Medieval painting, in fact, is not, in his opinion, caught within the conflict of the spiritual and the psychological, while the invention of perspective on the other hand is the result of that conflict. This rather obscure idea hints, I think, at the illusory and especially abstract character of the *representation* of reality in the technique of perspective. The essential task for Bazin is not to represent but to re-create or create anew. Such is the incantatory power of revelation. Niepce and Lumière can therefore be seen as redeeming the plastic arts, freeing them from what Bazin calls 'their obsession with likeness'. Photography jumps away from the original sin of Western painting, from the prejudices with which it affected our perception of the object, and, it can be added, from the subsequent sin of expressionism. Expressionism is in fact connected to the *a priori* of perspective, because it needs to transgress and deform it, and, by doing this, it reconfirms perspective's hegemony. Photography is silent and sober. It renounces the dream of likeness, focusing on what can be called the existential solitude of things and beings, their phenomenological density, their mysterious life. Photography is, for Bazin, the revelation of the *real*:

> The aesthetic qualities of photography are to be sought in its power to lay bare realities [Les virtualités esthétiques de la photographie résident dans la *révélation* du réel]. It is not for me to separate off, in the complex fabric of the objective world, here a reflection on a damp sidewalk, there the gesture of a child. Only the impassive lens, stripping its object of all those ways of seeing it, those piled-up preconceptions, that spiritual dust and grime with which my eyes have covered it, is able to present it in all its virginal purity to my attention and consequently to my love. By the power of photography, the natural image of a world that we neither know nor can see, nature at last does more than imitate art: she imitates the artist.[31]

Bazin's argument builds up dramatically, surveying human history, casting light on unconscious attempts and desires, sketching a compelling anthropology capable of finding the dazzling emotion that *reveals* the real. In that luminous moment of revelation photography moves away from the path of the visual arts and fulfils the quest for the object, giving the certainty that what has been photographed really existed in space and time. On this point, Bazin's intuition is similar to Benjamin's, despite their ideological differences, in that photography's revelation is close to Benjamin's tiny spark of chance which I commented on above.

But who can, looking a photograph, escape that shade of the nostalgia for the real? In his 1980 book *Camera Lucida*, Roland Barthes, from a structuralist-phenomenological perspective, reached an understanding of photography similar to Bazin's revelation (or to Benjamin's magic). Barthes is convinced that photography's essence relies in the *ça a été* (it has been). Following Sartre's work on the imaginary, Barthes insisted on the absence of the photographed object, finally realizing an

experience of hallucination that is not too far away from the revelation
Bazin talked about:

> The image, says phenomenology, is an object-as-nothing. Now, in the
> Photograph, what I posit is not only the absence of the object; it is
> also, by one and the same movement, on equal terms, the fact that
> this object has indeed existed and that is has been there where I see it.
> Here is where the madness is, for until this day no representation
> could assure me of the past of a thing except by intermediaries; but
> with the Photograph, my certainty is immediate: no one in the world
> can undeceive me. The Photograph then becomes a bizarre *medium*, a
> new form of hallucination: false on the level of perception, true on the
> level of time: a temporal hallucination, so to speak, a modest, *shared*
> hallucination (on the one hand 'it is not there,' on the other 'but it
> has indeed been'): a mad image, chafed by reality.[32]

The startling personal experience of Barthes researching the essence
and meaning of photography culminates in the astonishment of a resurrection, when, after his mother's death, contemplating (not unlike
Proust's narrator looking at his grandmother's picture) the photograph of
a 6-year-old girl, he *recognized* his dead mother as he had never really seen
her. Photography is a snapshot, in the technical and existential senses; it
catches the instant, fixing it for all time. In front of that picture, Barthes
is taken by cathartic revelation that blends the sorrow for an absence with
the melancholy beauty of time, of the time we have never lived but we
can long for in the faded light of the black-and-white image.

Discussing film history and its periodization in his essay 'The Existence
of Italy', Jameson rejects a simply linear or evolutionary chronology
progressing from realism, to modernism to postmodernism. He nevertheless considers that this 'three terms' trajectory is valuable 'at a more compressed tempo',[33] and, beyond the analogies between what has been
called the realist moment of film and nineteenth-century realist novel, he
faced 'realism' as a 'peculiarly unstable concept owing to its simultaneous, yet incompatible, aesthetic and epistemological claims, as the two
terms of the slogan, "representation of reality", suggest.'[34] Jameson
follows the conceptual tension implicit and explicit in that slogan, since
the strength of representational techniques undermines the truth
content, stressing the illusory character of realistic effects, while the
simple claim of a correct representation of the world – of reality –
annihilates the very existence of an aesthetic mode of representation,
exalting a documentary value beyond the realistic artifice, or art. But, in a

very anti-Bazinian way, Jameson insists that we cannot but take into account the conceptual instability posited by the simultaneity of the epistemological and the aesthetic claims, 'prolonging and preserving – rather than "resolving" – this constitutive tension and incommensurability'.[35]

Photography is condemned to be inextricably linked with reality and its fluctuations as it necessarily embodies the paradox of the phrase 'representation of reality'. But Jameson perceives photography as crucial to understanding something which is, I would say, at the basis of any historical research – namely the paradox of history itself. Both history and photography share a concern with the relationship of an event to the present, or with the presence of an event beyond its primary phenomenological appearance in that disquieting reinvention or re-enactment or rediscovery of it – a process that combines immediacy with representational distance.

Still photography remains, however, the archetypal embodiment of this process and of its paradoxes: in it even 'fiction photography' (nineteenth-century *mise-en-scène* and costumed poses) ultimately becomes 'realistic', in so far as it remains a historical fact that nineteenth-century bourgeois people did put on costumes to pose for such tableaux. On the other hand, one is also tempted to say that in another sense that there is no photographic *realism* as such – all photography is already 'modernist' in so far as it necessarily draws attention (by way of framing and composition) to the act by which its contents are 'endowed with form,' as we used to say in the modernist period. 'Realism', in this view, would simply consist in the space of the family photograph and the 'likeness' of some sheer personal association and recognition.[36]

Jameson's major point of interest is in film history, but he must investigate it through a reflection on photographic image and on what I would call the 'trembling', or the flickering, of the term *realism*, which is always logically (rather than chronologically) first, even in the compressed sequence of realism – modernism – postmodernism. Through photography and its use in certain kinds of cinema Jameson perceived the nostalgic character inevitably attached to the medium. The embodied possibility of nostalgia provokes a startling reversal: Jameson reads Benjamin as being on the side of nostalgia, in spite of what can sound a non-nostalgic slogan – Benjamin's idea that photography marked the end of art's aura of uniqueness. In the age of video and television, according to Jameson, we can identify in cinema a sort of return to the splendour of the work of art, the famous aura Benjamin saw as characterizing the artistic object before the advent of mass production. Because of this return, the 'good print' of a film acquires the value of a renewed authenticity.

Nostalgia also lingers in the immobility of photography, in the fading away of its nuances. What separates our perception of photography from Benjamin's is obviously a technical aspect: the glossy colour picture of our age that changes the meaning and perception of black-and-white photography. This glossiness is the presence itself of the postmodern, which can cast a nostalgic light on the melancholy technicality of black-and-white, somewhat blurring the distinction between realism and modernism, while marking the postmodern. Jameson tracks down the tie with the past:

> In photography, however, as Susan Sontag has pointed out, things are somewhat different, the marks of ageing – fading, yellowing, and the like – increase the value of a black-and-white print and heighten its interest as an object for us. Color prints, however, merely deteriorate with age ... The distinction is strikingly dramatized in the Cuban film, *The Opportunist!* (*Un Hombre de éxito*, Humberto Solas, 1986), which begins with streaked and faded black-and-white (fictional) newsreel footage of the return of the police chief figure to La Havana in 1932, wondrously transmuted into color while the camera pauses on the monumental interior of the palace.[37]

I would insist on Jameson's perspective and reinforce his non-linear understanding of the series realism–modernism–postmodernism, while maintaining that realism holds a primary position and can be mapped with different degrees of intensity and carry various values. Within his thesis on the nostalgic character of photography, which he argues from the standpoint of a materialist cultural history of cinema, I will draw attention to what I call his snapshot, or photographic, method in writing, in the sense that his argument is constructed not according to a narrative development, but is rather a mode of writing and thinking which escapes both the old-fashioned Hegelian analytical-synthetical endeavour, and the postmodernist taste for a sort of random jamming together of quotations. Rejecting any master narrative, Jameson presents neither a linear account of the history of film nor a theoretical system nor a one-sided ideological demystification. He himself probably gives a perfect definition of his non-historicist mode of writing through the term 'alternate accounts'.[38] He precipitates – in the chemical sense, as in photography – theoretical questions and cases: an interrogation of the status of the visual, or the problem of realism blended with the interpretation of some films or literary or critical texts. Moreover, the cases modify their exemplary value, because they are positioned according to different angles of vision, and trigger off in multiple clicks.

In the sequence realism–modernism–postmodernism there is no eternal value judgement, since the logical and the chronological level are interchangeable, and because Jameson's aim is not to stand for one type or school against the other – that, for example, modernism is better than realism, postmodernism is better than modernism, and so on. We cannot, like Bazin, argue that Italian neo-realism is better than expressionism, because, in the age of post-capitalism, our memory filled with films' reminiscences, we see films that mix all categories, or use them laterally. While there are undoubtedly moments in which its is clear that Jameson's battle is against what he calls 'high modernism', so ineluctably tinged with nostalgia, nevertheless a very cogent example of his research is the reading of Antonioni's *Blow-Up*, a classic in self-reflexive modernism because of course its subject is the modernist art technique *par excellence* – photography.

Jameson writes that photography is 'already a philosophically "existentialist" medium, in which history is subject to a confusion with finitude and with individual biological time; and whose costume dramas and historical records are therefore always close to the borderline between historicity and nostalgia'.[39] But he can never be said to advocate the cause of a triumphant and perfectly liberatory postmodernism, one which would finally get rid of history and its melancholia in the splendid glossiness of coloured images. For he understands too well the pressing question:

> Is this then to say that even within the extraordinary eclipse of historicity in the postmodern period some deeper memory of history still faintly stirs? Or does this persistence – nostalgia for that ultimate moment of historical time in which difference was still present – rather betoken the incompleteness of the postmodern process, the survival within it of remnants from the past, which have not yet, as in some unimaginable fully realized postmodernism, been dissolved without a trace?[40]

Jameson is always aware that any 'strange form of vision has formal and historical preconditions'.[41] Take for example his comments on the postmodern insight at the end of *Blow-Up*: whether 'by fulfilling the realist ontology – that is, by revealing Bazinian realism openly as ontology (and as metaphysics) – it can be seen as the inauguration of all those non-ontological impulses which will take its place and which we loosely term postmodern'.[42]

Perhaps the borderline, that 'borderline between historicity and nostalgia' Jameson talks about, is inevitably there in the term 'inauguration' (which recurs often in his essay to indicate the input of certain works). To invoke this idea of inauguration places one in the stormy position of *Angelus novus*, Benjamin's angel of history, which I discussed at length in Chapter 6. The angel's face is turned towards the past, while he is violently pushed forward by a storm, which 'is what we call progress'.[43]

The term 'inauguration' is charged with the momentum of a surprise, and points to the paradoxical position of all who cannot believe in the high modernist phenomenon of avant-garde, who reject any idealism of progress, of history conceived as progress, but nevertheless understand that techniques are framed by history and that our collective unconscious struggles with the debris, the remnants of the past. We critics remain at the borderline, like spectators of photography who inevitably look for that 'here and there' of the thing, the event, the theory, knowing that what we have is an image, a piece of what Jameson calls an 'alternate account'. The borderline between historicity and nostalgia is imprinted as in a black-and-white photograph in the very form of writing – black on white. Consequently, perhaps the only coherent postmodern position would be to give up writing altogether, to dissolve our bodies in gleaming letters breaking the flux of images. By writing we cannot avoid some lingering between historicity and nostalgia.

Nostalgia is not exactly nostalgia for the past; nostalgia is not only conservative (I would venture that the conservative type is not nostalgic at all, just moralizing about contemporary evil). There is also the ontological nostalgia of Bazin; the phenomenological variety of Barthes; and something I would call radical nostalgia, which is an impossible nostalgia for the future coloured by the past, as well as for the past readable only through the wind of its future. Radical nostalgia refers to the longing for the *ça a été* in the moment we face images, being inhabited by endless conjectures. Barthes felt this while looking at an old photograph of 1854: Charles Clifford's 'Alhambra' – an old house, a porch, a deserted street. Barthes felt he wanted to live there:

> This longing to inhabit, if I observe it clearly in myself, is neither oneiric (I do not dream of some extravagant site) nor empirical (I do not intend to buy a house ...); it is fantasmatic, deriving from a kind of second sight which seems to bear me forward to a utopian

time, or to carry me back to somewhere in myself: a double movement which Baudelaire celebrated in 'Invitation au voyage' and 'La
Vie antérieure'.[44]

But the 'alternate account' is at work. Barthes's perception is openly
inscribed in Baudelaire's modernism, in his interrogative and fantasmatic meditation about time in 'A une passante'. Nevertheless, this
double movement of being carried backward and forward in time is
symptomatic of some decentring, which is our historical condition,
our situation when we try to make a point on historical events –
exactly what Jameson has perceived as the paradox embodied in photography, the tension between immediacy and the representational
distance which prescribes some re-enactment of what happened.
Benjamin, on his side, seized history's tension, this double movement,
through the expressionist violence of Klee's painting.

But the condition of our thinking and being in the world today is
decentred, or – using the concept Jameson suggested in his brilliant
interpretation of Antonioni's *Blow-Up* – 'lateral':

> There is a crucial structure of laterality at work here (demonstrable
> elsewhere in contemporary literature), by which perception or experi-
> ence requires a kind of partial distraction, a lateral engagement or
> secondary, peripheral focus, in order to come into being at the first
> place. The empty common is therefore not an image in any of the full
> or even post modern senses of the word ... Indeed, in these supreme
> moments the screen defeats the Gestalt structure of normal percep-
> tion, since it offers a ground with a figure, forcing the eye to scan this
> grassy surface aimlessly yet purposefully in a spatial exploration that is
> transformed into time itself: there is nothing to be seen, and yet we
> are, for one long lost instant, looking at it, or at least trying to.[45]

Thanks to Jameson, via the ideas of Bazin, Barthes and Benjamin, I
believe that the technical strength of photography can be perceived
today in something other than the medium itself, but something
which carries the effects of that theory/history of photography I have
attempted to sketch in this paper. Writing takes place today in the
world of cinematography. To write in a certain way is not simply a
question of style: I would even say that it is not simply a question of
writing but also of seeing. Photography, cinema, television are in our
blood. The point is not just that of writing about contemporary media,
giving dignity to them, in the way Bazin fought a battle against a

stifling culture, pushing for the dignity of cinema. It is to write today within the world of media, and to write theory or criticism with the rhythm of media. Perhaps the crossed roads of photography, cinema, literature and criticism will launch us back to the crucial debate on photography which neither Barthes nor Bazin could fully articulate, since they were too busy searching for the real. Photography and cinema, like language, and writing itself, anchored in the figurative element, are driven into the symbolic world; they display the immense hieroglyph of a collective mirror stage, of the identification of a plural alienating *imago*, of a fiction line that puts the image at the crossing of symbols and reality. But did not Bazin get close to this insight by ending his essay on photography with the bare sentence: 'On the other end, of course, cinema is also a language'?[46]

Only the snapshot can help: there is no theory today that flows in a linear narration. Intermittence and intervals cannot be ignored; they offer new beginnings, another montage, another use of pieces where reminiscence is displaced into another meaning, and continuously decentred and decentring. Jameson offers a perfect example of his critical writing and a successful postmodern use of quotations in his essay 'On Magic Realism in Film'. Interrupting his concern with history with the consideration of some Latin American films and literary works, he suggests the importance of colour in postmodernism and focuses on a long quotation by Lacan concerning the distinction between the eye and the gaze. Lacan's point in the original passage (on Zeuxis's grapes) had the purpose of illustrating the Freudian concept of instinctual drive. But here Jameson displaces its theoretical input into his own argument – which is akin to the rotating curtain of the succession of photograms, moving on to another element: a wonderful quotation from Pablo Armando Fernandez's novel, *Los Niños se despiden*, about colour, where the whole spectrum of multiple colours is nuanced 'in a wide and varied register from almost pure white to jet black'.[47]

Photograms are at the basis of the filmic image. We must work like the protagonist of *Blow-Up*, with a host of shots, made and unmade by history, following the snapshots of language, of writing. We must be able to write – and to read – with the remote control, following pieces of different stories and histories at the same time, 'laterally', nevertheless knowing where we are, in a sort of dense, nervous journalism – aimlessly yet purposefully. Distracted and concentrated at the same time, we must see, in writing, through writing, the 'signatures of the visible' that shape our everyday experience, and condition the making of our experience and existence in the mass-media metropolis of our contemporary world.

8

The Image versus the Visible: From Baudelaire's *The Painter of Modern Life* to David Lynch's *Lost Highway*

Human perception in our contemporary world seems to be increasingly visual.[1] The overwhelming presence of the visual calls for a type of experience where physical sensation and the immediate feelings connected with it are constantly solicited. The richness of the visual is boundless: the gaze dominates every human activity. Cinema has magnified the power of the gaze. One need only think of Michael Powell's *Peeping Tom* (1960): the protagonist is obsessed by the camera, and his voyeurism turns him into a serial killer. According to Fredric Jameson in *Signatures of the Visible*, contemporary civilization 'has transformed human nature into this single protean sense, which even moralism can surely no longer wish to amputate'.[2] Media are the instruments of an 'all-pervasive visuality'; films 'are a physical experience, and are remembered as such, stored in bodily synapses that evade the thinking mind'.[3]

The argument developed by Jameson is constructed very generally on the basis of a Marxist approach. On one hand the inescapable presence of capitalism turns the visual into an addiction which bypasses the thinking mind: it is the most contemporary form of alienation. On the other hand, only a historical analysis can help us to resist this process: 'This book will argue the proposition that the only way to think the visual, to get a handle on increasing, tendential, all-pervasive visuality as such, is to grasp its historical coming into being.'[4] Against Jameson's proposition I shall argue that aesthetic experience itself furnishes the resistance Jameson has in mind, and always has done. It is there that we find what Jameson calls 'other kinds of thought' capable of replacing 'the act of seeing by something else'.[5] These different kinds of thought are actually already present in aesthetic apprehension, or more precisely in an aesthetic experience of *high* quality. While considering some of the assumptions of several modern or contemporary critics, this chapter will focus on the analysis of two examples which show an unexpected similarity: Baudelaire's aesthetic principles and David Lynch's aesthetic implications in *Lost Highway*.

It is probably time to rethink the whole problem of aesthetic value and stop being afraid of evaluating works of art as good or bad, even if, of course, in the free-market society under capitalism, the art-object circulates like any other product (as Jameson reminds us in the first chapter of *Signatures of the Visible*, 'Reification and Utopia in Mass Culture'). If production affects aesthetics, this does not mean that the appreciation of aesthetic values has to be completely condemned. High-quality aesthetic experience calls for a type of attention that resists the absolutism of consumption. Historical analysis can indeed get to grips with the increasingly addictive power of visuality as such, but philosophical reflection is equally urgent, reflection which can overcome the simple opposition between the radical consciousness and the so-called 'traditional aesthetic philosophy'.

While emphasizing the 'force of application' of the theory of reification so important to Max Weber and the Frankfurt School, Jameson insists on the contrast between this new notion and the traditional definition of art as 'a goal-oriented activity which nonetheless has no practical purpose or end in the "real world" of business or politics or concrete human praxis generally'.[6] But disinterested contemplation is not the sole or even the most important tradition of aesthetics and, crucially, there is more than one traditional aesthetic philosophy. Two contrasting attitudes can be identified in Western thought: one separates the world of emotions from the world of reason (*der Geist*, spirit; *die Vernunft*, the intellect); the other insists that emotions and thought are inseparable, and that both are part of the *Geist*. The first attitude is found in the Kantian tradition and is still popular in philosophy and theories of culture; the second goes back to Shaftesbury and his heirs, and to Austro-German philosophers influenced by Brentano, such as Robert Musil. It is time to consider this philosophical tradition seriously in the field of aesthetics, too. The study of the rationality of emotions has been an important achievement in the last 20 or 30 years within analytical philosophy, political philosophy, ethics.[7] From this perspective, the artistic product can be appreciated as having a critical power comparable to that revealed by historical analysis.

The consequences of Kantian dualism are unfortunately widespread. In philosophy, the irrationality of emotions is often taken for granted;

while in literary and artistic works the obsession with feeling and the heart has created, and continues to create, much confusion. Finally, in everyday life the identification of emotion with strong, merely physical impulses (sex and violence) seems inescapable and hides many subtle affective phenomena. The overrating of the sentimental is typical of the nineteenth-century Western romantic attitude (for example, German Romanticism, the English romantic poets, the American Transcendentalists or Chateaubriand[8]). Even the Freudian and post-Freudian concentration on drives and instincts helps to make many affective phenomena invisible, since drives are nothing like as rich as the infinite gamut of emotions.[9] Some contemporary critical fashions which cultivate obscurity, jargon and an overall nihilist flavour also derive from old dualist habits. Postmodern criticism – whether enthusiastic or negative – is often based on an anti-rational impulse, anti-logocentric (to use the canonical term) response, with a simplistic association of reason and bourgeois cultural hegemony. The opposition between low and high culture is often based on the division between the heart and the head, the rational and the irrational.

Against all these sharp, simplistic divisions, the analysis of the work of art, its effects, and its composition as a form, can offer an alternative to the all-pervasive visuality of today's world. The work of art and the aesthetic experience can actually oppose the divorce between body and mind, while revealing the strong link between rationality and emotion.

The Marxist postmodern approach of Jameson simply presupposes the two separate realms: on one side, the sensationalist, addictive, completely physical and totalitarian domination of sight; on the other side, fully rational behaviour within the process of rationalization in commodification. Here the forms of human activity 'are instrumentally reorganized and "taylorized," analytically fragmented and reconstructed according to various rational models of efficiency'.[10] But a proper understanding of the imagination and its activity through different works of art can clarify the real interrelation between the emotional and the rational. The work of imagination participates in that specific emotion, which is the aesthetic emotion, as well as all the emotions that are represented by the work of imagination itself. A work of art does indeed represent something – a claim all the struggle against representation which has preoccupied avant-garde criticism over the last 30 years has not overturned. The aesthetic approach understands representation not as a way of reinstating the concept of a supposedly stable reality simply reproduced by art, but, rather, as something capable of suggesting models of human mental behaviour.

Imagination, even in its most specific expressions, is a faculty imply-
ing human emotions and mental mechanisms that are not separated
from the rational, even if they are unconscious (in the sense that they
do not depend directly on the will). Imagination can elucidate several
aspects of human behaviour in general. Here I would like to draw
attention to Gilberto Freyre who, in several of his many editions of
Casa-Grande e Senzala, talked in a similar vein of the value of art. He
speaks of his pioneering work in sociology and anthropology as similar
to that of Picasso in plastic arts. He concentrated on the study of
'human behaviour, both the primitive and the civilized, the rational
and the irrational'.[11] He mentioned also the examples of Marcel Proust
and Henry James whose fiction is 'sometimes the equivalent of a social
history that could be also a scientifically psychological history'.[12]
Human behaviour is in his opinion both objective and imaginative.

The re-reading of Freyre can help today's theory and criticism to
maintain some distance from the approaches of the 1960s and 1970s,
and their postmodern re-enactment. The recent massive rejection in
European universities of the study of literature and art – as is clearly
evident in the treatment by systems of public funding of the humanities – often assumes the uselessness of art. But the analysis of aesthetic
experience shows that it is not solely concerned with some supposedly
specific and autonomous realm of art. An important assumption of an
aesthetic approach, in line with Walter Benjamin's *The Work of Art*
(1936), is the belief that we can understand more about society, contemporary or not, if we look at ways of imagining human behaviour,
understanding and feeling. It seems a matter of particular urgency to
understand the value of the imagination in today's cyberworld as a
conscious resistance against the devaluing of images, since, paradoxically, the effect of the frantic post-capitalist circulation of images is
profoundly iconoclastic:[13] images do not mean anything any longer.
Understanding works of the imagination can clarify the dangers of
complete human catastrophe described by several thinkers, such as
Guy Debord or Paul Virilio. In a world of spectacle where images
become the ultimate objects of consumption, a reflection upon art
should accompany the historical perspective suggested by Jameson.

The main assumptions of postmodern criticism inevitably lead to the
complete loss of a structuring principle, for example the assumption
that the victory of commodification is total (so total that even the
rationalizing principle of reification is completely debunked: as in
Schumpeter's vision of capitalism, where reification grows beyond any
control). But the analysis of aesthetic experience shows that emotional

and intellectual life is an open bundle that is nevertheless structured rather than scattered at random – because some artistic objects, while embodying in their form and content the commodification process to which they inevitably belong, nevertheless avoid being entirely dissipated by it, and focus on the interplay between the rational and the irrational, openness and structure, the head and the heart. When Freyre talks about Picasso's unitary art (*'arte unitaria'*), he means precisely such holding together as opposed to all scattering. He finds, in fact, that in spite of the dismembering of human bodies in his paintings, Picasso shows a strong sense of unity.

In the internet age, commodification has reached a level of globalization that even the most futuristic thinkers of the postmodern condition could not fully foresee. Jameson has suggested, following Guy Debord's *The Society of the Spectacle*,[14] that 'the ultimate form of commodity reification in contemporary consumer society is precisely the image itself. When we buy the new model car, we consume less the thing itself than its abstract idea, open to all the libidinal investments ingeniously arrayed for us by advertising.'[15] But, as we know, along with the negative visions of a society of all-pervasive visuality, there are some thinkers who express enthusiasm for its liberating qualities. Gianni Vattimo, for example, criticized the utopia of a transparent society dear to Jürgen Habermas and Karl-Otto Apel, pointing out the positive values of the *non-* transparency of the society of spectacle. The technological society is non-transparent because it is manipulated by power, since technological development constitutes the object of propaganda and of the conservation and enhancement of ideology. But Vattimo's non-transparent society is also a world where reality takes on a soft and mobile character, where experience is marked by constant change and the ludic attitude is pervasive.[16] The chaos of the non-transparent mass-media society, he tells us, is not a phenomenon to be opposed or rejected; on the contrary, such chaos comprehends the very change that makes possible the liberation of minorities. The new form of human experience in the non-transparent society is to be the key to cultural pluralism.

The general aesthetic approach as well as the examples discussed below argue against both the tragic pessimism of Debord and the floating free-associations of postmodern experience. Some artistic productions involve a critical power which does not correspond to the old-fashioned radical avant-garde hope of total subversion. Some works of art are consciously shaped by the contemporary circulation of images but resist fashionable views of that circulation. They might illustrate what Jameson calls 'the anti-social and critical, negative (although not generally revolutionary) stance of much of the most important forms of modern art'.[17] But these works of art embody the rejection of the Kantian dualism between reason and emotion. They manifest an important affinity with some of Baudelaire's major intuitions about modern art or with some of the main ideas of Robert Musil.

Baudelaire's works obviously furnish the classic example of many modern aesthetic principles; let these illustrate what I have called the 'aesthetic approach'. Baudelaire felt the need for art to respond to the modes of life of the present, which meant metropolitan life and its consequences in and for human perception. The conditions of subjectivity and experience in the modern big city are a constant concern in his poems and in his writings on painting. While searching for an art capable of integrating in its own form and content the real conditions of modernity, he insisted on the abstract aspect of art, thus anticipating the contemporary idea of the persistence of the vision in the retina and therefore in the mind – as suggested by Paul Virilio. We see, and the image that we see lingers in our memory while other images roll in front of our eyes. In order to be able to see, we must abstract, remember and understand images.

As I have suggested in other chapters, Delacroix's painting was in Baudelaire's opinion the product of thought and intelligence. Memory requires speedy execution, if the artist is not to lose his ideas. Baudelaire had seen the connection between memory and speed already in his *Salons* of 1845 and of 1846, where he comments on the works of Delacroix. Later, *The Painter of Modern Life*, inspired by the work of the painter Constantin Guys, came to be his fundamental text on this issue. Baudelaire's firm belief is that painting needs thought, strength of conception, and the power to express. For him expression becomes more important than the ability to represent. Imagination is that power, and it is based on memory: the recollection of landscapes, of other paintings, and of personal impressions. For the poet of metropolitan life, nature is not a pastoral dream nor the object of imitation, but a *dictionary* which the good painter knows how to consult. The art of painting consists not in copying or reproducing the visible world, but rather in translating mental states onto the canvas.

In *The Painter of Modern Life*, Baudelaire is particularly interested in the need for quick execution in works representing everyday life. Low-cost techniques were crucial: 'For the sketches of manners, the depiction of bourgeois life and the pageant of fashion, the technical means that is the most expeditious and the least costly will obviously be the best.'[18] After pastel, etching and aquatint, lithography appeared the best way for the modern artist to adapt to the 'daily metamorphosis of external things', and to distribute images of 'that vast dictionary of modern life'. Techniques changed the mode of production and circulation of the artistic object, which then ceased to be a *unicum*, something unique and irreplaceable.

But what is most important for my purpose, which is to show the link between Baudelaire's intuitions and film aesthetic, is that imagination is perceived as a moment of struggle between two types of memory: the one would be capable of repeating the entire range of real experience, the other selects its main outstanding features. Imagination does not exist in a sort of *vacuum*; it implies the artist at work with his pencils, brushes and all the other material instruments that should, as Baudelaire suggested with regard to Delacroix, 'translate the idea as quickly as possible, otherwise it fades away'.

In *The Painter of Modern Life*, Baudelaire invents a beautiful story: he imagines Constantin Guys at work. The painter is a real man of the crowd:

> The crowd is his element, as the air is that of birds and water of fishes. His passion and his profession are to become one flesh with the crowd. For the perfect *flâneur*, for the passionate spectator, it is an immense joy to set up house in the heart of the multitude, amid the ebb and flow of movement, in the midst of the fugitive and the infinite.[19]

The painter spends every night wandering around Paris in order to observe and absorb with all his senses the external world. Then, at dawn, instead of sleeping, he sets to work, putting down on paper his previous night's impressions, 'skirmishing with his pencil, his pen, his brush, splashing his glass of water up to the ceiling, wiping his pen on his shirt, in a ferment of violent activity, as though afraid that the image might escape him ...'[20] Memory must work together with imagination, it cannot be reduced to a mere bodily impression. And hence the struggle takes place between the two types of memory, the one capable of recalling the general contour, and the other concerned with capturing details. The only way in which the painter can resolve the tension between the temptation of a total reconstruction and the principle of selection, is to execute the work as quickly as possible.

Thus two elements are to be discerned in Monsieur G.'s execution: the first an intense effort of memory that evokes and calls back to life – a memory that says to everything, 'Arise, Lazarus'; the second, a fire, an intoxication of the pencil or the brush, amounting almost to a frenzy. It is the fear of not going fast enough, of letting the phantom escape before the synthesis has been extracted and pinned down; it is that terrible fear that takes possession of all great artists and gives them such a passionate desire to become masters of every means of expression so that the orders of the brain may never be perverted by the hesitation of the hand and that finally execution, ideal execution, may become as unconscious and spontaneous as is digestion for a healthy man after dinner.[21]

Time is therefore an essential factor in the relationship between memory and aesthetic experience. But here time is not crucial as existential recollection (it is not Proustian time), since it is the real time of artistic execution; it is the short period in which the artist produces under the pressure of the struggle between the two types of memory. It is the time of the actualization of imagination. With *The Painter of Modern Life*, art entered the age of speed. Contemplation was typical of a past, agrarian world, while metropolitan life demanded on one hand the slow and solitary accumulation of data, on the other the frantic introjection of various impressions whose rhythm had to reflect that of metropolitan life.

The importance of the time factor in film is obvious: 24 images per second are impressed on our retina, and any movie is divided into sequences lasting for a certain amount of real time. Benjamin defined film as the form of art that corresponds to the ever-increasing danger of losing one's own life – and he would make it clear that film is the form that realizes he essence of any art in the contemporary world. In film, there is no *Geborgenheit*, or security, no reconciliation, but only precariousness, disorientation, in the continuous flux of images, recalling the situation described in the famous poem interpreted by Benjamin, 'A une passante' (which I comment in Chapter 7): the metropolitan passer-by is perceived in a glimpse and then disappears equally quickly. Existence in general is precarious. The aesthetic experience – its frantic absorption of impressions of the external world and its speed – becomes the model for life in general. The extreme solicitation of our senses and an increasing quickness shape our lives and our perception in the cyber-world. From modern art as understood by Baudelaire, to film and to the internet, speed has become the central issue.

Paul Virilio, deeply concerned with the possibility (now already a reality) of technology's tyranny, insists on the question of speed. He reminds us of the totalitarian and military dimension of new technologies since the nineteenth century and of the revolution in transportation. He points to a major feature of our cyber age: speed resembles more and more the speed of light. It has the divine characteristics of ubiquity and instantaneity.[22] Speed can make everything visible – all at once and immediately. Virilio calls speed 'a vision machine'. Photography and cinema in the nineteenth century offered a vision of the world that was objective; television and computers give a vision that is flattened, like the horizon on-screen. The vision of the world today is compressed, crushed in the close-ups of time and space.

Virilio therefore identifies the period of modernity as stretching from the industrial revolution to the contemporary electronic age, and talks about the coming into being, already in the nineteenth century, of 'an aesthetic of disappearance'. This aesthetic can of course be identified with cinema itself and the disappearing of images in the sequences which follow one another. It is the opposite of 'the aesthetic of appearance' in, for example, sculpture and painting, where forms emerge from their supports, while the persistence of what holds the image is essential to its appearance. The snapshot already initiated the aesthetic of disappearance and speed; from the snapshot to the filmic image, human perception has been integrating the response to rapid images. The 24 images per second in film represent a great impact on perception: images disappear in front of us, while they are kept in the retina. An abstract mental activity is substituted for concrete holders. The conditions of seeing have switched from the persistence of marble or canvas or any such-like matter to the cognitive persistence of vision.

Memory, indispensable for the cognitive process, is involved in the process of acceleration. The points made by Virilio were already present in Baudelaire's intuitions, and are manifest in the work of David Lynch, whose film *Lost Highway* (1997) exemplifies what I have suggested about the aesthetic approach.

Speed and vision are but one: at the beginning of *Lost Highway* (1997) the spectator sees for more than three full minutes the tar on a road flashing by, rhythmically lit up by gleams. The dividing yellow line frantically folds in the night up to the point that vision itself becomes difficult. We understand that this two-lane highway is seen from a car driven fast, but neither the car nor the hypothetical driver appear on the screen. The aesthetic of disappearance becomes extraordinarily vivid: nothing but an image running away, which is almost the vision of speed itself materialized on the road's moving surface. The image is forced on our eyes to the limit of the retina's endurance, almost as if the abstraction of the persistence of vision has become tangible. Rather than seeing, our eyes are touching the grey substance of the pavement's tar as it runs away. Speed is described in its totally dehumanized essence: just bare matter hitting the eye and moving beyond the possibility of fixing vision either on a stable object or on a movable one. The traditional technique of representing movement, such as a rapidly travelling camera, is set aside, since the point of vision is not really above the road, but inside it – as if it were inside speed itself. Lynch has chosen a magnified close-up on the road. The close-up, the very means used in general to linger on a human face (or on an important object) is used to grasp the ungraspable: speed itself. The Baudelairean passer-by aesthetic has reached the paroxysm of total hallucination. The hallucinatory atmosphere is increased by the violent music which accompanies the cast-list and credits ('I'm Deranged', performed by David Bowie). Hearing and touch are summed up by sight.

After this breath-taking beginning, the visual-auditive-mental hallucina-tion is interiorized in the features of human anxiety: the protagonist's face appears in darkness and in total silence. We can scarcely distinguish the walls of a room, but we can indeed see the expression of suffering, while our brain cannot reconcile itself to the silence of this scene, since the impression of the previous shot and its soundtrack persists in our mind.

A complete reading of many elements of *Lost Highway* would confirm the interpretation of the aesthetic of disappearance: the story of the male protagonist, Fred, is continued by another character, Pete, while the female protagonist splits into two women, Renee and Alice. But, more importantly, already from the very first cut, the overwhelming power of the visual – and the visual as speed – is put in question pre-cisely because of the exaggeration of the image. The 'visible' has, so to speak, such a strong signature that it calls for other senses, highly solicited in our age, such as hearing. But it also calls for an understand-ing: the utterly physical moment envisioned by Jameson's negative utopia of the visible, is actually the quick shortcut between vision and the mind since the perception of the image is contracted into some inevitable questioning about the events in the film.

The most perfect representation of our cyberworld is not the computer itself, nor a story where some secret file on a drive is the object of dispute, as we have been seeing now for almost 20 years in so many TV series. The most perfect representation of cybernetics is the portrait of its effects on the eyes and the mind. Baudelaire did not so much describe the big city as show its imprint on human perception. In a similar way, almost at the end of the twentieth century, Lynch composes a filmic image, which, without showing any computers, shows the screen-like electronic movements of the greyish particles of a road flattened in such an extreme way that it resembles a TV or a computer screen.

Lynch succeeds in condensing the history of roads and speed into the history of the world of television and computers. At the beginning of *Lost Highway* our eyes are surfing on something that looks like a screen. With that daring, dreadful close-up, Lynch renders the internet in our brains. The film-maker is especially capable of *expressing* the equivalent of its hallucinatory effect on our vision and in our minds. Thanks to this crucial first scene also, the usual contemporary cocktail of sex and violence, so important in this film too, becomes much more than merely physical. The images that we see constantly in all movies here contain a double meaning which challenges the view of them as mere objects of consumption. They are, we may say, therefore presented iron-ically. *Peeping Tom*, in the early 1960s, hinted at the pornographic and violent aspect of the visual; *Lost Highway*, in the 1990s, sketches a pro-found meditation on the visual through what might at first appear to be its pornographic and violent essence. Our guts are not solicited *per se*, since the spectator is forced to think through images. Images address intelligence and memory, and become the means to criticize our society of the spectacle. All the elements of a history of the audiovisual appear in the film: videotapes, sound-track, photographs, cameras, portable telephones and portable TVs. They are not simply ornamental, but suggest a reflection on film, in the same way that Baudelaire's lyrics point to a reflection on the very form of lyrical poetry.

If a typical feature of postmodernism is the inclination to quote, Lynch's film is fully postmodern, but with a major difference. Its resist-ance to the postmodern taste for citations can be retraced in the con-tinuous attempt to recontextualize the world from which quotations come or could come. Many elements – setting, clothes, hair-style etc. – bring into the scene the 1940s and, even more, the 1950s; that is to say the age of the blooming of film and of the spread of television. The two levels of that epoch and our contemporary age blend without nos-talgia. The 1950s and the 1990s are periods of major changes in com-munication techniques, and in the way in which we live and feel. The spectators cannot completely free-float on clichés as if they were empty images of a pure postmodern world. The spectators must be active, must interpret; they have to put their own memory into a historical context, understanding the interplay of different epochs. Lynch's style is indeed postmodern, but not its intention, since he aims exactly to show up the conditions of existence of postmodern style.

As with another major film by Lynch, *Blue Velvet* (1984), which makes use of images and music from the 1950s in the USA, the spectator is led into the world of imagination that the film-maker has made, and comes to grasp what Jameson calls the 'historial coming into being' of the all-pervasive character of the visual. A cultural or social historian would have to write chapters analysing the conditions of communication in the 1950s, and draw comparisons with our present technological revolution; an artist can contract everything into an image.

Let us cast our minds back to the road in the opening sequence. While projecting speed in a most contemporary spasm of vision, this cut alludes not only to the general recurring filmic motif of the road, but to other films. It obviously works as a quotation from Lynch himself, since the frantic road constituted a motif in *Blue Velvet*. Already in that film, he suggests, through the double reading of the present time and the 1950s (songs and images), that we are in the age of the intrusion of film and TV into real life. That is the condition of our mind today. But, in the *Lost Highway* road scene, one can also detect a reference and re-enactment of the first minutes of a famous film of the fifties: *Kiss Me Deadly* by Albert Aldrich. Imagination elaborates elements of memory; it translates, updates them. Road and speed are not the same in the 1950s and in the 1990s: in order to show the jump from one period to the other, the motif needs to be emphasized, accelerated. Aldrich is an acrobat of the camera, Lynch shows a similar deftness, already with the initial powerful close-up, and in quoting and deforming Aldrich's images in several other scenes: the garage, the burning house on a Californian beach, some female voices and tones, the mystery of identities – all these elements recall *Kiss Me Deadly*.

Lynch obviously uses many features of B-movies but his aim is to overcome their addictive, purely physical impact. Through the importance of music and the elaboration of his cuts, he definitely contests the iconoclastic primacy of the purely visual, claiming for the power of the image as an experience of thought. Through cinematic effects he displays the work of artistic imagination intermingled with memory and creates a complex composition that transcends the mere stereotype giving it the depth of film history. Above all, he continues that chapter of modern aesthetics for which art should be a critical response to the demands of its own time.

Lynch, like Baudelaire, shows us how the aesthetic experience is capable not only of placing itself historically but also of displaying what an intelligent interplay of imagination, emotion and thought might be. The image lays claim to more than the merely visible.

9
Martin Scorsese and the Rhythm of the Metropolis

> Cities, like people, can be recognized by their walk ... So let us not place any particular value on the city's name. Like all big cities it was made up of irregularity, change, forward spurts, failures to keep step, collision of people and interests, punctuated by unfathomable silences; made up of pathways and untrodden ways, of one great rhythmic beat as well as the chronic discord and mutual displacement of all its contending rhythms. All in all, it was like a boiling bubble inside a pot made of the durable stuff of buildings, laws, regulations, and historical traditions.
>
> Robert Musil, *The Man Without Qualities*

How could we possibly think of the cinema without images of cities springing to mind? Throughout the past century, cities have been caught by the camera in documentaries and in fictions, continuing the tradition of the literary works that represent people, events and feelings in a metropolitan environment. For a whole century urban landscapes have been coming and going on screens in no particular order and with no recognizable development or thematic unity, since cities have been the canvas for a story as often as they have been the main subject, the protagonist of the whole film. Ever since René Clair's *Paris qui dort* (1924), which has so much in common with Guillaume Apollinaire's visions of Paris, and Fritz Lang's *Metropolis* (1926), which has so much in common with an expressionist painting or a constructivist project, films and cities have been an irresistible combination, proving that architecture and film-making have as close a relationship as cinema and theatre or painting or literature – the arts which have most typically been associated with film (one need only think of André Bazin's essays on these topics).[1]

186

New York, Little Italy, the streets and the buildings of Manhattan, feature a great deal in Martin Scorsese's work. Paris is essential for Baudelaire, Vienna for Musil. In a similar way, it is impossible to understand Scorsese's films, their ethos, without understanding the American metropolis, which, like many European cities, is also a village, a complex of neighbourhoods. An architect, an urban historian or a sociologist could learn much from Scorsese: his camera dips into the skyline, stones, colours, atmosphere, violence, people and emotions of New York. No distinction is drawn between the city and its inhabitants. At the very beginning of *Taxi Driver* (1976) we see a white cloud and, from it, the lower body of a yellow taxi emerges with its bumpers. The typical white steam of Manhattan's streets, a yellow cab, a driver with his story, solitude, obsessions, they are all one. The protagonist, Travis Bickle (in the wonderful interpretation of Robert De Niro), is a Vietnam veteran who becomes a taxi driver: it could be anywhere in the big city, at any season, at any time of the day or the night; it could be anybody; it could also be in any metropolis. *Taxi Driver* is so real in every detail that it could almost be a documentary of New York in the 1970s; but it is also the allegory of the metropolis, and of any big city. Scorsese comments:

> There's a shot where the camera is mounted on the hood of a taxi and it drives past the sign 'Fascination', which is just down my office. It's that idea of being fascinated, of this avenging angel floating through the streets of the city, that represents all cities for me.[2]

The same mixture of documentary about the city and fiction can be found in Roberto Rossellini's *Voyage en Italie* (1953). All the images of Naples showing street life, museums, excavations, hotels, restaurants, capture the reality of local life in the 1950s and blend with the personal story of a British man and his wife, who live through a critical time in their marriage. It is hard to tell if the film is more about the two people than about Naples, since the city and the nearby landscape are not always perceived through the eyes of the protagonists; they often become so central that the protagonists are just an excuse to show the city. One can think of even more tantalizing examples from Rossellini, such as what might be called the city and war trilogy, *Roma, città aperta* (1945), *Paisà* (1946), and above all *Deutschland im Jahre Null* (1947). This film shows that, like Rome at the end of the war in *Rome, Open City*, or Florence during the war in one of the most unforgettable episodes of *Paisà*, the bombed city of Berlin is not simply the background against which a terrible story takes place. The devastated streets and buildings seem to be made of the same matter as the actions and souls of the people. A child has to learn to steal and even to poison his grandfather in order to survive the extreme poverty in which his family lives at the end of the Second World War. He wanders through streets, buildings, along railway lines, among stone ruins. He embodies Berlin's misery and despair. The physical and moral destruction is quite overwhelming in the last terrible sequences of the film: the child jumps from the top of a wrecked building from which the only view is a deadly urban landscape. This landscape is actually both exterior and interior. The ruins of brick, marble, concrete in Rossellini's Berlin can speak and feel as if they were human, as if they were flesh and blood.

The American poet and film critic Vachel Lindsay, recently republished thanks to Martin Scorsese, gave some examples of urban landscapes as they are used in films in a chapter on 'Architecture-in-Motion' in his 1922 book *The Art of the Moving Picture*. He points out that peculiar cinematic phenomenon whereby inanimate matter is given as much significance as people, and significance of the same sort:

> I have said that it is a quality, not a defect, of the photoplays that while the actors tend to become types and hieroglyphics and dolls, on the other hand dolls and hieroglyphics and mechanisms tend to become human. By extension of this principle, non-human tones, textures, lines, and spaces take on a vitality almost like that of flesh and blood.[3]

For examples, the immense machines operated by workers in *Metropolis* embody metropolitan and industrial life as much as the buildings or the urban skylines themselves: they are living monsters. Or think of the buildings and the street shot by Lang in *M* (1931), where the protagonist looks for shelter when he is identified as the killer of little girls: in the contrast of light and darkness and in shades of black and white, the walls, the windows, the street-lamps on the screen tell us as much about the pursuit as the very faces of both the criminal and the pursuers. The pavement and the stones, the urban space, all give material substance to the fear and suspicion, the waiting, the hope and despair.

The steam, the yellow metal and the mirror at the beginning of *Taxi Driver* are also flesh and blood. The principle set forth by Vachel Lindsay helps us to understand that some objects or details are not simply décor but acquire meaning. The list of such objects is, of course, potentially infinite, from mirrors to guns, doors, windows; in the first moments of *Taxi Driver* it is possible to see in the cab's bumpers and rear-view mirror what Lindsay calls 'the vitality of objects'. This shot from wheel-level perspective is like a huge hieroglyphic, as if a detail in a dream were taking shape and becoming more important than anything else.[4] The steam rising from the pavement is a very real characteristic of Manhattan's avenues. It can also be an almost involuntary reference to Lang's Moloch in *Metropolis* as it appears in white clouds of smoke, endowing matter with powerful physical and symbolic features, as if it were in hell. The steam, the bumpers and the car's body appear in a huge close-up, like the following one showing the face of the driver inside his cab, reflected in the rear-view mirror. The slow, mechanical movements of his eyes are shot in a camera speed which recalls Eisenstein's editing (or, as Scorsese explains, the effect he had seen in 'the Venitian episode' of Powell and Pressburger's *The Tales of Hoffmann*). Thanks to the technique of the close-up, mainly used to show the human face and its expression, the objects themselves have acquired something human and embody the spirit of the metropolis. New York and the yellow cab are protagonists just as the main character is.

The presence of New York

In the same way that the metropolis incorporates various aspects of human life and activity, cinema encompasses various modes of expression, from image to voice, sound, music and dance. Similar to a big city made up with what Musil, in the epigraph of this chapter, calls 'the chronic discord and mutual displacement of all its contending rhythms',[5] cinema is a multifaceted, complex world. Moreover, in spite of the suburban movie-houses and home videos, is not the most mythical, and perhaps nostalgic, image of cinema itself connected with urban life, theatres, crowds, traffic, city lights, social interaction, night life?

Bernardo Bertolucci said that, when he was living in the countryside near Parma, cinema meant going to the city and the fascination of the cinema began to be associated with that of the city.

> For me film meant to leave the country, where I lived since I was a child, and go to the city. Undoubtedly, I identified the city and a real change in my life with cinema, that meant an expressive universe different from the one at home, and therefore it meant poetry.[6]

Parma's streets, squares, parks, opera house and outskirts are everywhere in his first film, *Prima della rivoluzione* (1964). Martin Scorsese,

who so much admires Bertolucci and especially this first great achievement, often talks, in interviews and articles, about his own childhood
in New York. He recalls his neighbourhood with its violence and
family outings, when he went to the movies with his father, mother
and brother. Scorsese often describes his life in Little Italy, when he
watched European films on television, against all the different noises
from the street and from the building where his family occupied a
small four-room flat in Elisabeth Street.[7] In Scorsese's interviews and
writings, his memories and comments often refer to New York, as if the
city and its life formed the substance of his imagination. He insists on
the importance of the city for *Taxi Driver*: 'The whole film is very much
based on the impressions I have as a result of my growing up in New
York and living in the city.'[8] Manhattan is also there as an overwhelming presence during the shooting of his films:

> When one shoots in New York, one gets more than he asked for.
> This is what I learned while shooting *Taxi Driver* ... There is some-
> thing in New York, a feeling that penetrates the subject one is
> working on (whatever it is), and ends up affecting the behaviour of
> your characters. This feeling – a sort of buzzing – cannot be defined
> but all those who live in this city know what I mean ... New York
> can be called so many names – vulgar, magical, scarring, dynamiz-
> ing, tiring, prosaic – that every time one must evoke it in a movie,
> even incidentally, the city ends up imposing its presence. New York
> refuses to be just a vague setting, like Los Angeles in so many films.[9]

Scorsese likes to remember the first time he saw Eisenstein's
Alexander Nevsky on a summer afternoon in Manhattan, on 96th
Street, in a movie theatre: 'I noticed they were showing *Alexander
Nevsky*, which I had read about in a magazine, and I walked in half-
way through, as usual.'[10] In this recollection, the rhythm of metropolitan life – hearing the city noises, strolling in the streets, going to
the movie, walking in half-way through, reading magazines – and the
effect of watching the battle on ice in 1242 as edited by Eisenstein in
1938 are jammed together. In the unpredictability of the metropolis
one can enter a cinema and go back in time thanks to the magic of
film. In the metropolis there is no clear-cut beginning or end, since
anything can take place anytime and anywhere. ('Anytime, anywhere': this is the phrase that Travis, in *Taxi Driver*, constantly repeats
when interviewed for his job.) As in Poe's *The Man of the Crowd*, the
life of the big city has no beginning, middle or end; it can start at any

point in time and space and continue like an infinite narrative; it implies repetitions, going back and forth. A linear sequence of time and events is totally inadequate to represent time in the metropolitan space.

In many ways, Scorsese is the counterpart in cinema of Aldo Rossi in architecture, who associated the idea of architecture itself with the city and claimed that, among all the cities he loved, the experience of New York was important for his understanding of architecture. Film is by its very nature movement, while Rossi's projects emphasize the static atmosphere typical of design. Nevertheless, both Rossi and Scorsese confirm the insistent motif in Baudelaire's aesthetics, which is born out of metropolitan experience: memory is crucial for the imagination of the artist, and images dwell in memory. Like many artists, both Rossi, the architect, and Scorsese, the film-maker, consider the images that struck them when they were children as essential to their work. In his *Scientific Autobiography*, Rossi writes of the importance of some films, and of Bertolucci's in particular, for his vision of the city. Rossi also describes the same experience mentioned by Scorsese when talking about *Alexander Nevsky*: that of getting to the cinema when the film has already started. Arriving 'half-way through', or even towards the end, is one of the chances of metropolitan life, and can influence our perception of a film. Rossi compares his early fascination with the statues of some Mannerist chapels in Lombardy to watching a film that is 'half-way through':

> As in the statues of the Sacri Monti of S., which I passed almost every day, what I admired was not their art; rather I pursued the relentlessness, the story, the repetition ... It is like seeing the same film or play many times and thus being free from the desire to know the end. To experience this effect I often go to cinema when the film is half over or just ending; in this way one meets the characters in their conclusive moments, and then one can rediscover the action that happened earlier or imagine an alternative.[11]

These important aesthetic phenomena are also crucial for the film-maker: the role of memory, the act of 'walking in half-way through', and a particular sense of time, which composes and unfolds the narrative regardless of the sequence of events. The effect of the work of art is enriched by repetition and liberated from the wish to know the end or the beginning of a story. In this way it encourages the spectator to imagine alternatives.

Scorsese mentions a feeling of repetition similar to that described by Rossi. He tells about his habit of watching the same film over and over again on a TV programme in the 1950s:

> I remember seeing Powell and Pressburger's *The Tales of Hoffmann* on this programme: it was in black and white, cut and interrupted by commercials (it was not until 1965 that I saw it in colour). But I was mesmerized by the music, the camera movements and the theatricality of the gestures by these actors who were mostly dancers. There's a lot to be said against *The Tales of Hoffmann*, yet I've always said that those repeated views on television taught me about the relation of the camera and the music: I just assimilated it because I saw it so often. Even now there is hardly a day when the score of the picture doesn't go through my mind, and of course it had an effect on the way in which I handled the musical sequences in *New York, New York* and the fight in *Raging Bull*. There was another lesson I learned from it too: when we were doing the close-ups of De Niro's eyes for *Taxi Driver*, I shot these at 38 or 46 frames per second to reproduce the same effect that I'd seen in the Venitian episode of *The Tales of Hoffmann*, when Robert Helpmann is watching the duel on a gondola.[12]

Repetitions and alternatives are therefore fundamental both to the life of a big city and to the imagination which is based on some very deep impressions imprinted on the memory (dating from childhood or other experiences). Repetitions and alternatives imply a temporal dimension which is cyclical or at least disrupts simple sequences, since parallel events are taking place either in the physical vastness of urban space or as conjectures of the mind. Possibility is added to reality – and not opposed or subtracted from it.

An imaginative person must be aware of possibilities. The life of any metropolis is constituted by the summing up of reality and possibility. At the beginning of his novel, Musil describes a car accident in Vienna. In his usual ironic style, the narrator speculates on the sense of possibility:

> It is reality that awakens possibilities, and nothing would be more perverse than to deny it. Even so it will always be the same possibilities, in sum or on the average, that go on repeating themselves until a man comes along who does not value the actuality above the idea. It is he who first gives the new possibilities their meaning, their direction, and he awakens them.[13]

Reality and possibility give the rhythm to any big city. The treatment of space-time in *Taxi Driver* is a good example of metropolitan rhythm. The story does indeed take place within a precise sequence of days, punctuated by the journal that Travis writes and reads in a tempo which both may and may not coincide with his writing, and both may and may not correspond to the protagonist's oral narration. But all the rides in the cab through the streets, at the beginning and at the end of the film, place the time of the story in the continuous traffic of New York: 'any time, anywhere', according to Travis's words. His exceptional story, which for a while makes him a hero in the newspaper – he has saved the life of a young prostitute – is just one piece in the jigsaw of the metropolis, in the vast network of actual and potential events. But time belongs more to the city than to people.

The urban experience of watching a movie which may or may not start at the beginning is often imprinted on Scorsese's mind: his narrative is his way of dealing both with time in the metropolis, and with the conjectures of imagination. For example, at the very beginning of *GoodFellas* (1989), the three protagonists – Henry, Tom and Jim, interpreted by Ray Liotta, Joe Pesci and Robert De Niro – are startled by a thumping noise coming from the trunk of their car. They open the trunk and the face of a wounded man becomes visible. They finish him off with a knife and a round of gun-shots. When Henry shuts the trunk, the image freezes and Henry's voice-over begins the story: 'As far back as I can remember, I always wanted to be a gangster.' The whole film follows Henry's narration from the glorious period of the 1950s up to the big raids of the 1960s and 1970s, and finally to the decadence of the 1980s. More or less in the middle of the film, after 'the wise guys' have already achieved some successful raids, we see them in a bar on Queens Boulevard, at night, at a very precise date, on 11 June 1970. There is a fight. Tom and Jim beat Billy Batts savagely. Then, after a stop-off at Tom's mother's, we see the first scene over again, with the three friends and Billy Batts horribly wounded but still alive in the trunk.

This repetition of the initial cut in *GoodFellas* is modelled precisely on a type of vision that starts 'half-way through', as if the spectator happens to enter the movie-house just as that very scene is taking place, and he/she has then to reconstruct the narrative. A similar type of repetition is played though in *Casino* (1996), which begins with the explosion of the protagonist's car while he tells his own story. Ace (Robert De Niro) becomes a minuscule image whirling in flames, spectacularly shooting up into Las Vegas's phantasmagoria of lights, a visual counterpart of the way the notes in Bach's *Saint Matthew Passion* leap up.[14] The sequence of the car explosion is resumed towards the end of the film and the voice of Ace explains that he survived the attack thanks to his metal seat.

Urban and suburban motifs: Scorsese and Lynch

Repetitions or interrupted temporal sequences are typical features of Scorsese's work, and are very disturbing for anybody who likes a simple narrative.[15] They are based on the metropolitan tempo and not on the random shifts of a remote control that jumps here and there, joining different pieces together and jeopardizing any possibility of reconstructing the story or the stories. Time in Scorsese's movies is the result of both the rhythm of the city and the technical characteristics of cinema; short-cuts, cross-cutting, sequence shots, subtle graphic skills in the cast and credits are the tools that the film-maker uses in order to give cohesion to his narrations. Scorsese sometimes chooses to construct the story in a very classical way, within a short, concentrated period of time, or reduced to a few days, as in the adventures of Charlie and Johnny Boy in *Mean Streets*. Sometimes, on the contrary, he tries the long period of time in a novel-like form, like *GoodFellas*, where the dates shown at the beginning of the four sections go from the 1950s to the 1980s. Within these large temporal structures, time is treated unevenly, according to the pattern of repetition and interruption, and there are often discrepancies or ellipses between what is shown in the cut and what is said by the narrating voice. For example, in *GoodFellas*, towards the end, the voice-over of Henry explains that he was worried that Tom, in his excessive violence, would also murder a friend, Morrie, and confesses his relief: 'It was like a load off my mind. Poor bastard. He never knew how close he came to getting killed. Even if I told him he would have never believed me.' But immediately after, without voice-over, we see Jim, Tom, Frank Carbone and Morrie in a car: suddenly, in the middle of the conversation, Tom kills Morrie with an ice pick in his neck. In the brief spasms of time and events typical of urban life – and in the tense schedule of the shooting of a film – the film-maker does not need to lose time explaining every detail, to have everything fit neatly. A spectator who is quick on the uptake, as anyone entering half-way through needs to be, can connect the pieces and guess at events and feelings. Why should any narration block the intelligent and free rein of the imagination?

Scorsese translates into his films the experience of New York, of its external, concrete presence, which is of course interiorized. His colours, adventures and marvellous soundtrack disrupt any simplistic, linear sequence of time and events, and create a flexible structure. The city-dweller knows how to put together elements in order to make sense of them and, at least partially, must reconstruct a narrative: it is a question of life and death, like crossing a street or understanding where noise and danger are coming from. And this capacity to reconstruct and comprehend rapidly is interiorized by the inhabitants of the city. (As I mentioned in the previuos chapters, Walter Benjamin spoke of the interiorization of shock in metropolitan life, and George Simmel of 'nervous life' as the basis of perception in urban life.) As in Stendhal's novels, elliptical narration in Scorsese's films helps to produce a fast rhythm, not lingering on description. Ellipsis enhances the pace of action and emotion; it demands intelligence to understand short-cuts and compose the elements of a story – or an argument.

Ellipsis implies mobility, flexibility, areas of particular density, changes, irregularities, like the rhythm of a metropolis as suggested by Musil in the quotation at the beginning of this essay. But ellipsis does not imply lack of structure. The fragmentation or random piecing together so typical of postmodernism is a very different phenomenon from the abrupt narrative which is moulded by urban rhythm. The contrast between David Lynch and Scorsese might be illuminating. Lynch likes 'fragments of narrative', such as those he finds in Bacon's paintings.[16] He cleverly builds his images on what can be called the postmodern suspicion of narrative. His fragments of stories are highly suggestive: they recall the way in which images come and go in dreams – both when we are asleep and when we are awake. In *Lost Highway* (1997), the characters (Fred and Pete, Alice and Renee) have parallel identities. Their substitution can also be understood as the composition of images through skipping around with the remote control, or the winding and unwinding of a video cassette – the winding and unwinding of a mysterious cassette is in fact an important element of the film, and even the scene of Fred killing his wife Renee seems to be shown from a video at the police office. David Lynch is intimately inspired by suburban life: a mixture of nature and technology – *The Machine in the Garden*, as remarkably summed up in the title of a 1960s book by Leo Marx[17] dealing with nineteenth-century anti-urban American ideology. Media and technology have shaped the minds of the inhabitants, they have taken the place of real relationship with the world. In the suburbs, images are the substitute for reality, while in the metropolis, images and reality are continuously responding to each other, at a frantic pace. New York is the ground for Scorsese's imagination. California, Los Angeles, which is like an immense suburb, or any

Midwestern suburb, such as the fictional Lamberton in *Blue Velvet* (1986), form the background of the glossy colours, the splendid sound-track, and the maverick adventures of Lynch's films.

Scorsese and Lynch can be considered two of the contemporary film-makers who most effectively master their art with the complete under-standing that cinema is composed of both image and sound. But Scorsese feeds his imagination with urban life, while Lynch does it with suburban life (and that infinite suburb that is LA). The initial cut of the road in *Lost Highway* (which I discussed in the previous chapter) and the road in a scene that takes place 15 minutes from the beginning of *Taxi Driver* will be examples of the difference between the urban and suburban imagina-tion, or between the New York and the Los Angeles imprint.

The asphalt rolling in front of our eyes in *Lost Highway* can be described as the visual hallucination of speed; it is not a specific road but almost the image of speed imprinted on the retina. The cut of the two-lane highway is followed next by a cut with the interior of a villa where the face of the protagonist appears in the darkness. He looks ter-ribly distressed. Later the exterior of a Los Angeles villa is shown in full daylight (it is actually the Lynch's Pasadena house where he edits the music for his films). The road at the beginning is an isolated object, just as the protagonist is isolated in his white villa: within the sub-urban motif objects are singled out thanks to their plain, glossy colours: for example the flowers, the grass and the sky at the beginning of *Blue Velvet*. Lynch talks about the blue sky with aeroplanes as the substratum of his personal memory, from his childhood in 'deep America', in Montana, where he was born, to Boise, Idaho, and Spokane, Washington State, where he moved with his family when he was about 14 years old: 'It was a world of dream, blue sky, planes which passed over the fences, green grass, cherry-trees ...'[18] Of course, this dream is not absolute, untouched: Lynch is fully aware of that. He mentions in fact the presence of industrial dust on every leaf and tree; this broken pastoral ideal shows that Nature is not as pure as it seemed in the forests of Montana where he used to go with his father when he was a child.[19] Actually, Lynch's irony about the American dream is based on the contrast between the ideal of Nature and industrial reality. It should also be said that Nature itself is a complex reality: Lynch likes to show how insects are swarming under what seems the purity and perfect smoothness of a tree-trunk or the grass (in the first minutes of *Blue Velvet*, after the image of the idyllic blue sky and sub-urban life, we see dark insects moving in a piece of brown thick earth while their noise comes amplified to our ears).

A long tradition of art longing for Nature shows that industrialization undermines Nature's wholeness. Hence the terrible noises of the
railroad and factories in *Eraserhead* (1976), or, in *The Elephant Man*, the
reconstitution of London as its appears in Dickens's novels (with a
memorable long scene in Victoria Station where people chase the elephant man). In any event, the urban-industrial landscape is perceived
from outside, as horror, fear and surprise, almost what Lynch himself
felt when he went to New York as a child: 'Because my grandparents
on my mother's side lived in Brooklyn, I would go to New York City ...
And it scared the hell out of me. In the subway I remember a wind
from the approaching train, then a smell and a sound. I had a taste of
horror every time I went to New York.'[20] The urban milieu, which can
produce a maverick fascination, is connected with monstrosity, with
deformed nature, such as the elephant man and the strange baby-
monster in *Eraserhead*.[21]

In *Taxi Driver*, a few minutes from the beginning, the road appears in
a close-up lasting for almost 30 seconds: the shot comes after New York
has already been introduced as a presence, and not simply as a backdrop, with its thoroughfares, lights, rain, noise, people in the street,
cab-station, and the endless journeys of Travis's yellow cab. The real
macadam of a New York avenue is there, with its holes and bumps, in a
slow-motion huge close-up on the grey matter. As suggested by Musil,
every city is made of its own rhythm, of events taking place or suscep-
tible of taking place, and of 'the durable stuff' of buildings and history.
In *Taxi Diver*, the 'stuff' of New York boils up as if from a pot. And New
York becomes an allegory for all cities, as suggested by Scorsese
himself, precisely because it has a fully concrete existence from which
meaning can be developed. Spectators grasp the documentary dimension of the shot on the macadam together with the allegorical one,
and, having been able to identify areas in Manhattan, impelled by a
taste for the realistic representation of place and time (don't we all like
to recognize what we have already seen and what we know?), they
could even be tempted to try and identify the avenue shown in the
shot. In *Taxi Driver*, as in many of Scorsese's films, the metropolis is
perceived from within, since the shot on the road forms part of the
complex network of material and mental relations that constitute the
big city. Even the solitude and the madness of the protagonist is represented within the multiple pattern of the city: we see Travis looking for
a job, speaking with the employee in the interview, and the whole
story follows an election campaign. In the big city lots of people meet,
bump into each other, talk, drive cars, go to the movies, to bars. Even

the anonymity of the crowd is a real presence and creates a network of relations, however transient they may be. Images, words and urban reality merge. When Travis is alone in his apartment getting ready with his guns, the social dimension is not diminished, since his silent gestures are accompanied by the noise of the city – a different noise from that of insects in *Blue Velvet* or from the terrible screaming inside the heads of Fred and Pete, the male protagonists of *Lost Highway*, whose identities blend in an incomprehensible way. In Lynch, the external world is a projection of the internal frame of mind; in Scorsese any mental state is a response to reality, even if this reality is dream-like. Scorsese's films have a lot in common with Baudelaire's *Fleurs du Mal*, with his peculiar, intense way of combining the most concrete and the most abstract elements in his poetic images.

Nothing can be really isolated in the city, since the city is the social space *par excellence*. Family, group, community, neighbourhood, friends and enemies, ethnic definitions and accents, circulation of money – all these elements are crucial for Scorsese. The circulation of money is visible and almost tangible in his movies. So many scenes in *Mean Streets, Taxi Driver, GoodFellas* show dollars bills passing from one hand to another. The sequence in which, in *GoodFellas*, the young Henry meets Jimmy for the first time shows the wise guys playing cards. Henry's voice-over tells: 'It was a glorious time', and, after a whole account of the bills the legendary Jimmy gives to everybody in the room, we see him slipping a 20-dollar bill into Henry's pocket. A freeze-frame on Jimmy underlines the unforgettable character of this episode. In *Casino*, where money plays in a spectacular way the usual central role in human relationships, an extraordinary sequence shows the accumulation of money in its most material aspect: cash. Ace, the narrator who runs a Las Vegas casinos, tells at the beginning of the film about his thrilling enterprise 'that's like selling people dreams for cash', while in the casino's most secret room tons of coins quickly pile up like objects in an assembly line, and the empoyees count and separate packages of bills.

Even the apparently most trifling scene in Scorsese's movies can be rich in social information: the brief words uttered by Mike in the first minutes of *Mean Streets* while a truck is unloaded indicate the Italian-American community; a certain intonation in the voice of Karen (Lorraine Bracco) in *GoodFellas* when she asks policemen if they want some coffee, reminds us that she is Jewish. And Catherine Scorsese, the film-maker's mother, appears in several films, talking in a mixture of American and Sicilian dialect, as when she speaks about a spaghetti-sauce recipe in Scorsese's documentary *Italianamerica* (a 1974 film financed by a bicentennial award from the National Endowment for the Humanities, which became part of a TV series about immigrants and ethnic minorities[22]).

Similar episodes in public spaces have different flavours in Scorsese and Lynch. The bars, restaurants, clubs and cafés in *Mean Streets, Taxi Driver, Raging Bull, GoodFellas* etc. show a social network, a strong sense of neighbourhood in spite of violence – Mafia, family parties, young people hanging out together in the same parts of the city. Every individual, whoever they are and whatever their problem, is steeped in that social atmosphere and, however uncommunicative or violent they may be, they indicate some urban cohesion, even if it is problematic. Also, violence in a Scorsese film has a culturally urban quality: its dynamics are those of a group, however secluded the group or isolated the individual may be – even Travis's mad project takes shape through the words of one of his fellow taxi drivers and through a 'business' transaction with the salesman (in a wonderful scene where the salesman displays all his guns in front of Travis, in an apartment from whose windows is visible a corner of the parkways and roads at the foot of Brooklyn Bridge).

By complete contrast, in Lynch's films, bars and restaurants seem like the cinematic equivalent of Edward Hopper's forlorn bars and restaurants (Hopper is one of the painters Lynch most admires, together with Bacon). In the jazz-lounge in *Blue Velvet* where Dorothy (Isabella Rossellini) sings the famous Bobby Vinton song which gives the film its title, we feel that all the characters are contributing their separate lives through the contingency of the event – a murder, a mysterious ear found in the grass by the young protagonist, Jeffrey (Kyle MacLachlan), and Jeffrey's determination to discover the enigma. The humour with which Lynch colours the whole scene rests upon a sort of advertisement for American and imported beers: Jeffrey drinks Heineken, but the daughter of the detective, Sandy (Laura Dern), only knows the beer her 'daddy' drinks, Budweiser.

Violence and sex in Lynch's film are isolated, crazy, surreal outbursts of colour and movement that subtly recreate the well-known stereotypes of television and B-series and porno films. Suburban life erases social and historical connections. Facts, people, dreams and events float around unrelated to time or space, isolated from the impact of the reality and continuous metamorphosis of the big city. Violence in Scorsese is a product of social tension: if the brutality of westerns is imprinted on his memory, his tough scenes always carry some documentary flavour. Indeed, Scorsese likes to remind us of reality – for example in the notice following the title *GoodFellas*: 'This film is based on a true story' (from Nick Pileggi's book *Wise Guy*). But, above all, Scorsese believes that the true violence of some people 'ought to be used in a film in order to affirm an ethical point of view'.[23] Lynch, on the contrary, likes to stress the dream component in his films, as much as in his paintings. He thinks, for example, that the first section of *Lost Highway* is like being 'just on the border of consciousness – or on the other side of that border', 'in someone else's bad dream'.[24]

The contrast between love scenes as constructed by the two film-makers can also be seen in terms of the opposition between urban and suburban. First of all, lovers are rarely alone in Scorsese's films; in *Mean Streets*, in one of the most open sex scenes, deeply inspired by Godard, Teresa and Charlie are alone in a hotel room, and Teresa gets up, naked, and moves towards the window, from which comes the roar of the traffic outside, overwhelming the conversation between the two young people. In Lynch, we can see another splendid declination of the formula 'the machine in the garden': Pete and Alice drive at night to a mysterious isolated cabin, then they make love on the beach, in a long scene shot in overexposed light, while the golden sand scatters around their bodies.

Scorsese's imagination does not find inspiration in nature or wilderness: in *Mean Streets*, in a rare scene near the sea, in Long Island, Teresa and Charlie are flirting. The cut, where colour is greatly diminished in favour of a very white light, recalls the sea as it appears in Truffaut's *Les 400 coups*, and it provides an opportunity to spell out Charlie's dislike for nature. 'I hate the ocean, and I hate the beach, and I hate the sun ... And the grass and the trees ...' When Teresa asks him what he likes, his ironical answers are unmistakably urban, Italian-American, New York: 'I like spaghetti and clam sauce ... John Wayne ...' Mountains are for him Manhattan's 'tall buildings'. Nature is present in *Casino*, but it is just the desert surrounding the area where Las Vegas has been built: nothing but dust and rocks, and the same violent light that can be seen above skyscrapers and stone. The protagonist, Ace, is sent to Las Vegas from New York; Scorsese's Vegas harbours the same type of Mafia life as the big city, with Italians and Jews. The contrast between the city and the country is also fundamental in Scorsese's first film when he was 25 years old, *Who's That Knocking at My Door* (1967).

Lynch and Scorsese are profoundly interested in the soundtracks of their movies. Few film-makers have been able to use so intelligently the music of the 1950s and 1960s. Even when they choose the same type of music, they end up proving the difference between the urban and the suburban. Bobby Vinton's 'Blue Velvet' is sung by Dorothy in that forlorn lounge very appropriately called Slow Club. In a composition showing Lynch's taste for strong contrasts, the languorous notes and theme of Roy Orbison's 'In Dreams' accompany the beating-up of Jeffrey, who has been driven to an isolated house where the group of thugs meet. But the performance of the song is faked by the actor, who uses a torch as a microphone and pretends to sing while the record plays. In a violent scene of *Blue Velvet*, suburban elements emerge as though they were in a painting by Edward Hopper: car, road, violence, music from the car's radio playing. One of the women of the group is dancing on the car's roof while Frank (Dennis Hopper) and his friend hit Jeffrey, and Dorothy screams and cries. The machine is really in the garden, and the garden is not an idyllic one. By contrast, Scorsese's music is closely connected with urban life: the singer Jerry Vale appears live in *GoodFellas*. The world of entertainment, from cinema to restaurants, bars, juke-boxes, and shows of any kind, is part of city life, of crowds, of people going out, meeting up with each other. According to Baudelaire, the painter of modern life should choose his subjects from everyday existence in the city: traffic, crowds, theatres and night-life. The painter of modern life must immerse himself in urban life.

Scorsese belongs to the line of great artists who express the complexity of urban reality, and consider that the imagination composes by freely combining and putting together elements of the world. We might say of him what Baudelaire said about Delacroix: 'Nature, for Eugène Delacroix, is a vast dictionary whose leaves he turns and consults with a sure and searching eye.'[25] The big city is for the film-maker a vast dictionary. Scorsese believes in the existence and significance of the external world as an immense source of inspiration, and tries to represent its effect on the lives and minds of people, convinced as he is that the history of cinema is a treasure as rich as the world itself. Actually, for him, there is continuity between the real world and cinema, again not in the postmodern sense, but in what can be called the classical modern sense, exactly as in Baudelaire's poetry where the abstract and the concrete can never be separated, and external and internal life respond to each other.

Scorsese's films are full of action, and could never imply that everything is mere rhetoric or a series of empty images meaning nothing. In the way he uses his camera, he proves his intense passion for reality, for matter, for the flesh. This is well illustrated by a famous cut in *GoodFellas*: Henry, the Irish-Italian boy who finally, at 21, becomes part of Paulie Cicero's Italian Mafia group, takes Karen to his restaurant, the Copacabana. This extraordinary cut, which lasts three minutes, engages many of the spectator's emotions and senses (from sight to hearing, even smell – or the conjuring up of smell through the visual): the sixties music 'Then He Kissed Me' (performed by the Crystals) spreads the joy of an evening of conquest amidst food, wine, dollar bills and tips, various activities, entertainment and flirtation. The young couple take a thrilling walk through the basement and the kitchens of the restaurant to their dining table set near the stage, where the humorist Henry Youngman himself tells his jokes. The soundtrack with 'Look in My Eye' (performed by the Chantels) continues into the following cut where Henry and Tommy succeed in stealing $420,000 'without using a gun' from the Air France cargo area at Idlewild airport. The overlapping of the soundtrack on this image enhances the rhythm of the story as it is remembered and told with excitement by Henry: remembrance becomes as intoxicating as the success of the operation in the moment it takes place.

Henry and Karen are, during their walk through the basement and the kitchen, shot from behind: in contempt of Hollywood, Scorsese's camera disdains any cosmetic operation on the human body, any of the hygienic perfection of photography or film, and the flesh of the actress is as real as flesh can be, especially with the effect of the typical New York grey and red paint of the restaurant's basement. The food displayed on the kitchen's counters is as real as if Scorsese were shooting the hustle and bustle of a busy restaurant. As in a novel by Balzac, matter is acknowledged in all its density. It is as if centuries of Western painting and baroque art were concentrated in this shot which, far from denying the strength of cinema, allows it to integrate the characteristics of different arts,[26] stressing also what Scorsese relentlessly affirms, that music is not a sort of ornamentation of the image but has an equally central role. It is as if New York had stamped its physical reality onto cinema: isn't the metropolis perceived equally through the eyes and through the ears (and through the mind)?

Scorsese is fully aware of the blending of fiction with reality, but the lesson of his films could never be that of Lynch's almost surrealist taste for dreams, nor could it be reduced to the postmodern belief that all reality is just fiction. For Scorsese, our internal world is shaped by the external one, and imagination helps us to understand and hold onto reality. As in Poe's 'The Man of the Crowd', or in Baudelaire's 'Les Sept Vieillards', reality and hallucination blend, but reality remains the spark which fires hallucination. Cinema is the art that translates this phenomenon into its language: 'Much of *Taxi Driver*' – said Scorsese – 'arose from my feeling that movies are really a kind of dream-state, or like taking dope.'[27]

Not unlike Baudelaire – not unlike many artists mesmerized by big cities – Scorsese is hungry for the external world and tries to find an artistic form that can quickly translate its features and its effects on the human mind. In a similar way to the painter Constantin Guys in *The Painter of Modern Life*, Scorsese likes to get immersed in the reality of the city, what can be called its carnal presence. Then he selects and creates images that carry the fullness of his impressions.

Above all, as indicated by the scenes I have analysed, the city is present in the rhythm of Scorsese's films, at the level both of sounds and of music. Rhythm might vary: it might be slow or quick; it might alternate slowness and rapidity, or it might show a type of slowness that is already the translation of real time into human perception and feeling. But what is typical of Scorsese is syncope – exactly what characterizes the rhythm of the jazz or pop music in his soundtracks. This musical syncope is mimetic of the noise of modern urban life. But it is also expressive of a state of mind, of what may be called the emotional structure of modern life. Baudelaire announced in his foreword to *Spleen de Paris* his ideal of a poetic prose:

> Which one of us, in his moments of ambition, has not dreamed of the miracle of a poetic prose, musical, without rhythm and without rhyme, supple enough and rugged enough to adapt itself to the lyrical impulses of the soul, the undulations of reverie, the jibes of conscience?[28]

This prose, Baudelaire insisted, should be the equivalent of the metropolitan rhythm that generated it: 'It was, above all, out of my exploration of huge cities, out of the medley of their innumerable interrelations, that this haunting ideal was born.'[29]

Syncope, nervous rhythm, irregularities can sometimes result in that incredible acceleration Scorsese can give to some of his sequences in a frantic editing of images and sound. Towards the end of *GoodFellas*, after the killing of Tom and the disruption of the group, the pulsing rhythm of 'Jump into the Fire' (performed by Harry Nilsson) hits the spectator together with the black screen indicating the date and the hour: these are the last stormy moments of Henry's life as a gangster, just before the epilogue when he gives the police the names of his friends. The challenge for Henry is that of keeping a grip on many different things: his drugs trade in Pittsburgh, his ill brother, his wife and children, his mistress who mixes dope, some dealers in Queens, a family dinner party where he has to cook. He has to drive here and there, while a helicopter is following him. The challenge for the film-maker is to master real time in film – the actual duration of visual cuts as much as that of the sound – and the represented time of the action, through the timing of Henry's voice-over describing the events. Scorsese succeeds in composing a most breathtaking 10 minutes of editing. His cross-cutting intermingles places, people, voices, noises and an immensely large number of musical segments, sometimes repeated, sometimes only instrumental, sometimes interrupted and reiterated later– such as Muddy Waters' powerful blues voice followed by the amplified guitar sound in the famous 1955 'Mannish Boy', the words 'Yeah, everything, everything will be all right' emerging in an overly light-blue sky where the helicopter hovering over Henry's car spreads the syncopated noise of its propellers. The instant is, so to speak, caught with all its charge: it is the event both in its absolute contingency and within a network of possibilities, premises and con-sequences; it is action to the uttermost degree, together with the feeling of fear or urgency that spurs on action. What could be more quintessentially metropolitan?

Cinema as a metropolis

Two universes then offer Scorsese the vast dictionary from which he selects and composes through 'the jibes of consciousness', of memory and invention: one universe is New York, with its infinite life; the other is the gleaming metropolis that is cinema itself. Scorsese observes and absorbs the real world and the world of cinema in order to trans-late his ideas with his camera. He remembers – more or less precisely, more or less consciously – images from other films. Cinema does not copy the real world: it dreams of the world. It adds to the impressions coming from the external world the most intimate, internal feelings and thoughts. The city for Aldo Rossi was a concrete city – Parma, Milan, Trieste, Venice, Belo Horizonte, Seville, etc. – with the addition of what he called the analogous city: pieces of other cities lingering in the memory of the architect or imagined by him. In a similar way, the world of cinema for Scorsese is composed of the films he has seen and those he has imagined, dreamed of. When talking about his early passion for the cinema, he remembers that, as an adolescent, he borrowed from the New York public library a book by Deems Taylor,

A Pictorial History of the Movies, which is a history of film from silent cinema to the talkies up to 1949: 'It was the first course in my film education. Its beautiful black-and-white images recreated the visions and emotions of the movies I'd already seen, and allowed me to dream about the others.'[30] Scorsese is a real *cinéphile* and likes to pay homage to cinema: in his *A Personal Journey with Martin Scorsese through American Movies*, he declares: 'I am talking to you about some of the films that coloured my dreams, that changed my perceptions, and even my life in some cases. Films that prompted me, for better of for worse, to become a film-maker myself.'[31]

The urban imprint on time, which I have discussed in the first part of this chapter, is very clear in *Mean Streets*. I will now return to this urban element to look at how important the world of cinema is for Scorsese – as important as New York. The metropolis is full of potential as well as actual events that take place; in a similar way, a film results from editing but so many rushes could offer alternatives (the inclusion of what has been excluded either by the director or by the producer is increasingly today the principal reason for the re-editing of films – such as Kubrick's *2001: A Space Odyssey*, or Coppola's *Apocalypse Now*). Where does the story of *Mean Streets* start? Where does it end? During the first minutes we see a young man suddenly waking up in his bed surrounded by the noise of the city. As suggested in *Taxi Driver*, it might be any day, any time, at the beginning or middle or end of the story. It might be anyone living in the metropolis. Immediately, at the sound of 'Be My Baby' (The Ronetts, 1963), a few photograms run rapidly across the screen, showing church, marriage, and a new-born baby. These images could be, already at the beginning, a happy epilogue softening the violence of the last part of the movie.[32] This anticipated happy end could also be the imagined alternative version of the story. After all, the tough story that takes place in Little Italy could be treated with irony: it is just a bunch of young people, and the neighbourhood Mafia in *Mean Streets* is not a big enterprise like the Mafia in Coppola's film.[33] One could start watching the film 'half-way through'– for example, when there is an outbreak of violence in the group – and then, after the terrible shooting-down of Charlie, Johnny Boy and Teresa, see the opening images of the film. The beginning of *Mean Streets* suggests that one should be free from the temptation to know the end of the film, and that an alternative end is possible. Conjectures are part of any storytelling.

The ruthless young protagonists in *Mean Streets* are adolescents dreaming of cowboy and gangster movies, and living the ethos of some songs from the 1960s, the era when pop music became big business, a widespread industrial phenomenon establishing quick contacts between cities, countries, musical traditions and cultures. The last cuts of the film concentrate on the car in which Charlie, Johnny Boy and Teresa are badly wounded by Michael (who carries out his revenge against Johnny Boy, who has insulted him). In a frantic cross-cutting, in these tragic final minutes, Scorsese juxtaposes scenes taking place at the same time in different areas of the city: the three young people are talking and singing in their car, while speeding at night on the highway from downtown Manhattan to Brooklyn; Michael and the killer (played by Scorsese himself) are speeding in another car chasing after them; Tony is, as always, in the bar he owns, where so many episodes take place; in the street festival in Little Italy an elderly crowd dances and listens to old Italian songs; Charlie's uncle, who is part of a rather inoffensive Mafia, switches on his television and quietly watches a film in his flat.

The scene on television comes from Fritz Lang's *The Big Heat* (1953): the protagonist takes his dead wife out of his car. This scene constitutes a turning-point in the life of the protagonist, and introduces an ethical dimension to the events. From the uncle's room, the cross-cutting jumps to the terrible image of Johnny Boy, wounded in the neck, limping along a wall, then to Teresa as she is taken out from the car by the police. Quickly the camera moves to Charlie as he falls to his knees, his arm bleeding. Chance, coincidences, events taking place at the same time, mixing fiction and reality – all this is part of the every-day pulse of the city. Cinema can be documentary and fiction at the same time. The way in which metropolitan life solicits human percep-tion is not very different from the way in which cinema does: our senses and nerves are constantly forced to a high degree of attention, so high that at some point this nervous excess is integrated in our minds and constitutes the precondition of our experience.

Scorsese's reference to Lang is important for another reason: it stresses the presence of the universe of film. The scene from *The Big Heat* is the third and last quotation in the film: the first one was a fero-cious scene in a western, and the second a sequence from *The Tomb of Ligeia* by Roger Corman (the hyperactive film-maker and Scorsese's mentor who financed *Mean Streets*).[34] The image taken from *The Big Heat* alludes to the circulation of images through different media, from cinema to television; the two previous quotations come from the screen of movie-theatres, where Charlie and his friend like to spend time. Scorsese's generation became acquainted with films also – and sometimes only – through television. Besides the similarity of a car and a woman being taken out of it, and the fact that in *Mean Streets*, too, the scene marks a turning-point in the adventures of the protagonists, the short dramatic scene from *The Big Heat* appears as a statement about the type of cinema Scorsese seeks. In this way, he openly acknowledges his multifold European influences, and the link between the United States and Europe in the 1960s. Cities are space, time and culture, or, more exactly, a mixing of cultures; audiovisual technology increases the possibility of cultural exchanges; and the rapidity with which the image and the sound can be diffused can enhance the urban dimension of cultures. Metropolises are where cultures cross, constant movement back and forth characterizes the cultural network: the meeting of cultures happens in time and space, following not the model of evolution but that of contagion. Cultures do not develop like plants, they spread like viruses.

Mean Streets, which has been seen as the most autobiographical of Scorsese's works, proves indeed that his childhood and adolescence in New York, in Elisabeth Street, is important for him. But that presence of New York can be felt also as a cinematic phenomenon – it belongs to the film-maker's intellectual biography, to his cinephilia. Scorsese's ideals about film are infused with his life in the Village, in the 1960s, at the time when he was a film student at New York University. It was the period, as he said, of 'the height of the French New Wave, the international success of the Italian art cinema and the discovery of the new Eastern European cinema'.[35] The New Wave was part of the recent heritage; the minds of young film-makers from New York and from Los Angeles (such as Francis Coppola) were filled with images of American films from their childhood. Then they discovered Truffaut, Resnais, Rivette and Godard who, in their turn, had appreciated American cinema, contrary to the general response in France in the 1950s. The young crowd who wrote in the *Cahiers du cinéma* loved westerns, thrillers, American comedies, gangsters and cowboys. They loved Howard Hawks and Alfred Hitchcock, and they were deeply influenced by American cinema when they started making films. Scorsese often recalls the sense of freedom that the first two minutes of Truffaut's *Jules and Jim* gave and still give to him – a sense of freedom similar to what one can experience in the first minutes of *Mean Streets:* the thrill of making a film, of thinking and feeling through the camera, 'of using the camera as a pen', as Truffaut said. The camera is actually shown in *Mean Streets* towards the end of its cast and credits list, as it is shown at the beginning of Godard's *Le Mépris*, and so many times in Michael

Powell's *Peeping Tom*. And, as in *Jules and Jim*, at the beginning of *Mean Streets* the rhythm of images is accelerated as if re-enacting the motion typical of a silent movie.

The young American avant-garde in the sixties was formed by the 'underground' international movement, by the experimental cinema of the New York group 'Independent Cinema', and by journals like *Film Culture* and *The Village Voice*: critics like Andrew Sarris and Jonas Mekas, the founder of the New York Film-makers' Cooperative in 1962 – and himself a film-maker – were receptive to the French New Wave and its aesthetics.[36]

The Big Heat had been condemned in Europe as a banal American thriller; those who admired the German period of Lang found it very disappointing. But François Truffaut wrote an enthusiastic review in an important issue of the *Cahiers du cinéma*, while at the same time his long article 'Une certaine tendance'[37] ('A Certain Tendency') criticized the so-called 'réalisme poétique' (poetical realism) typical of French cinema. The young writers of the *Cahiers du cinéma* were committed to the defence of cinema as a true art; they launched what they called 'la politique des auteurs' (the authors' politics) – a 1963 issue of *Film Culture* was devoted to this question. For the New Wave artists, a film is not an isolated work but belongs fully to a series of works by the same author, developing certain themes, a certain style and technique.

Today, postmodern correctness makes it seem criminal to take authorship into account in a critical study, as if by so doing the critic would not be a true follower of the dogma of 'the death of the author', so fashionable in the structuralist and post-structuralist critical approaches of the 1970s and 1980s. But we have moved on since then. Authorship is not simply a historical and ideological construction, but also an aesthetic phenomenon. To talk about authorship does not mean that one considers the artist to be either endowed with divine power or full of subjective, old-fashioned beliefs; it simply allows one to take into account the imagination without which artistic production is impossible (even if we are in the era of absolute consumption and technological reproduction). In any event, for those who wanted to make films in the 1960s, the theories of the New Wave were essential, and did not in the least contradict the commercial aspect of cinema. And well-intentioned academics should rest easy: the most avant-garde tendency in film and film criticism in the 1950s and 1960s was *not* influenced by Maurice Blanchot's nihilism. Godard claimed the values of classicism.

An author is an artist who through time and effort tries to define his/her themes, manners, even obsessions. To be an author means having a certain style. In a film, the spectator must be able to recognize a signature, a style, an atmosphere, something that accounts for the unity of a project. *The Big Heat* does not, Truffaut insists, betray the essence of Fritz Lang, who focused on the conflict between the individual and society, on 'the moral solitude' of a hero who 'becomes the justice-dispenser of himself'. 'The favourite theme of Lang is moral solitude: a single individual fighting alone against a half-hostile, half-indifferent universe.'[38]

The Big Heat is not a simple thriller but a real drama about the corrupted world of the Chicago Mafia and police in the 1950s. Not unlike the protagonist of *The Big Heat*, Charlie in *Mean Streets* experiences an internal conflict in the Little Italy of the early 1970s: he lives and tries to find his way through an atmosphere of small juvenile Mafia combined with the pop music of the 1960s and even the 1950s, old-fashioned Neapolitan songs, gun shots, everyday racism, and the Catholic themes of sin and penitence.[39]

New York is defined by different perspectives: as a concrete reality, an allegory, and a cultural network. Streets, bars, apartments, public spaces, noises, people, violence are filmed by a young artist who has been influenced by the documentary and low-budget narratives typical of the New York Film-makers Group, and by a New York artist who understands the New Wave and their aesthetic preferences. Scorsese often translates ideas from the French directors into his New York reality and allegory. Again, think of the famous sequence in *Taxi Driver*: Travis, in his miserable flat in Manhattan, practises his skills on all the guns he has bought. His hands move deftly, testing the guns, and, using wooden and metal bits and pieces he takes from a drawer, he patiently puts together an extraordinary machine. This scene indeed recalls an atmosphere typical of Robert Bresson, of his 'transcendental style', to use the expression that Paul Schrader, the screenplay writer for *Taxi Driver*, stigmatized in the title of his important 1972 book on Ozu, Bresson and Dryer.[40] In the wonderful performance by De Niro (another New Yorker whom Scorsese met in his neighbourhood when they were young),[41] the protagonist is totally absorbed in his work: he does not speak, there is no music, only some sounds coming from the objects and the outside world. There is no psychological digression, only the bare facts which constitute an activity with a very precise aim. One can juxtapose, as is done in the illustrations to *Scorsese by Scorsese*, this scene from *Taxi Driver* with some shots from

Bresson's *Pick Pocket* (1959), when the main character is taught by an accomplice how to move his hands quickly and delicately.

Think, too, of Bresson's *Un condamné à mort s'est échappé* (1956): Lieutenant Fontaine, imprisoned near Lyon by the Germans in 1943, is determined to escape and, day after day, with the help of a spoon, he tries remove the nails holding his cell door. In the sequence from *Taxi Driver*, it is as if Scorsese had transposed that patient work from the French prison during the war, into another prison, the American metropolis in the years following the Vietnam war. Travis's room does in fact resemble a prison-cell, with grids, dim light and noises coming from outside. Travis himself is a prisoner of his suffering and obsessions, and of the toughness of Manhattan life. This metropolitan cowboy, as the character has often been defined, is haunted by the idea of salvation, like the character portrayed by John Wayne in John Ford's *The Searchers* (1956), who succeeds in 'saving' his niece from the Indians and bringing her back to her family. Actually, Travis, in the streets of Manhattan, experiences a battle similar to the Vietnam war: in fact, towards the end of the film, when he is going to accomplish his project, his head is shaved, as if he belonged to the Mohawk squad, the most fearsome group in Vietnam, specializing in guerrilla warfare.

Besides direct quotations or allusions to other films, Scorsese cannot but integrate in his mind some cinematic effects and re-elaborate them according to his own invention. The famous scene of Travis's massacre in the hotel where the young prostitute Iris meets her clients can be interpreted as an extraordinary example of the way in which the universe of cinema offers Scorsese the dictionary from which he freely develops his imagination. Travis wants to save Iris (the adolescent Jodie Foster); almost unrecognizable in his Mohawk hair-cut, he gets back to the building where he had previously met Iris's pimp (Harvey Keitel). After a short conversation, Travis shoots him and enters the hotel to find the young girl. He shoots everyone he meets. They shoot back at him; blood glistens on the staircase and on the walls. In spite of his wounds, Travis continues to go up the staircase to the room where Iris is with a man: the interior looks very much like a small baroque altar in Sicily or in Spain. The shooting goes on incessantly, as in Hawks' *The Red River*; blood flows everywhere, Iris cries among the dead bodies, and finally Travis sits, bleeding, on an old couch, after having tried unsuccessfully to kill himself with his last empty revolver.

Suddenly, after all that shooting and screaming, there is a terrible silence, which inevitably slows down the rhythm of the scene. This impression is emphasized by the camera's movement while a policeman enters cautiously, his arm outstretched and pointing his gun. At this moment the soundtrack starts up again, with Bernard Herrmann's jazz-blues sounds. As the notes rise, the image catches their movement: the music goes higher and higher and the image moves up to that extra-ordinary, completely vertical shot of the massacre. The camera turns slowly above the room. Its movement is as slow and ample as the circular expansion of the music. Slowly, terribly slowly, objects and bodies become visible. Furniture, bodies and blood are seen from above. The camera, always slowly and from above, flattens down the heads and the shoes of the policemen, the threshold of the room and the corridor, where finally the usual horizontal angle of vision is re-instated.

Fully vertical high-angle shots are unusual.[42] When they are used, the aim is normally to offer a realist perspective – as it would be, for example, from the height of a building or of an aeroplane. But in *Taxi Driver*'s massacre scene the viewpoint cannot correspond to the per-spective of any character. It can only be an intellectual intervention that recalls the allegorical presence of the city and the real presence of the camera and the work of film-making. Obviously, a considerable amount of practical, costly work has gone into shooting that scene: drilling the floor in the apartment above the one where the massacre took place, constructing a sort of rail where the camera could turn to embrace the whole scene down below. In fact, Paul Schrader and other people working on the film were strongly opposed to Scorsese's idea.

Where does that urgency of the imagination come from? It comes from the layers of memory, from the immense universe that is cinema. The film-maker can consult both voluntarily and involuntarily the dic-tionary of cinema. And cinema, like architecture and the city, has to do with matter (very probably, cinema is facing today yet another epoch in its history: after the silent movie, and the talkies, now special effects and images constructed with the aid of the computer are making an ever stronger impact). When we look at a film, we some-times try and perceive the other side of the iceberg, the work that went into realizing the smooth dance of images that is now in front of our eyes: where, when and how did the shooting take place? It seems impossible, for example, to look at the famous Odessa steps scene in Eisenstein's *Battleship Potemkin* without thinking of the work it implied (Eisenstein himself recounts all this in detail in his writings).

The argument of my chapter can now go back to its beginning. The imagination of Scorsese has stored striking cinematic effects since his childhood and adolescence. He has lived, so to speak, with those effects. We know that Scorsese was deeply impressed by

Eisenstein when he entered 'half-way through' in a Manhattan theatre where *Alexandre Nevsky* was showing. The famous battle on the ice filled his eyes and imagination: 'It was like being in a time machine, as if I were there watching the battle on the ice in 1242! Seeing the design of the film, I fell under the spell of Eisenstein and his style of editing.'[43] In the last part of this battle on the ice, a long series of shots that lasts for more than three minutes shows the German warriors as they are swallowed by the ice that breaks under their weight. This cut is spectacular: from an almost completely vertical perspective, we see men and horses falling through the cracks in the ice. After a useless struggle, in a frantic scramble of swords, spears, helmets, legs, arms and hooves, they are sucked down into the pitiless icy-cold water. At the end of this scene, the Russian warriors appear at the top of a hill, looking down over their white, chilling ice-victory.

The magic of Eisenstein's editing is re-enacted by Scorsese, who exaggerates the conditions of vertical vision. *Taxi Driver*'s massacre is not observed by any human eye, but only by the camera as it moves along the rail on the smashed floor of the flat from which the scene is shot. Scorsese goes further than Eisenstein: the presence of the cinema itself is stronger than that of people – in the same way as the presence of New York is stronger than that of the characters (and the camera can be an allegory of the city looking at itself). In his immense theoretical work, the Russian film-maker had criticized the narrow-minded position of those who thought that a high angle could only be justified by the presence of a person looking from above. Eisenstein thought that any excessive perspective and light could be justified by the attempt to express the intensity of a character's perception and consciousness.[44] But in Travis's massacre everything is beyond human perception and consciousness.

The camera, and nothing but the camera, has the possibility of being ubiquitous. The camera can see what no human gaze can see. The camera can realize all dreams, fantasies; it can be the instrument of an incommensurable voyeurism, and of a visual dance in which human physical limitations are defied. Sight can be from above, from below, from beneath, defying the boundaries of space and light and movement. The visible and the invisible are equally reachable. Godard's message in *Le Mépris* was right: the camera is to the modern world what the gods were to the ancient world. As I have mentioned, the camera is actually visible throughout the cast and credit listing for *Mean Streets*. The camera is a tool, a material object which has to deal with a *mise-en-scène* composed by objects and bodies. If the camera is an instrument of thought, one should not forget the amount of matter that is necessary for making a film. An important sequence in *Taxi Driver* points to the work of the camera and the film-maker: in a black-humour scene where Scorsese himself plays one of the many clients for Travis's cab, Travis has to listen to a madman who frantically talks of killing his wife. He wants the cab to stop in front of the building where his wife is with her lover, and look through a window where a light is on. Clearly the window looks very much like a screen.

Scorsese, influenced by Powell's voyeuristic camera and by the 'caméra stylo' of the New Wave, is paying tribute to Eisenstein's talent with his own invention, with his audacious high-angle shot in Travis's massacre scene. Poe said that the new is the result of a different combination of known elements. In Travis's massacre many sources of inspiration are condensed to brilliant effect: the lessons of Hawks, Powell, Truffaut and Orson Welles,[45] and especially that almost unconscious recollection of *Alexander Nevsky*'s impressive battle on the ice. No words, no long explanations are necessary: Scorsese may mention Eisenstein only a couple of times, but films speak the language of images, and Eisenstein's editing has worked its spell on Scorsese's mind.

In his *Voyage through American Movies*, Scorsese advises young film-makers to study the great masters (which does not mean simply to copy them). They can explain what cinema is. They can teach one how to be daring. All tricks are possible to achieve one's end: such as altering the floor of an apartment to obtain a straight vertical vision. No one understood and felt more fully than Eisenstein, the great pioneer of the beginning of the twentieth century, that cinema is a wonderful artifice, an extravagant machine which has to respond to the orders of the imagination.[46] The shooting of *Alexander Nevsky* required that nature be turned upside down: the torrid heat of Siberia's summer had to be transformed into the chilling winter of the 1242 war between the Russians and the Germans. All that vast expanse of thick, white ice that we see on the screen was completely artificial: piles of grass pressed together and pasted with plaster.

Scorsese does not quote Eisenstein in the scene I am analysing, as he clearly quotes Lang's *The Big Heat*; nor does he directly allude to Eisenstein, as he does to Bresson in the gun sequence in Travis's apartment. Scorsese has interiorized a cinematic effect from Eisenstein. I would call this phenomenon exacerbation or amplification (as pop music amplifies sounds). There is no resemblance between Travis's massacre and the 1242 battle on the ice. What is comparable is the effect, the impact on the spectator, thanks to the intuition of a certain way the camera is made to operate through artifice. Variation is a full right of the imagination: the fall into the broken ice in *Alexander Nevsky* takes place in the open air, while Travis's massacre happens totally in the interior of an apartment. This fact radicalizes Scorsese's vertical shot: it is as if a huge, Kafkaesque insect were moving about on the ceiling, casting an absent-minded glance over the bloody event. The slow-motion view of objects, people and décor increases the sense of absurdity. It appears to be the end; it is the end, even if the story goes on and the film continues with the sardonic bouncing back of Travis as a hero, and with his return to his usual business of driving around the city.

Amplification can give new impetus to cinematic effects, and push even further the parallelism between Eisenstein and Scorsese. The making of *Alexander Nesvky* realized an important idea in Eisenstein's film practice – that the very close relationship between image and soundtrack, which he called 'vertical montage', was different from what he called 'intellectual montage', which has to do with the way in which fragments of montage direct the meaning of images. The Russian film-maker collaborated with the composer Sergei Prokofiev, as is well documented by the rich correspondence between the two artists. In vertical montage, music cannot be reduced to its most obvious ornamental role. Music has the power of forging the image. Eisenstein explained how the vertical movement of swords and spears in the battle was totally inspired by Prokofiev's ascending notes. The opposite could also be true: sometimes the visual rhythm of an image could direct the sound of musical instruments, and Prokofiev would translate the language of Eisenstein's images into the language of music. Many variables are possible, since what really matters is the vital relationship between the sound and the image.

Taxi Driver is unthinkable without its Bernard Herrmann score.[47] Scorsese wanted him to work on the film. He describes how he tried very hard to convince him. Herrmann accepted after having seen the scene of De Niro pouring whisky on his cereals. The rhythm of Herrmann's notes inspired the splendid credits accompaniment where the yellow cab drives through Manhattan's streets in the rain. The city lights, as they are visible through the car's windshield covered with raindrops, recur in the film, and at some length at the end when Travis resumes his driving along the avenues, among red lights, people crossing the streets, and many other cars with their lights. The traffic moves like a long river, both fitful and flowing, with steady, melancholy stops and starts along with Herrmann's rhythm, which is somewhere between cool jazz and blues. Actually his notes *are* those lights and raindrops: they move forward, follow one another, connect up, leap and spread on the screen, into our ears and eyes. Herrmann's notes are pure sound vibrations that become visual matter, as in a famous passage from Sartre's *Nausea*, jazz notes are described by words, become words. Sartre's 'existential novel' was well known to Schrader and Scorsese.[48] This passage can illustrate the 'aesthetic of dissapearance' typical of metropolitan impressions, of film and music:

> For the moment, the jazz is playing; there is no melody, only notes, a myriad of tiny jolts. They know no rest, an inflexible order gives birth to them and destroys them without even giving time to recuperate and exist for themselves. They race, they press forward, they strike me like a sharp blow in passing and are obliterated. I would like to hold them back, but I know if I succeeded in stopping one it would remain between my fingers only as a raffish languishing sound.[49]

Scorsese has been thinking through very thoroughly the relationship between image and sound, ever since he saw *The Tales of Hoffmann*, long before making those of his films whose main subject is music (*New York, New York* (1997), *The Last Waltz* (1978)), and maybe since the time he edited *Woodstock* (1969), Mike Wadleigh's documentary of the three-day legendary rock concert. With *Taxi Driver* Scorsese successfully tries his own vertical montage, like Eisenstein. Cinema and its effects are like a metropolis where one can stroll, stopping here and there. The possibility of various relationships is immense: Herrmann had written scores for Orson Welles and Alfred Hitchcock, and for Scorsese's friend Brian De Palma (for *Obsession*, 1976). Herrmann's tune penetrates *Taxi Driver*'s massacre room: it carries in its rhythms Iris's sobs, the useless click of Travis's trigger, the 'psch, psch, psch' sound that issues from his lips when, his fingers covered with blood against his temple, he imitates the noise of a gun – like a child who plays cowboys. Herrmann's tune rises up, pours out, invades the space, spreads its strangely muffled boom; the notes approach inexorably, but nevertheless slowly, like the vertical slow-motion on the scene. The sound goes back to the theme of the beginning of the film, amplifying the mixing of brass and drums. The music is insistent, hammering, repetitive: it becomes one with the comings and goings of the metropolis, with its eternal life.

Scorsese has captured the rhythm of New York: city, cinema, music and image hold together.

Notes

Chapter 1: Edgar Allan Poe

1 This chapter develops one of the arguments of my book *Edgar Poe et la Modernité: Breton, Barthes, Derrida, Blanchot* (Birmingham, AL: Summa Pubications, 1985), pp. 7–67. All translations, in all chapters, are mine, unless otherwise indicated. Bibliographical references for texts frequently cited and for other key texts are listed in the 'General Bibliography'.

2 Edgar Allan Poe, 'Marginalia', *Essays and Reviews* (New York: Library of America, 1984), pp. 1382–3. As Mallarmé said, 'meditating, without leaving any traces, becomes evanescent'; Stéphane Mallarmé, 'Crise de vers', *Oeuvres Complètes* (Paris: Gallimard, Bibliothèque de la Pléiade, 1945), p. 369. Mallarmé translated several poems by Poe.

3 Georges Bataille, *The Story of the Eye*, trans. J. Neugroschel, with essays by R. Barthes and S. Sontag (Harmondsworth: Penguin Books, 1982), pp. 70–4.

4 Roland Barthes, 'The Metaphor of the Eye', trans. J. A. Underwood, published as an appendix to Georges Bataille, *The Story of the Eye*, pp. 119–27.

5 Poe, 'Annabel Lee', *The Complete Tales and Poems* (New York: Modern Library, 1938; repr. New York: Vintage, 1975), p. 958. My emphasis.

6 'To Helen', *The Complete Tales and Poems*, p. 950. My emphasis.

7 'Eleonora', *The Complete Tales and Poems*, p. 651.

8 'Ligeia', *The Complete Tales and Poems*, p. 656.

9 See Ralph Waldo Emerson, 'Each and All', *The Complete Works, Poems*, vol. 9 (Boston: Houghton, Mifflin, 1903–4; repr. New York: AMS Press, 1968), p. 4–6.

10 Samuel Taylor Coleridge, *Aids to Reflection* (London: W. Pickering, 1848), p. 5.

11 Emerson, 'Nature', *The Complete Works*, vol. 1, p. 10. My emphasis.

12 'The Transcendentalist', ibid., p. 330–1.

13 'Ligeia', *The Complete Tales and Poems*, p. 661.

14 Ibid., p. 656.

15 Ibid., p. 657.

16 'Morella', *The Complete Tales and Poems*, p. 668.

17 See Allen Tate, 'Our Cousin, Mr. Poe', *Essays of Four Decades* (Chicago: Swallow Press, 1968), pp. 385–400.

18 'Ligeia', *The Complete Tales and Poems*, p. 657.

19 Ibid., p. 654.

20 'Morella', *The Complete Tales and Poems*, p. 667 .

21 Ibid.

22 Emerson, 'Plato; or, the Philosopher', *The Complete Works*, vol. 4, p. 41.

23 One effect of Poe's approach was his constant fear of plagiarism and of those who appropriate phrases and ideas without admitting it. For that would bring about the same monstrosity as 'Morella', namely the identical or the homogeneous.

24 Hermann Melville, *Moby Dick, or the White Whale* (New York: Oxford University Press, 1947), p. 122.
25 'The Domain of Arnheim', *The Complete Tales and Poems*, pp. 607–8.
26 Ibid., p. 607.
27 Ibid., p. 609.
28 'Ligeia', *The Complete Tales and Poems*, pp. 665–6.
29 Marie Bonaparte, *Edgar Poe, sa vie et son oeuvre: Etude analytique* (Paris: Presses Universitaires de France, 1958), vol. 2, p. 287.
30 Ibid.
31 'The Black Cat', *The Complete Tales and Poems*, p. 224. My emphasis.
32 Ibid. My emphasis.
33 'The Philosophy of Composition', *Essays and Reviews*, p. 19.
34 Stéphane Mallarmé, 'Préface. Avant-dire au *Traité du verbe*', *Oeuvres complètes*, p. 857.
35 Ibid., p. 858.
36 'Marginalia', *Essays and Reviews*, p. 1331.
37 Ibid.
38 'Berenice', *The Complete Tales and Poems*, p. 643
39 'James Russell Lowell', *Essays and Reviews*, p. 809.
40 'Marginalia', *Essays and Reviews*, p. 1451.
41 'Berenice', *The Complete Tales and Poems*, p. 643–4.
42 Ibid., p. 646.
43 'The Tell-Tale Heart', *The Complete Tales and Poems*, p. 303.
44 'Marginalia', *Essays and Reviews*, p. 1418.
45 Ibid., p. 1459.
46 'Rufus Dawes', *Essays and Reviews*, p. 492. Poe criticizes 'the queer tone of philosophical rhapsody' of Dawes' poem 'Geraldine': 'There is now much about Kant and Fichte; about Schelling, Hegel and Cousin (which is made to rhyme with *gang*)' (p. 495).
47 'The Tell-Tale Heart', p. 303.
48 Ibid.
49 See M. Bonaparte, *Edgar Poe, sa vie et son oeuvre*, vol. 1, p. 38.
50 'A Few Words on Secret Writing', *Essays and Reviews*, pp. 1277–91.
51 'Marginalia', *Essays and Reviews*, p. 1343.
52 'A Tale of the Ragged Mountains', *The Complete Tales and Poems*, p. 686–7.
53 *The Narrative of Arthur Gordon Pym*, in *The Complete Tales and Poems*, p. 883.
54 Ibid., p. 882.
55 Ibid.
56 Ibid., p. 878.
57 Ibid., p. 882.
58 'Berenice', *The Complete Tales and Poems*, p. 646.
59 Ibid., p. 642.
60 Ibid., p. 648.
61 Emerson, 'Language', 'Nature', *The Complete Works*, vol. 1, p. 25.
62 Ibid.
63 See Francis Otto Matthiessen, *American Renaissance: Art and Expression in the Age of Emerson and Whitman* (New York: Oxford University Press, 1941), pp. 134–5.

64 Emerson, 'Nature', *The Complete Works*, vol. 1, p. 1.
65 See H. Melville, *Pierre, or the Ambiguities* (New York: New American Library, 1964), p. 65.
66 Emerson, 'History', *The Complete Works*, vol. 2, pp. 5–6.
67 'Marginalia', *Essays and Reviews*, p. 1384. One of his tales, taking the form of a dialogue, is entitled 'The Power of Words' (*The Complete Tales and Poems*, pp. 440–3).
68 'The Poetic Principle', *Essays and Reviews*, p. 75.
69 Georges Poulet, *Les Métamorphoses du cercle* (Paris: Gallimard, 1979), pp. 295–319.
70 'The Power of Words', *The Complete Tales and Poems*, p. 442.
71 'Marginalia', *Essays and Reviews*, p. 1340.
72 Ibid., p. 1409.
73 Emerson, 'The Poet', *The Complete Works*, vol. 3, p. 7.
74 Ibid., p. 8.
75 Ibid., p. 26. My emphasis.
76 'Elisabeth Barret Browning', *Essays and Reviews*, p. 139.
77 Emerson, 'The Poet', *The Complete Works*, vol. 3, p. 26.
78 'Marginalia', *Essays and Reviews*, p. 1363.
79 Ibid., p. 1364.
80 'The Murders in the Rue Morgue', *The Complete Tales and Poems*, p. 141.
81 Ibid.
82 Paul Valéry, *Monsieur Teste*, in *Oeuvres*, vol. 2 (Paris: Gallimard, Bibliothèque de la Pléiade, 1960), p. 11.
83 Ibid., p. 67.
84 'Marginalia', *Essays and Reviews*, p. 1392.
85 'Nathaniel Hawthorne', *Essays and Reviews*, p. 572.
86 Ibid., p. 571.
87 Coleridge, cited by F. O. Matthiessen, *American Renaissance: Art and Expression in the Age of Emerson and Whitman*, p. 133.
88 Coleridge, cited by F. O. Matthiessen, ibid., p. 134.
89 Ibid.
90 Ibid.
91 'Nathaniel Hawthorne', *Essays and Reviews*, p. 572.
92 Poe, 'Ligeia', *Tales*, p. 661. No wonder Poe is admired by the decadent hero *par excellence* in the French novel of the late nineteenth century: Des Esseintes, in Joris Karl Huysmans' *A rebours*.
93 E. T. A. Hoffmann, 'The Sandman', *Tales*, trans. R. J. Hollingdale (Harmondsworth: Penguin Books, 1982), p. 116.
94 Ibid., p. 117.
95 'The Man of the Crowd', *The Complete Tales and Poems*, p. 481. As is well known, Walter Benjamin comments on this tale in his essay 'On Some Motifs in Baudelaire', *Illuminations*, trans. Harry Zohn (New York: Schocken Books, 1969, 1985), pp. 170–2.
96 'The Man of the Crowd', *The Complete Tales and Poems*, p. 481. This edition and some others give 'er lässt sich nicht lesen'; other edition give the pronoun 'es'.
97 Coleridge, *Biographia Literaria* (New York: Putnam & Wiley, 1848) vol. 1, p. 205.

98   Ibid.
99   Ibid., pp. 205–6.
100 Ibid., p. 370.
101 Ibid., p. 378.
102 Poe, 'Marginalia', *Essays and Reviews*, p. 1451.
103 Poe, 'Thomas Moore', *Essays and Reviews*, p. 334.
104 'The Murders in the Rue Morgue', *The Complete Tales and Poems*, p. 142.
105 Ibid.
106 Ibid.
107 Ibid.
108 Ibid., p. 143.
109 'The Black Cat', *The Complete Tales and Poems*, p. 223.
110 'The Imp of the Perverse', *The Complete Tales and Poems*, p. 283.
111 Ibid.
112 'The Black Cat', *The Complete Tales and Poems*, p. 228.
113 'The Imp of the Perverse', *The Complete Tales and Poems*, p. 281.
114 Ibid., p. 283.
115 'The Black Cat', *The Complete Tales and Poems*, p. 223.
116 Ibid., p. 230.
117 'The Tell-Tale Heart', *The Complete Tales and Poems*, p. 303.
118 Ibid.
119 'Marginalia', *Essays and Reviews*, p. 1383.
120 'The Murders in the rue Morgue', *The Complete Tales and Poems*, p. 141.
121 'The Tell-tale Heart', *The Complete Tales and Poems*, p. 303. My emphasis.
122 'The Man of the Crowd', *The Complete Tales and Poems*, p. 481.
123 'Berenice', *The Complete Tales and Poems*, p. 646.
124 Ibid.
125 'Ligeia', *The Complete Tales and Poems*, p. 656.
126 'The Tell-Tale Heart', *The Complete Tales and Poems*, p. 304.
127 Ibid.
128 Ibid.
129 'Nathaniel Hawthorne', *Essays and Reviews*, p. 571.
130 Marie Bonaparte, of course, interpreted the story in terms of the mythical act of killing one's own father, as in the legend of Chronos and Saturn, or in the eternal narrative of Oedipus.

Chapter 2: Van Gogh and Hofmannsthal

1   A different version of this chapter was given as a lecture at a colloquium entitled 'La modernité', at the Musée Rodin, Paris, in 1982.
2   Charles Baudelaire, *Les Fleurs du Mal*, in *Oeuvres complètes*, vol. 1 (Paris: Gallimard, 1975), p. 134.
3   Baudelaire, *Le Peintre de la vie moderne*, *Oeuvres complètes*, vol. 2 (Paris: Gallimard, 1976), p. 684. *The Painter of Modern Life, and other Essays*, trans. Jonathan Mayne (London: Phaidon, 1964, 1995), p. 3.
4   Ibid., p. 13.
5   *Salon de 1845*, *Oeuvres complètes*, vol. 2, p. 353. *The Salon of 1845, Art in Paris, 1845–1862. Salons and Other Exibitions Reviewed by Charles Baudelaire,*

trans. and ed. Johnathan Mayne (London: Phaidon Press, 1965; Ithaca, New York: Cornell Paperbacks, 1981), p. 3.

6 Baudelaire, *The Salon of 1846, Art in Paris*, p. 65.

7 Georg Trakl, *Selected Poems*, trans. R. Grenier, M. Hamburger, D. Luke and C. Middleton (London: Cape, 1968), pp. 18–19.

8 Baudelaire, 'The Life and Works of Eugène Delacroix', *The Painter of Modern Life and Other Essays*, p. 44.

9 Ibid.

10 Vincent Van Gogh, *Lettres à son frère Théo* (Paris: Grasset, 1982), pp. 34 and 37 (letter dated July 1880).

11 Hugo von Hofmannsthal, 'Colours', from 'The Letters of the Man Who Returned', *Selected Prose*, trans. Mary Hottinger and Tania and James Stern (New York: Pantheon Books, 1952), pp. 146–7.

12 Baudelaire, *The Salon de 1846, Art in Paris*, p. 418.

13 Hofmannsthal, 'Colours', *Selected Prose*, p. 149.

14 See the chapter 'Gustav Klimt: Painting and the Crisis of the Liberal Ego', in Carl Shorske, *Fin-de-siècle Vienna* (New York: Knopf, 1980), pp. 208–78.

15 Hofmannsthal, 'The Letter of Lord Chandos', *Selected Prose*, pp. 132–4.

16 Hofmannsthal, 'Colours', *Selected Prose*, pp. 142–3.

17 Hofmannsthal, 'Die Bühne als Traumbild', *Reden und Aufsätze I (1891–1913)*, *Gesammelte Werke* (Frankfurt am Main: Fischer Taschenbuch, 1979), pp. 490–1.

18 Walter Benjamin, *Briefe*, vol. 2 (Frankfurt am Main: Suhrkamp, 1978), p. 852.

19 Van Gogh, *Lettres*, p. 202 (Aug. 1888).

20 Ibid., pp. 215–16 (Sept. 1888).

21 Ibid., p. 214.

22 Hofmannsthal, 'Colours', *Selected Prose*, pp. 148–9.

23 Hofmannsthal, 'The Letter of Lord Chandos', *Selected Prose*, p. 136.

24 Ibid., p. 137.

25 Hofmannsthal, 'Colours', *Selected Prose*, p. 147.

26 Hofmannsthal, 'The Letter of Lord Chandos', *Selected Prose*, p. 138.

27 Ibid., p. 137.

28 Ibid., p. 139–40.

29 Hofmannsthal, 'Colours', *Selected Prose*, p. 148.

30 Hofmannsthal, 'Balzac', *Selected Prose*, p. 273.

31 Hofmannsthal, 'The Letter of Lord Chandos', *Selected Prose*, p. 136.

32 Hofmannsthal, 'Der Dichter und diese Zeit', *Reden und Aufsätze I*, *Gesammelte Werke*, p. 78.

Chapter 3: Baudelaire, Haussmann, Fustel de Coulanges

1 This chapter was first published in Suzanne Nash, ed., *Home and its Dislocations in Nineteenth-Century France* (Albany: State University of New York Press, 1993), pp. 147–65.

2 See Edgar Allan Poe, 'The Man of the Crowd', *The Complete Tales and Poems* (New York: Modern Library, 1938; reprint New York: Vintage, 1975), pp. 480–1.

3 Charles Baudelaire, *Les Fleurs du Mal*, in *Oeuvres complètes*, vol. 1, pp. 87–9.

4 Ibid., p. 75.

5 'In Baudelaire allegory's illusory character is not confessed and declared, opposite from the baroque.' Walter Benjamin, 'Zentralpark', *Charles Baudelaire. Ein Lyrkler im Zeitalter des Hochcapitalismus, Gesammelte Schriften,* vol. 1, pt 1 (Frankfurt am Main: Suhrkamp, 1974), p. 659.

6 Bertolt Brecht, 'Uber den Realismus 1937 bis 1941', *Schriften zur Literatur und Kunst 2, Gesammelte Werke,* vol. 19 (Frankfurt am Main: Suhrkamp, 1967), p. 299.

7 Ibid., p. 309.

8 Ibid., p. 312.

9 Benjamin, 'Zentralpark', p. 658.

10 *Les Fleurs du Mal, Oeuvres complètes,* vol 1, p. 11.

11 Ibid., p. 1025.

12 P. B. Shelley, 'Peter Bell and the Third Part', quoted by Benjamin, 'Das Paris des Second Empire bei Baudelaire', *Gesammelte Schriften,* vol. 1, pt. 2, p. 562.

13 Brecht, *Gesammelte Werke,* vol. 19, p. 346.

14 Baudelaire, 'Puisque réalisme il y a', *Oeuvres complètes,* vol. 2, p. 58.

15 Ibid., p. 1123.

16 Ibid., p. 80.

17 *Oeuvres complètes,* vol. 1, p. 424.

18 See Roland Barthes, *Writing Degree Zero,* trans. Annette Lavers and Colin Smith (New York: Hill and Wang, 1978), p. 5.

19 Barthes said in *Leçon* that one is uni-dimensional and the other multi-dimensional. Literature always tried to come to terms with this discrepancy between language and reality, therefore 'literature, whatever the school in whose name it declares itself, is absolutely, categorically, realist'. See 'Inaugural Lecture, Collège de France', in *A Barthes Reader,* trans. Richard Howard, with an introduction by Susan Sontag (New York: Hill and Wang, 1981), p. 18. This realism coming out of the discrepancy between language and reality is what I call allegorical realism.

20 *Les Fleurs du Mal, Oeuvres complètes,* vol. 1, p. 92.

21 'The masses had become so much a part of Baudelaire that it is rare to find a description of them in his works.' Benjamin, 'On Some Motifs in Baudelaire', *Illuminations,* trans. Harry Zohn (New York: Schocken books, 1985), p. 167.

22 Benjamin, 'Zentralpark', *Gesammelte Schriften,* vol. 1, pt 1, p. 548.

23 Georg Simmel, 'The Metropolis and Mental Life', *The Sociology of Georg Simmel,* trans. Kurt H. Wolff (New York: Free Press, 1964), p. 410.

24 P. B. Shelley, 'Peter Bell and the Third Part', quoted by Benjamin, 'Das Paris des Second Empire bei Baudelaire', *Gesammelte Schriften,* vol. 1, pt 2, p. 562.

25 Baudelaire, *The Painter of Modern Life, The Painter of Modern Life and Other Essays* (London: Phaedon Press, 1964, repr. 1995), p. 4.

26 Thomas Carlyle, 'Signs of the Time', *Selected Writings* (London: Penguin, 1980), p. 65.

27 See Max Weber, *The City,* trans. D. Martindale and G. Neuwirth (New York: Free Press, 1958), p. 65–89.

28 Baron Haussmann, *Mémoires,* vol. 1 (Paris: Victor-Havard, 1890–3), p. 32.

29 Ibid.

30 Ibid., vol 3, p. 55, quoted by Sigfried Giedion, *Space, Time, and Architecture* (Cambridge, MA: Harvard University Press, 1967), p. 649.

31 *Les Fleurs du Mal, Oeuvres complètes*, vol. 1, p. 86.

32 Benjamin talks about Baudelaire's social awareness in 'Zentralpark', p. 88.

33 *Les Fleurs du Mal, Oeuvres complètes*, vol. 1, p. 87.

34 I mean here radical in the intellectual sense, and not in the narrowly political sense, since Baudelaire moved quite easily from the 1848 barricades to
his scorn for militant literature. See Baudelaire, *Oeuvres complètes*, vol. 1,
p. 679 and 691.

35 Baudelaire, *The Salon de 1845, Art in Paris*, p. 32.

36 On the ambiguity of the modern see Antoine Compagnon, *Les Cinq paradoxes de la modernité* (Paris: Editions du Seuil, 1990).

37 *Oeuvres complètes*, vol. 1, p. 275–6. *Paris Spleen*, trans. Louise Varèse (New
York: New Directions, 1947), p. ix–x. Benjamin quotes these famous passages in *Gesammelte Schriften*, vol. 1, pt 2, p. 617.

38 The bibliography could be endless. See Fritz Stern, ed., *The Varieties of
History from Voltaire to the Present* (New York: Vintage Books, 1973), p. 57.
For a brilliant discussion of the dictum, see Stephen Bann, *The Clothing of
Clio* (Cambridge: Cambridge University Press, 1984), pp. 8–14.

39 Fustel de Coulanges, in François Hartog, 'Choix de textes de Fustel de
Coulanges', *Le XIXe siècle et l'histoire: le cas Fustel de Coulanges* (Paris: Presses
Universitaires de France, 1988), p. 341.

40 Haussmann, *Mémoires*, vol. 1, p. xi–xii.

41 See Arnoldo Momigliano, 'The Ancient City of Fustel de Coulanges', *Essays
in Ancient and Modern Historiography* (Oxford: Blackwell, 1977), p. 329. For
the most illuminating reading of Fustel de Coulanges, see Hartog, 'La Cité
antique et la cité moderne', *Le XIXe siècle et l'histoire*, pp. 23–95. See also his
foreword to Fustel de Coulanges, *La Cité antique* (Paris: Flammarion, 1984),
pp. v–xxv.

42 *La Cité antique*, p. 2.

43 Jean-Jacques Rousseau, *Discours sur l'origine et les fondemens de l'inégalité*, and
Fragments politiques, Oeuvres complètes, vol. 3 (Paris: Gallimard, Bibliothèque
de la Pléiade, 1964), pp. 113 and 550.

44 *La Cité antique*, p. 2.

45 Ibid., p. 307.

46 Momigliano, 'The Ancient City', p. 336.

47 *La Cité antique*, p. 26. Momigliano maintains that 'the *Cité antique* would be
inconceivable without the arrival of the Aryans on the scene of ancient
history. The Celts and the Slavs entered Fustel's mental horizon later on'
('The Ancient City', p. 333).

48 See Momigliano, 'The Ancient City', p. 339.

49 He was wrongly perceived as a Catholic although he tried to make clear
that he was not a Christian. See ibid., p. 411, and Hartog, *Le XIXe siècle et
l'histoire*, p. 17.

50 His notion of *patrie* was close to Renan's idea that a nation is 'a spiritual principle resulting from some deep historical complications'. (*Qu'est-ce qu'une
nation?, Oeuvres complètes*, vol. 1 (Paris: Calmann-Lévy, 1947), p. 902.) Hartog
exhaustively discusses the connections between Fustel and Renan, *Le XIXe
siècle et l'histoire*, pp. 44–61.

51 *La Cité antique*, p. 8.

52 Momigliano, 'The Ancient City', p. 415.

53 Baudelaire, *Le Spleen de Paris, Oeuvres complètes*, vol. 1, p. 356.
54 *Les Fleurs du Mal*, ibid., p. 130.
55 Ibid., p. 134.

Chapter 4: Trieste as Frontier

1 This chapter was first published as 'Lieu de retour ou lieu de fuite? De Slataper à Bazlen', *Critique* ('Les mystères de Trieste'), 435–6 (1983), pp. 653–69.
   Scipio Slataper was born in Trieste in 1888. His father Luigi, a Triestino of Slovak origin, was a tradesman; his mother, the daughter of a German woman, was the cousin of Scipione de Sandrinelli, who held public office in Trieste up until 1909, as a representative of the national (liberal) party. In 1899, in the aftermath of a period of nervous depression, and of a serious financial crisis suffered by his family, the young Scipio spent six months on the Carso, the high plateau around Trieste. In 1908, he went to Florence, and to the Istituto di Studi Superiori. While there, he published regularly in the review *La Voce*. In 1911, he travelled for two months in central Europe, visiting Vienna, Prague, Dresden and Berlin. In 1913, he obtained a post as reader in Italian at the Colonial Institute in Hamburg. He was in Trieste in 1914 when war broke out. He immediately voiced his support for Italian intervention. On December 1915 he fell in battle, on the Podgora Mt., near Trieste. He published *Il mio carso*, in 1912; a translation of Hebbel's journal, also in 1912; a study of Ibsen, based upon his thesis, in 1916. Posthumous writings: *Scritti letterari e critici* (Rome: La voce, 1920), *Scritti politici* (Rome: La voce, 1925), *Lettere* (Turin: Buratti, 1931) and *Appunti e note di diario* (Milan: Mondadori, 1953).
2 Slataper, *Il mio carso* (Rome: Editori Riuniti, 1982), p. 31.
3 *La voce*, the first number of which appeared in December 1908, was an exceptionally important review for Italian intellectual life in the early years of the twentieth century. Founded by Giuseppe Prezzolini and Giovanni Papini, on essentially Crocean lines (Croce himself had suggested entitling it *La cultura italiana*), it may be considered an expression of the liberal intelligentsia in crisis. Intellectual commitment was seen as a remedy for the political degeneration of the country.
4 *Il mio carso*, p. 31.
5 The use of the epithet 'barbaric' in relation to poetry derives from the poet Giosué Carducci. In 1889, having already written in Italian in Latin metres, he published the *Odi barbare*, in which he employed a metre founded not on quantity, as is the case with classical Latin metre, but on the tonic accent. Thus, to the ears of their putative Latin audience, these poems would have sounded barbaric. In this way Carducci forged his own brand of classicism, reconciling it with modern notions of rhythm. Gabriele D'Annunzio followed his example. Slataper's barbarism entailed rejecting verse altogether, so as to discover a harsh rhythm in prose.
6 *Il mio carso*, p. 90
7 Ibid., p. 56.
8 Ibid., p. 104.
9 Bazlen, *Note senza testo* (Milan: Adelphi, 1970), p. 72.

10 Ibid., p. 144.
11 Ibid., p. 132.
12 Ibid., p. 70.
13 Ibid., p. 39.
14 Ibid., p. 34.
15 Ibid., p. 119.
16 See Italo Calvino, 'Afterword', Del Giudice, *Lo stadio di Wimbledon* (Torino: Einaudi, 1982), p. 127
17 Bazlen, *Note senza testo*, p. 41.
18 *Lo stadio di Wimbledon*, p. 29.
19 Bazlen, *Note senza testo*, p. 42.
20 *Lo stadio di Wimbleton*, p. 106.
21 Ibid., p. 108.
22 Ibid., p. 44.
23 Ibid., p. 119.
24 Bazlen, *Note senza testo*, p. 48.
25 *Lo stadio di Wimbledon*, p. 124.

Chapter 5: Aldo Rossi

1 A shorter version of this chapter was first published in 'Piazza d'Italia: l'architecture d'Aldo Rossi', *Critique* ('E l'Italia va'), 447–8 (1984), pp. 681–92, as a review article of Aldo Rossi, *A Scientific Autobiography*, postscript by Vincent Scully, trans. Lawrence Venuti (Cambridge, Mass.: MIT Press, 1981), and *Il libro azzurro. I miei progetti 1981* (Zurich: Jamileh Weber Galerie-Edition, 1981).
   The quotation is from *A Scientific Autobiography*, p. 78.
2 Ibid., p. 2.
3 Aldo Rossi, *L'architettura della città* (Padua: Marsilio, 1966), p. 11.
4 Rossi wrote the preface to *Adolf Loos* (Milan: Electa, 1982).
5 *A Scientific Autobiography*, p. 44.
6 Ibid., p. 75.
7 Ibid., p. 66.
8 'The *Sacri Monti*, characteristic forms of Lombard mannerism, were series of chapels with depictions of sacred history, which pilgrims followed in their narrative order culminating in the reproduction of a view of the Holy Sepulchre.' A. Tomlison, 'Sacri Monti', *The Architectural Review*, 116 (Dec. 1954), quoted in a note to *A Scientific Autobiography*, p. 2.
9 *A Scientific Autobiography*, p. 53.
10 Ibid., p. 55.
11 Ibid.
12 Ibid., p. 35.
13 E. Bonfanti, R Bonicalzi, A. Rossi, M. Scolari and D. Vitale, *Architettura razionale* (Milan: Electa, 1973); on Rossi's rationalism, see A. Vidler, 'La troisième typologie', *Architecture rationnelle: la reconstruction de la ville européenne*, ed. L. Krier (Brussels: Editions des Archives d'architecture moderne, 1978).
14 *A Scientific Autobiography*, p. 72.

15 Ibid., p. 1.
16 Ibid., p. 54.
17 Ibid., p. 23.
18 Rossi, 'Nuovi problemi', in *Casabella-Continuità*, 264 (1962), p. 6. See Vittorio Savi, *L'architettura di Aldo Rossi* (Milan: F. Angeli, 1976).
19 *A Scientific Autobiography*, p. 23.
20 Ibid., p. 72.
21 Ibid., p. 78.
22 Ibid., p. 16.
23 Ibid., p. 57.
24 Ibid., p. 72.
25 Aldo Rossi, *Il libro azzurro. I miei progetti*, p. 32.
26 See the postscript to *A Scientific Autobiography* by Vincent Scully (pp. 114–15), who finds that the cemetery in Modena recalls the Fascist monument of the EUR in Rome.
27 *A Scientific Autobiography*, p. 82.
28 For Rossi's parallels with de Chirico, see Peter Eisenman, 'The House of the Dead as the City of Survival', in *Aldo Rossi in America, 1976 to 1979*, ed. Kenneth Frampton (New York: Institute for Architecture and Urban Studies, 1979), pp. 4–19.
29 Giorgio de Chirico, 'Rêves', *La Révolution surréaliste*, 1 (1 Dec. 1924).
30 *A Scientific Autobiography*, p. 81.
31 Ibid., p. 76.
32 Ibid.
33 Ibid.
34 Aldo Rossi has spent a long time in Trieste, especially in 1974 on the occasion of the competitions for the Palazzo della Regione and the Casa dello studente. He has made several journeys to the United States; in 1977 be was Mellon Professor at Cooper Union School of Architecture in New York.
35 *A Scientific Autobiography*, p. 65.
36 Aldo Rossi, *Teatro del Mondo*, (Venice: Cluva, 1982), p. 12. This book includes articles by Francesco Dal Co and Manfredo Tafuri; the photographs are by Antonio Martinelli.
37 Ibid.
38 *A Scientific Autobiography*, p. 29.
39 Ibid.
40 Ibid., p. 19.
41 Ibid., p. 25.
42 Ibid., p. 66.

Chapter 6: Massimo Cacciari

1 This chapter was first published as the introduction to Massimo Cacciari, *Architecture and Nihilism: On the Philosophy of Modern Architecture*, trans. Stephen Sartarelli (New Haven and London: Yale University Press, 1993), pp. ix–lviii.
2 Enrico Berlinguer, 'La politica che il paese esige dopo la caduta del governo Andreotti-Malagodi (comizio al Festival Nazionale dell'Unità a Venezia,

24 giugno 1973)', *La questione comunista, 1969–1975*, a cura di Antonio Tato, vol. 2 (Rome: Editori Riuniti, 1975), p. 584.

3 See Cacciari, *Metropolis. Saggi sulla grande città di Sombart, Endell, Scheffler e Simmel* (Roma: Officina, 1973). This essay, constituted by materials discussed in Manfredo Tafuri's seminars at Venice's School of Architecture, is the introduction to selected texts by the German sociologists and the German architect (August Endell) mentioned in the Italian title.

4 Cacciari, *Architecture and Nihilism*, p. 6.

5 Ibid., p. 30.

6 See Antonio Negri, 'La teoria capitalistica dello stato nel '29: John M. Keynes', *Contropiano*, 1 (1968), pp. 3–40; and Mario Tronti, 'Estremismo e riformismo', pp. 41–58. Works by Antonio Negri published in English include: *The Savage Anomaly: The Power of Spinoza's Metaphysics and Politics*, trans. Michael Hardt (Minneapolis: University of Minnesota Press, 1991); *The Politics of Subversion: A Manifesto for the Twenty-first Century*, trans. James Newell (Cambridge, UK; Cambridge, MA: Polity Press, Blackwell, 1989); *Marx beyond Marx: Lessons on the Grundrisse*, trans. Harry Cleaver, Michael Ryan and Maurizio Viano (South Hadley, Mass.: Bergin and Garvey, 1984).

7 Alberto Asor Rosa, one of the editors of two essential journals in the early 1960s – *Quaderni rossi* and *Classe operaia* – is a professor of Italian literature at the University of Rome, 'La Sapienza'. Among his most important works: *Intellettuali e classe operaia: Saggi sulle forme di uno storico conflitto e di una possibile alleanza* (Florence: La nuova Italia, 1973), *La lirica del Seicento* (Bari: Laterza, 1975), *Storia della letteratura italiana* (Florence: La nuova Italia, 1985).

8 On the question of economic development of the Veneto region, see Silvio Lanaro, ed., *Storia d'Italia: Le regioni dall'unità a oggi: Veneto* (Turin: Einaudi, 1984).

9 *Contropiano*, 2 (1968), p. 240.

10 Ibid., p. 241.

11 See Cacciari, *Ciclo capitalistico e lotte operaie. Montedison Pirelli Fiat 1968* (Padua: Marsilio, 1969), pp. 21–22.

12 Cacciari, 'La Comune di maggio', *Contropiano*, 2 (1968), p. 462.

13 Berlinguer addressed women, young people and a large section of the 'productive middle classes' as possible allies of the traditional basis of the PCI. See Enrico Berlinguer, 'Le masse femminili, forza di rinnovamento della società', *La questione comunista*, vol. 1, p. 301.

14 Alberto Asor Rosa, 'Rivoluzione e letteratura', *Contropiano*, 1 (1968), pp. 235–6.

15 Aldo Rossi, *Teatro del mondo*, p. 104.

16 Charles Baudelaire, *Les Fleurs du Mal*, *Oeuvres complètes*, vol. 1, p. 86.

17 Cacciari, *Architecture and Nihilism*, p. 4.

18 Alberto Asor Rosa and Cacciari, 'Editorial', *Contropiano*, 2 (1968), p. 238.

19 Ibid., pp. 239, 243.

20 In 1988 Alberto Asor Rosa wrote a preface to a new edition of the 1964 *Scrittori e popolo*, a controversial book that was seminal for an entire generation in Italy. He alluded to the weight of time and the changes in politics and expectations: 'Twenty years have gone by since that time [the publica-

tion of his book]: but they seem many more. Something of enormous importance happened in the meantime: at that time we thought that the factory working class would take power; today we think that, in the social displacements that took place in these twenty years, *no* class is able to take and control power: for the good reason that there *is no longer* a class that would be capable of taking power.' Alberto Asor Rosa, 'Vent'anni dopo', *Scrittori e popolo* (Turin: Einaudi, 1988), p. vii.

21 Cacciari, 'La Montecatini-Edison di Porto Marghera', *Contropiano*, 3 (1968), pp. 579–627, and 2 (1969), pp. 579–627; 'Sulla genesi del pensiero negativo', *Contropiano*, 1 (1969), pp. 131–200.
22 Asor Rosa, 'Prefazione alla seconda edizione', *Scrittori e popolo*, p. 9.
23 See Cacciari, *Krisis* (Milan: Feltrinelli, 1976); *Dallo Steinhof* (Milan: Adelphi, 1982); *Icone della legge* (Milan: Adelphi 1985); *L'Angelo necessario* (Milan: Adelphi, 1986); *Dall'Inizio* (Milan: Adelphi, 1990). Earlier works by Cacciari include his preface to Georg Lukács, *Kommunismus* (Padua: Marsilio, 1972), his preface 'Negative Thought and Rationalization', for Eugene Fink, *Nietzsche* (Padua: Marsilio, 1973), and *Pensiero negativo e razionalizzazione* (Venice: Marsilio, 1977).
24 See Walter Benjamin, 'On Some motifs in Baudelaire', *Illuminations*, p. 175.
25 Cacciari, *Architecture and Nihilism*, pp. 31–3.
26 Cacciari, 'Sulla genesi del pensiero negativo', *Contropiano*, 1 (1969), p. 138.
27 Ibid.
28 Ibid.
29 Ibid., p. 139.
30 Antonio Negri, 'La teoria capitalista dello stato nel '29: John M. Keynes', *Contropiano*, 1 (1968), p. 7.
31 'The "irrationalism"of the romantic period here analysed is only apparent.' Cacciari, 'Sulla genesi del pensiero negativo', *Contropiano*, 1 (1969), p. 133.
32 See Cacciari, 'Il problema del politico in Deleuze e Foucault', in Franco Rella and Georges Teyssot, eds, *Il dispositivo Foucault* (Venice: Cluva, 1977), pp. 57–69. Asor Rosa stressed his distance from Herbert Marcuse's position, which he labelled 'political romanticism'. See Asor Rosa, 'Dalla rivoluzione culturale alla lotta di classe', *Contropiano*, 3 (1968), pp. 472–4.
33 Cacciari, 'Eupalinos or Architecture', *Oppositions*, 21 (1980), p. 107, trans. Stephen Sartarelli.
34 See Pierre Bourdieu, 'Intellectual Field and and Creative Project', *Social Sciences Information*, 8 (1969), pp. 89–119; and Fritz Ringer, 'The Intellectual Field, Intellectual History, and the Sociology of Knowledge', *Theory and Society*, 19 (1990), pp. 269–94.
35 Baudelaire, 'Le Cygne', *Les Fleurs du mal*, in *Oeuvres complètes* vol. 1, p. 86. See my Chapter 3 above.
36 A critique, from a Nietzschean perspective, of the persistence of a redemptive ideology in the conception of art, is offered by Leo Bersani, *The Culture of Redemption* (Cambridge, MA: Harvard University Press, 1990).
37 *Architecture and Nihilism*, p. 111.
38 Ibid., p. 118.
39 On the question of alienation as the foundamental form on which is constructed the radical concept of the State during the Enlightenment, see Cacciari, 'Entsagung', *Contropiano*, 2 (1971), p. 411.

40 See Benjamin, 'On Some Motifs in Baudelaire', *Illuminations*, pp. 155–200; and 'Paris, Capital of the Nineteenth Century, *Reflections*, pp. 146–62.

41 *Cantata di Strapaese*, such is the title of a satyrical poem by the Tuscan poet Mino Maccari, who edited the review symptomatically titled *Il selvaggio* from 1934 until 1943. 'Selvaggismo' is the trend of some Italian twentieth-century literature (Papini, Soffici and Malaparte) completely focused on a rural, anti-urban ideology. On the Italian attachment to a rural tradition, see Asor Rosa's exhaustive *Storia d'Italia. Dall'unità a oggi*, vol. 4, pt 2 (Turin: Einaudi, 1975).

42 Antonio Gramsci, *Letteratura e vita nazionale*, quoted by Asor Rosa, *Scrittori e popolo*, p. 177.

43 Asor Rosa, 'La teoria marxista e le altre', *Le due società. Ipotesi sulla crisi italiana* (Turin: Einaudi, 1977), p. 88.

44 The Italian film critic Roberto Escobar wrote about *Ultrà*: Tognazzi 'looked for the story of an Italy that has never been loved by cinema: that metropolitan and violent Italy – so hard that ideology and good feelings cannot tame it. Then he developed that story privileging elliptical narration and montage technique' (*Il sole 24ore*, 31 March 1991).

45 Fredric Jameson, 'Architecture and the Critique of Ideology', *The Ideologies of Theory: Essays 1971–1986: Syntax of History*, vol. 2 (Minneapolis: University of Minnesota Press, 1988), p. 48.

46 Ibid., p. 49.

47 See Lewis Mumford, *The Culture of Cities* (New York: Harcourt, Brace & Co., 1938); and *The City in History: Its Origins, Its Transformations and Its Prospects* (New York: Harcourt, Brace & World, 1961).

48 See Raymond Williams, *The Country and the City* (New York: Oxford University Press, 1973). *Nuova Corrente*, a review where Cacciari published many of his articles, published several translations of Raymond Williams's work, and mainly of essays that became part of his *The Long Revolution* (London: Chatto and Windus, 1961).

49 See Stuart Hall, 'The Emergence of Cultural Studies and the Crisis of the Humanities', *October*, 53 (Summer 1990), pp. 11–23.

50 See Manfredo Tafuri, *Progetto e Utopia* (Bari: Laterza, 1973); *Architecture and Utopia: Design and Capitalist Development*, trans. Barbara Luigia La Penta (Cambridge, MA: MIT Press, 1976). See also 'Per una critica dell'ideologia architettonica', *Contropiano*, 1 (1969), pp. 31–79.

51 Alberto Asor Rosa, 'Vent'anni dopo', *Scrittori e popolo*, p. xiii.

52 Ibid. pp. ix–x.

53 Manfredo Tafuri, 'Austro-marxismo e città: *das Rote Wien*', *Contropiano*, 2 (1971), p. 259.

54 Manfredo Tafuri, *Teorie e storia dell'architettura* (Bari: Laterza, 1968). *Theories and History of Architecture*, trans. Giorgio Verrecchia (New York,: Harper and Row, 1980).

55 Manfredo Tafuri, 'Avvertenza alla seconda edizione', *Teorie e storia dell'architettura* (Bari: Laterza, 1973), p. 5.

56 See a similar argument in Roland Barthes, 'History or Literature?', *On Racine* (New York: Hill and Wang, 1964), pp. 154–5.

57 Fredric Jameson, 'Architecture and the Critique of Ideology', *The Ideologies of Theory*, vol. 2, p. 38.

58 Ibid.

59 Ibid., p. 39.
60 Ibid., p. 38–9.
61 Ibid., p. 40.
62 Ibid., p. 38.
63 Walter Benjamin, 'Theses on the Philosophy of History', *Illuminations*, p. 256.
64 Ibid., p. 262.
65 Ibid., pp. 262–3.
66 This essay was published in Massimo Cacciari and Francesco Amendolagine, *Oikos: Da Loos a Wittgenstein* (Rome: Officina, 1975). Officina published, among others, Giangiorgio Pasqualotto, Giorgio Ciucci, Georges Teyssot, Paolo Morachiello, and Donatella Calabi.
67 Giorgio Ciucci, Francesco Dal Co, Mario Manieri-Elia, Manfredo Tafuri, *The American City. From the Civil War to the New Deal*, trans. Barbara Luigia La Penta (Cambridge, MA: MIT Press, 1979), pp. x–xi.
68 Tafuri, *Teorie e storia dell'architettura* (Bari: Laterza, 1968), p. 25.
69 *Architecture and Nihilism*, p. 128.
70 Ibid., p. 130.
71 Carl Schorske, 'The Ringstrasse and the birth of Urban Modernism', *Fin-de-siècle Vienna*, p. 84.
72 Ibid., p. 85.
73 Ibid., p. 100.
74 *Architecture and Nihilism*, p. 130.
75 See Renato De Fusco, *Storia dell'architettura contemporanea* (Bari: Laterza, 1974, 1988) pp. 127–30. In 'Loos and His Angel', Cacciari writes that it is 'fundamentally impossible to assimilate him into the currents of progressive rationalism, in architecture and elsewhere' (Architecture and Nihilism, p. 173).
76 *Architecture and Nihilism*, p. 119.
77 Ibid., p. 132.
78 Ibid., p. 133.
79 Ibid., p. 134.
80 Ibid., p. 106.
81 Ibid., p. 107.
82 Ibid., p. 134.
83 Manfredo Tafuri, 'The Disenchanted Mountain', *The American City*, p. 403. Tafuri discusses the Chicago Tribune project also in *Theories and History of Architecture* (New York: Harper and Row, 1980), p. 85.
84 Aldo Rossi, *A Scientific Autobiography*, p. 76.
85 Aldo Rossi, Introduction to Adolf Loos, *Spoken into the Void, Collected Essays 1897–1900* (Cambridge, MA: MIT Press, Oppositions Books, 1982), pp. viii–xiii. Rossi perceives no contradiction between the Loos of 'Ornament and Crime' and the creator of the *Chicago Tribune* project, and feels in it the presence of that metropolis that Loos discovered in New York. Tafuri and Cacciari consider, in the words of Tafuri quoted by Cacciari, 'that in 1922 Loos seemed to have lost touch with the clarity of his prewar attitudes' (Manfredo Tafuri, 'The Disenchanted Mountain', *The American City*, p. 432). If we reread today Tafuri's words in *Theories and History*, we can say that, unlike Rossi, he hinted at a postmodern element of the *Chicago Tribune*: 'The Doric column planned by Loos for the *Chicago*

Tribune competition, as a first and violent experiment in extracting a linguistic element from its context and transferring it to an abnormally sized second context, is the anticipation of a caustic and ambiguous Pop Architecture' (p. 84).

86 *Architecture and Nihilism*, p. 154.
87 Ibid.
88 'Architects can no longer afford to be intimidated by the puritanical language of orthodox Modern architecture.' Robert Venturi, *Complexity and Contradiction in Architecture* (New York: Museum of Modern Art, 1966), p. 16.
89 *Architecture and Nihilism*, p. 107.
90 Ibid., p. 150.
91 Ibid. The horror of this figure – the architect-artist-dominator – appears in a satire by Loos that sounds almost like one of Baudelaire's *Prose poems*. The despotic architect does not even allow the poor little rich man to buy a painting at the Secession! See Adolf Loos, 'The Poor Little Rich Man', *Spoken into the Void*, pp. 125–7.
92 *Architecture and Nihilism*, p. 151.
93 The real loyalty to negative thought cannot be completed nihilismus, nor 'weak thinking', as Gianni Vattimo calls the postmodern thought that abandons any systematic attempt to organize the world. See Gianni Vattimo and Pier Aldo Rovatti, eds, *Il pensiero debole* (Milan: Feltrinelli, 1984).
94 'Desire is after all the desire to reconcile with the "naturality" of Desire.' Cacciari, 'Il problema del politico in Deleuze e Foucault', *Il dispositivo Foucault*, p. 66.
95 Ibid., p. 68.
96 *Architecture and Nihilism*, p. 152.
97 Massimo Caccciari, *Dallo Steinhof* (Milan: Adelphi, 1980), p. 31. At the end of a chapter on Trauerspiel, Cacciari quotes Roberto Bazlen: 'True life means: to invent new places on which to be able to shipwreck ... ; every new work is nothing but the invention of a new death' (p. 49).
98 See Charles Jencks, *The Language of Postmodern Architecture* (New York: Rizzoli, 1977). For a critique of this postmodernist immediacy, see Kenneth Frampton, *Modern Architecture: A Critical History* (New York: Oxford University Press, 1980), p. 292. See also Anthony Vidler, 'Academicism: Modernism', *Oppositions*, 8 (1977), pp. 1–5.
99 See *Architecture and Nihilism*, p. 187.
100 Cacciari, 'Eupalinos or Architecture', *Oppositions*, 21 (1980), p. 115.
101 Ibid.
102 Manfredo Tafuri, *La sfera e il labirinto: avanguardie e architettura da Piranesi agli anni '70* (Turin, Einaudi, 1980); *The Sphere and the Labyrinth: Avant-gardes and Architecture from Piranesi to the 1970s*, trans. Pellegrino d'Acierno and Robert Connolly. (Cambridge, MA: MIT University Press, 1987), p. 4. Cacciari expresses the same type of fear abour the sense of multiplicity when he talks about the *revêtement* character of linguistic games (*Architecture and Nihilism*, p. 163).
103 Tafuri, *The Sphere and the Labyrinth*, pp. 4–5.
104 See Tafuri, *Venezia e il Rinascimento* (Turin: Einaudi, 1985); *Venice and the Renaissance*, trans. Jessica Levine (Cambridge, MA: MIT Press, 1989).

105 See Michel Vovelle, *Idéologie et Mentalités* (Paris: François Maspero, 1982); *Ideologies and Mentalities*, trans. Eamon O'Flaherty (Chicago: Chicago University Press, 1990).
106 Tafuri, 'Réalisme et architecture', *Critique*, 476–7 (1987), p. 23. Tafuri posits the problem similarly to the historian Paul Veyne. See Paul Veyne, *L'Inventaire des différences* (Paris: Seuil, 1976), pp. 48–9.
107 On the question of orthodoxy, the conflict over expressionism between Benjamin and Lukács is important. See Ernst Bloch et al., *Aesthetics and Politics* (London: Whitstable, 1977), including Fredric Jameson's 'Reflections in Conclusion', pp. 196–209.
108 Lucien Febvre, 'Avant-propos', in Charles Morazé, *Trois essais sur histoire et culture* (Paris: Cahiers des Annales, 1948), p. vii.
109 *Architecture and Nihilism*, p. 147.
110 Benjamin, 'Theses on the Philosophy of History', *Illuminations*, pp. 257–8.
111 Nietzsche, *The Birth of Tragedy and the Genealogy of Morals* (New York: Anchor Press, 1956), p. 157.
112 Cacciari, *Dallo Steinhof* (Milan: Adelphi, 1980), p. 31.
113 *Architecture and Nihilism*, p. 157.
114 Ibid., p. 156.
115 Ibid., p. 205.
116 Cacciari, *Dallo Steinhof*, p. 13.
117 Ibid., p. 48.
118 Ibid., p. 29.
119 See ibid., pp. 76–80. Cacciari devoted an entire essay to the power of singing: see 'Il fare del canto', *Le forme del fare* (Naples: Liguori, 1987), pp. 47–74.
120 Cacciari, *Dallo Steinhof*, p. 31. One might also think of Cacciari's early fascination with Chomsky. See 'Vita Cartesii est simplicissima', *Contropiano*, 2 (1970), pp. 375–99.
121 This is the title of a chapter of Claudio Magris, *Il mito asburgico nella letteratura moderna* (Turin: Einaudi, 1963), pp. 185–260. See also Claudio Magris, *L'anello di Clarisse* (Turin: Einaudi, 1984), especially the essay 'La ruggine e i segni. Hofmannsthal e *La lettera di Lord Chandos*', pp. 32–62.
122 Cacciari, 'Intransitabili utopie', in Hugo von Hofmannsthal, *La Torre*, trans. Silvia Bortoli (Milan: Adelphi, 1978), p. 158.
123 Roland Barthes, 'Longtemps, je me suis couché de bonne heure', *The Rustle of Language* (New York: Hill & Wang, 1986), p. 286.
124 Alberto Asor Rosa, *Scrittori e popolo*, p. 10.
125 *Architecture and Nihilism*, p. 90.
126 Cacciari, 'Eupalinos or Architecture', *Oppositions*, 21 (1980), p. 114.
127 See Carl Schmitt, *The Concept of the Political* (New Brunswick, NJ: Rutgers University Press, 1976), and George Schwab's introduction, pp. 3–16.
128 Leo Strauss, 'Comments on Carl Schmitt's *Der Begriffe des Politischen*', in Carl Schmitt, *The Concept of the Political*, p. 81.
129 Cacciari et al., 'Sinisteritas', *Il concetto di sinistra* (Milan: Bompiani, 1982), p. 12.
130 Tafuri, 'The Historical Project', *The Sphere and the Labyrinth*, p. 5.
131 See Cacciari, 'Eupalinos or Architecture', *Oppositions*, 21 (1980), pp. 113–14.
132 Georg Simmel, 'Roma, Firenze e Venezia', translated into Italian in Cacciari, *Metropolis*, p. 197.

Chapter 7: Absence and Revelation

1 This chapter was first published in Colin MacCabe and Duncan Petrie, eds, *New Scholarship from BFI Research* (London: British Film Institute, 1996), pp. 58–85.

2 Raymond Williams, *Culture and Society* (London: Chatto and Windus, 1963), p. 285.

3 Ibid.

4 The Birmingham Centre institutionalized the existence of a new discipline, communication or cultural studies, with its emphasis on cinema and television.

5 See Christian Metz, 'A propos de l'impression de réalité au cinéma', *Cahiers du cinéma*, 166–7 (1965), pp. 75–82.

6 Walter Benjamin, 'A Short History of Photography', *Screen*, 13(1) (Spring 1972), pp. 5–6.

7 Williams, *Culture and Society*, p. 290.

8 Ibid.

9 Ibid., pp. 290–1.

10 Charles Baudelaire, *Les Fleurs du Mal*, *Oeuvres Complètes*, vol. 1, p. 93. Benjamin commented on this poem in 'On Some Motifs in Baudelaire', *Illuminations*, p. 167.

11 Jacques Lacan suggests that the human subject, aquainted with the world, has forgotten the inaugural scene of the discovery of his/her own image. Yet that scene is formative and dictates the function of the self. In a famous 1949 paper, 'The Mirror Stage', Lacan, deeply influenced by Jean Piaget, draw the attention to the euphoric, foundational moment in which the child – when it is approximateley six months old and is as yet unable to walk or talk – recognizes with exultation its own *imago* in the mirror, as well as the image of its reflected environment, and enjoys the repetition of this scene. See Jacques Lacan, 'Le stade du miroir comme formateur de la fonction du Je', *Ecrits* (Paris: Editions du Seuil, 1966), pp. 93–100.

12 Benjamin, 'A Short History of Photography', p. 6.

13 Ibid.

14 One should also investigate the distinction between the eye and the gaze. Lacan sketched this distinction, as noticed in a remarkable analysis of colour and glossiness by Fredric Jameson, 'On Magic Realism in Film', *Signatures of the Visible* (New York; London: Routledge, 1990), pp. 139–40.

15 Some psychoanalysts maintain that the era of neurosis is over and psychosis is much more representative of our age. Wouldn't this be confirmed by the psychic effects of the contemporary plethora of images? See Contardo Calligaris, *Introduction à une clinique différentielle des psychoses* (Paris: Editions du Seuil, 1992).

16 Baudelaire, 'A une passante', *Les Fleurs du Mal*, in *Oeuvres complètes*, vol. 1, p. 92.

17 Fredric Jameson, Introduction, *Signatures of the Visible*, p. 1.

18 Laura Mulvey, 'Visual Pleasure and Narrative Cinema', *Visual and Other Pleasures* (Houndmills: Macmillan, 1989). This article, written in 1973, was first published in *Screen* (1975).

19 Ibid., p. 18.

20 Ibid.

21 Jameson, 'The Existence of Italy', *Signatures of the Visible*, p. 186.

22 See Bertold Brecht, 'Uber den Realismus 1937 bis 1941', *Schriften zur Literatur und Kunst 2, Gesammelte Werke*, vol. 19. On this point see my Chapter 3. Jameson made a Brechtian argument when he wrote: 'Returning now to the historical issue of realism itself, the most obvious initial way of estranging and renewing this concept would seem to consist in reversing our conventional stereotype of its relationship to modernism. The latter, indeed, we celebrate as an active aesthetic praxis and invention, whose excitement is demiurgic, along with its liberation from content; while realism is conventionally evoked in terms of passive reflection and copying, subordinate to some external reality... . Something will certainly be gained, therefore, if we can manage to think of realism as a form of demiurgic praxis; if we can restore some active and even playful experimental impulses to the inertia of this appearance as a copy or representation of things.' ('The Existence of Italy', *Signatures of the Visible*, p. 162.)

23 To speak of the real is already to be in the symbolic order, because 'the real, whatever disruption we might operate, is always and in any event at its own place.' (Jacques Lacan, 'Le séminaire sur "La Lettre Volée"', *Ecrits*, p. 25.) The real will be there even after the most devastating atomic explosions; the real is always at its place, insists Lacan.

24 Baudelaire, *Les Fleurs du Mal, Oeuvres Complètes*, vol. 1, p. 87.

25 André Bazin, 'An Aesthetic of Reality', *What Is Cinema?*, trans. Hugh Gray (Berkeley: University of California Press, 1972), vol. 2, p. 26.

26 Ibid., pp. 26–7.

27 Dudley Andrew stressed in his study on Bazin the importance of the intellectual atmosphere around the Catholic and Bergsonian journal *Esprit*, and the influence of the Catholic critic Albert Béguin. Béguin believed in a double reality where things have a natural relationship to mystery and spirituality, not unlike the medieval religious tradition where reality is the revelation of a spiritual sense. See Dudley Andrew, *André Bazin* (Oxford: Oxford University Press, 1978).

28 Jameson, 'The Existence of Italy', *Signatures of the Visible*, p. 178.

29 Ibid, p. 209.

30 Bazin, 'In Defense of Rossellini', *What is Cinema?*, vol. 2, p. 98.

31 Bazin, 'The Ontology of the Photographic image', *What Is Cinema?*, vol. 1, p. 15.

32 Roland Barthes, *Camera Lucida: Reflections on Photography*, trans. Richard Howard (London: Vintage, 1993), p. 115.

33 Jameson, 'The Existence of Italy', *Signatures of the Visible*, p. 156.

34 Ibid., p. 158.

35 Ibid.

36 Ibid., p. 191.

37 Ibid., p. 217.

38 'What has been absent from these *alternate accounts* of realism – the experimental-oppositional, Hollywood, documentary, and photographic-ontological – is any trace of the older valorization of a realistic "work" within a dominant stylistic or narrative paradigm' (ibid., p. 197, my emphasis).

39 Ibid., p. 191.

40 Ibid., p. 229. It is the end of this essay provocatively entitled 'The Existence of Italy'.
41 Ibid., p. 196. Jameson wrote this sentence while analysing Antonioni's *Blow-Up*.
42 Ibid., p. 194.
43 Walter Benjamin, 'Theses on the Philosophy of History', *Illuminations*, p. 258.
44 Barthes, *Camera Lucida*, p. 40.
45 Jameson, *Signatures of the Visible*, pp. 195–6.
46 Bazin, 'The Ontology of the Photographic Image', *What Is Cinema?*, p. 16.
47 See Jameson, 'On Magic Realism in Film', *Signatures of the Visible*, pp. 139–41. This quotation from Fernandez is on p. 140.

Chapter 8: The Image versus the Visible

1 A version of this chapter was given as a lecture at the International Colloquium entitled 'Os limites do imaginario', Candido Mendes University, Rio de Janeiro, May 2000.
2 Fredric Jameson, *Signatures of the Visible*, p. 1.
3 Ibid.
4 Ibid.
5 Ibid.
6 Ibid., p. 10.
7 See Jon Elster, *Alchemies of the Mind: Rationality and the Emotions* (Cambridge, UK; New York: Cambridge University Press, 1999); *Strong Feelings: Emotion, Addiction, and Human Behavior* (Cambridge, MA: MIT Press, 1999). Ronald De Sousa, *The Rationality of Emotion* (Cambridge, MA: MIT Press, 1987); 'Fetishism and Objectivity in Aesthetic Emotion', in Mette Hjort and Sue Laver, eds, *Emotion and the Arts* (New York: Oxford University Press, 1997); Martha C. Nussbaum, *Love's Knowledge: Essays on Philosophy and Literature* (New York: Oxford University Press, 1990).
8 This passage from the *Génie du Christianisme* is eloquent: 'By what incomprehensible fate is man an exception to this law (harmony) which is so necessary for the order, conservation, peace and happiness of human beings? The lack of unity of qualities and movements in man is as striking as their harmony is visible elsewhere in nature. There is a perpetual clash between his intellect and his desire, between his reason and his heart. When he reaches the highest degree of civilization, he is morally on the lowest rung; if he is free, he is coarse; if he refines his manners, he makes chains for himself. If he is scientifically distinguished, his imagination dies; if he becomes a poet, he loses his ability to think. His heart profits at the expense of his head, his head at the expense of his heart.' René de Chateaubriand, *Essai sur les revolutions. Le Génie du Christianime* (Paris: Gallimard, Bibliothèque de la Pléiade, 1978), p. 534.
9 The obsessive use of Freudian categories disturbed Roberto Rossellini. In an essay he wrote a few months before his death in 1977, 'La société du spectacle', the film-maker attacked contemporary society and its use of media. He also meditated on what happened to Freud's discovery of the unconscious, regretting that 'it has been condemned, by means of a huge reduction, to

became the sole platform on which is based today's whole intellectual exercise.' (Roberto Rossellini, *Fragments d'une autobiographie* (Paris: Ramsay, 1987), pp. 21–2.)

10   Jameson, *Signatures of the Visible*, p. 10.

11   Gilberto Freyre, *Casa-grande e Senzala* (Rio de Janeiro: José Olympio, 1973), p. 11.

12   Ibid., p. 2.

13   As suggested by Luis Castro Nogueira in his talk at the Colloquium 'Os limites do imaginario'.

14   Guy Debord, *La Société du spectacle* (Paris: Buchet-Chastel, 1971); *Society of the Spectale*, trans. Donald Nicholson-Smith (New York: Zone Books, 1994).

15   *Signatures of the Visible*, pp. 11–12.

16   See Gianni Vattimo, *La società trasparente* (Milan: Garzanti, 1989), p. 83.

17   Jameson, *Signatures of the Visible*, p. 9.

18   Baudelaire, 'The Painter of Modern Life', *The Painter of Modern Life and Other Essays*, p. 4.

19   Ibid., p. 9.

20   Ibid., p. 11.

21   Ibid., p. 17.

22   See Paul Virilio, *La Vitesse de libération* (Paris: Galilée, 1995).

Chapter 9: Martin Scorsese and the Rhythm of the Metropolis

1   See André Bazin, 'Théâtre et cinéma', 'Peinture et cinéma', *Qu'est-ce que le cinéma?* (Paris: Editions du Cerf, 1990), pp. 129–78 and 187–92.

2   David Thomson and Ian Christie, eds, *Scorsese on Scorsese* (London: Faber and Faber, 1990), p. 54.

3   Vachel Lindsay, *The Art of the Moving Picture* (New York: Modern Library, 2000), p. 95. The editor of the series is Martin Scorsese.

4   This phenomenon is described by Poe in 'The Sphinx'. See Chapter 1 above.

5   Robert Musil, *The Man Without Qualities*, vol. 1, trans. Sophie Wilkins (London: Picador, 1995), p. 4.

6   Bernardo Bertolucci, 'Entretien', in Aldo Tassone, *Parla il cinema italiano* (Paris: Elig, 1982), p. 47.

7   See *Scorsese on Scorsese*, pp. 4–6.

8   Ibid., p. 54.

9   Scorsese, 'New York', *Cahiers du Cinéma*, 500 (March 1996), p. 41.

10   *Scorsese on Scorsese*, p. 8.

11   Aldo Rossi, *A Scientific Autobiography*, p. 38.

12   *Scorsese on Scorsese*, p. 6.

13   Robert Musil, *The Man Without Qualities*, vol. 1, p. 12.

14   See Scorsese, *Interviews*, Peter Brunette, ed. (Jackson: University Press of Mississippi, 1999), p. 234.

15   Scorsese remembers the objection expressed by many critics to his way of narrating. See Scorsese, *Interviews*, pp. 140–1.

16   Chris Rodley, ed., *Lynch on Lynch* (London: Faber and Faber, 1997), p. 17.

17   Leo Marx, *The Machine in the Garden* (London: Oxford University Press, 1964).

18 Lynch, 'Interview', *Premiere*, vol.4, 1 (1990). Quoted by Michel Chion, *David Lynch* (Paris: Cahiers du cinéma, 1998), p. 16.
19 See Chris Rodley, *Lynch on Lynch*, p. 5. See also Michel Chion, *David Lynch*, p. 17.
20 *Lynch on Lynch*, pp. 7–8.
21 Obviously this monster has been interpreted as anguish about fatherhood.
22 See *Scorsese on Scorsese*, pp. 51–3.
23 Martin Scorsese, '*Casino*. Entretien avec Thelma Shoonmaker', *Cahiers du Cinéma*, 500 (March 1996), p. 19.
24 *Lynch on Lynch*, p. 225.
25 Baudelaire, *The Salon de 1846. Art in Paris, 1845–1862*, pp. 58–9.
26 Of course David Lynch is also a painter.
27 *Scorsese on Scorsese*, p. 54.
28 Baudelaire, 'To Arsène Houssaye', *Paris Spleen*, p. ix.
29 Ibid., p. x.
30 Scorsese, 'Introduction to Modern Library: The Movies', in Vachel Lindsay, *The Art of the Moving Picture*, p. v.
31 Martin Scorsese and Henry Wilson, *A Personal Journey with Martin Scorsese Through American Movies* (New York: Hyperion, 1997), p. 2. Beside this illustrated book, Scorsese also made a documentary of the same title with BFI, produced by Colin MacCabe.
32 On violence see Jake Horsley, *The Blood Poets: A Cinema of Savagery 1958–1999* (Lanham, MD: Scarecrow Press), 1999.
33 'It [*GoodFellas*] is Scorsese's antidote to the romanticized Mafia of the Godfather.' Lawrence S. Friedman, *The Cinema of Martin Scorsese* (New York: Continuum, 1999), p. 171.
34 Scorsese tells the whole story in a 1975 interview, in a style that sounds like the dialogue of a film: 'I said, "Can we do it?" Roger said, "Marty, I understand we got a script from you and everybody here says it is one of the best scripts we've ever received. However I would like to ask you one thing." He said, "I haven't read it. Has it got gangsters?" I said, "Yes, it's got gangsters." He said, "Has it got guns?" I said, "Yes, it's got guns." He said, "Has it got violence? Has it got sex?" I said, "Yes." He said, "My brother just made a picture called *Cool Breeze*, which is the first time that my brother Gene is making money. It's making a lot of money." He said, "Now if you're willing to swing a little, I can give you $150,000, and you can shoot it all with a non-union student crew in New York.' (Scorsese, *Interviews*, p. 22.)
35 *Scorsese on Scorsese*, p. 14.
36 See ibid., pp. 21–2.
37 See François Truffaut, 'Une certaine tendance du cinéma français', *Cahiers du Cinéma*, 31 (Jan. 1954), pp. 15–29.
38 François Truffaut, 'Aimer Fritz Lang', *Cahiers du Cinéma*, 31 (Jan. 1954), p. 52.
39 See Michael Bliss, *The Word Made Flesh: Catholicism and Conflict in the Films of Martin Scorsese* (Metuchen, NJ: Scarecrow Press, 1995).
40 See Paul Schrader, *Transcendental Style in Film: Ozu, Bresson, Dreyer* (Berkeley: University of California Press, 1972).
41 'Robert De Niro was introduced to me by Brian De Palma, who'd discovered him in the early sixties and cast him in *The Wedding Party* ... He'd heard

that I had made a film about his neighborhood – *Who's That Knocking at My Door?* – though he used to hang out with a different group of people, on Broome Street, while we were on Prince Street. We had seen each other at dances and said hallo.' (*Scorsese on Scorsese*, pp. 41–2.)

42 A powerful high-angle shot appears in Welles' *Touch of Evil* (1955) (on Quinlan and his friend); and after *Taxi Driver*, at the beginning of De Palma's *The Untouchables* (1987). Some brief high-angle shots on New York streets are already used by Scorsese both in *Who's That Knoking at My Door* and in *Mean Streets*.

43 *Scorsese on Scorsese*, p. 8.

44 See S. M. Eisenstein, 'El Greco y el cine', *Cinématisme*, ed. François Albéra (Brussels: Editions Complexe, 1980), pp. 57–58.

45 Besides the high-angle scene in *Touch of Evil*, the low ceiling effect typical of *Citizen Kane* and *Touch of Evil*, which plays an important role in *Mean Streets* and *Raging Bull*.

46 See Baudelaire on Delacroix: 'He [Delacroix] professes a fanatical regard for the cleanliness of his tools and the preparation of the elements of his work. In fact, since painting is an art of deep ratiocination, and one that demands an immediate contention between a host of different qualities, it is import-ant that the hand should encounter the least possible number of obstacles when it gets down to business, and that it should accomplish the divine orders of the brain with a slavish alacrity; otherwise the ideal will escape.' (Baudelaire, 'The Salon of 1846', *Art in Paris*, p. 58.)

47 Herrmann died the night 'he had finished the score' for *Taxi Driver*. See *Scorsese on Scorsese*, p. 63. On *Taxi Driver* and Herrmann's score, see Leighton Grist, *The Films of Martin Scorsese 1963–1977*, pp. 130–2.

48 Schrader was in those years highly influenced by Sartre. See *Scorsese on Scorsese*, p. 53.

49 Jean-Paul Sartre, *Nausea*, trans. Lloyd Alexander (New York: New Directions, 1964), p. 21.

General Bibliography

Asor Rosa, Alberto, *Scrittori e popolo: il populismo nella letteratura contemporanea* (Roma: Samonà e Savelli, 1972).
——, *Intellettuali e classe operaia: Saggi sulle forme di uno storico conflitto e di una possibile alleanza* (Florence: La nuova Italia, 1973).
Barthes, Roland, *On Racine*, trans. Richard Howard (New York: Hill and Wang, 1964).
——, *Writing Degree Zero*, trans. Annette Lavers and Colin Smith (New York: Hill and Wang, 1978).
——, *A Barthes Reader*, trans. Richard Howard, introduction by Susan Sontag (New York: Hill and Wang, 1981).
——, *The Rustle of Language*, trans. Richard Howard (New York: Hill & Wang, 1986).
——, *Camera Lucida: Reflections on Photography*, trans. Richard Howard (London: Vintage, 1993).
Bataille, Georges, *The Story of the Eye*, trans. J. Neugroschel, with essays by R. Barthes and S. Sontag (Harmondsworth: Penguin Books, 1982).
Baudelaire, Charles, *Oeuvres complètes* (Paris: Gallimard, Bibliothèque de la Pléiade, 1975–6, 2 vols).
——, *The Painter of Modern Life, and Other Essays*, trans. Jonathan Mayne (London: Phaidon, 1964, 1995).
——, *Art in Paris, 1845–1862*, trans. Johnathan Mayne (London: Phaidon, 1965, 1981).
——, *Paris Spleen*, trans. Louise Varese (New York: New Directions, 1970).
Bazin, André, *Qu'est-ce que le cinéma?* (Paris: Editions du Cerf, 1990). *What Is Cinema?*, trans. Hugh Gray (Berkeley: University of California Press, 1967–71, 2 vols).
Benjamin, Walter, *Briefe* (Frankfurt am Main: Suhrkamp, 1978, 2 vols).
——, *Gesammelte Schriften* (Frankfurt am Main: Suhrkamp, 1974, 7 vols in 14).
——, *Illuminations*, trans. Harry Zohn (New York: Schocken Books, 1969).
——, *Reflections*, trans. Harry Zohn (New York: Schocken Books, 1986).
Bersani, Leo, *The Culture of Redemption* (Cambridge, MA: Harvard University Press, 1990).
Bonaparte, Marie, *Edgar Poe, sa vie et son oeuvre: Etude analytique* (Paris: Presses Universitaires de France, 1958, 2 vols).
Brecht, Bertolt, *Schriften zur Literatur und Kunst 2, Gesammelte Werke* (Frankfurt am Main: Suhrkamp, 1967).
Cacciari, Massimo, *Metropolis. Saggi sulla grande città di Sombart, Endell, Scheffler e Simmel* (Rome: Officina, 1973).
——, and Amendolagine, Francesco, *Oikos: Da Loos a Wittgenstein* (Rome: Officina, 1975).
——, *Architecture and Nihilism: On the Philosophy of Modern Architecture*, trans. Stephen Sartarelli, intro. by Patrizia Lombardo (New Haven and London: Yale University Press, 1993).

Carlyle, Thomas, *Selected Writings* (London: Penguin Books, 1980).

Ciucci, Giorgio, Dal Co, Francesco Manieri-Elia, Mario and Tafuri, Manfredo, *The American City. From the Civil War to the New Deal*, trans. Barbara Luigia La Penta (Cambridge, MA: MIT Press, 1979).

Coleridge, Samuel Taylor, *Aids to Reflection* (London: W. Pickering, 1848, 2 vols).

——, *Biographia Literaria* (New York: Putnam & Wiley, 1848).

Compagnon, Antoine, *Les Cinq Paradoxes de la modernité* (Paris: Editions du Seuil, 1990).

De Fusco, Renato, *Storia dell'architettura contemporanea* (Bari: Laterza, 1974, 1988).

Del Giudice, Daniele, *Lo stadio di Wimbledon* (Torino: Einaudi, 1982).

De Sousa, Ronald, *The Rationality of Emotion* (Cambridge, MA: MIT Press, 1987).

Debord, Guy, *La Société du spectacle* (Paris: Buchet-Chatel, 1972; repr. Gallimard, 1992).

——, 'Fetishism and Objectivity in Aesthetic Emotion', in Mette Hjort and Sue Laver, eds, *Emotion and the Arts* (New York: Oxford University Press, 1997).

Eisenstein, S. M., *Cinématisme*, ed. François Albéra (Brussels: Editions Complexe, 1980).

Elster, Jon, *Alchemies of the Mind: Rationality and the Emotions* (Cambridge, UK; New York: Cambridge University Press, 1999).

——, *Strong Feelings: Emotion, Addiction, and Human Behavior* (Cambridge, MA: MIT Press, 1999).

Emerson, Ralph Waldo, *The Complete Works* (Boston: Houghton, Mifflin, 1903–4; reprint New York: AMS Press, 1968, 12 vols).

Freyre, Gilberto, *Casa-grande e Senzala* (Rio de Janeiro: José Olympio, 1973).

Fustel de Coulanges, Numa Denis, *La Cité antique* (Paris: Flammarion, 1984).

Giedion, Sigfried, *Space, Time and Architecture* (Cambridge, MA: Harvard University Press, 1967).

Hall, Stuart, 'The Emergence of Cultural Studies and the Crisis of the Humanities', *October*, 53 (1990).

Hartog, François, *Le XIXe siècle et l'histoire: le cas Fustel de Coulanges* (Paris: Presses Universitaires de France, 1988).

Haussmann, Baron Georges, *Mémoires* (Paris: Victor-Havard, 1890–3, 3 vols).

Hoffmann, E. T. A., *Tales*, trans. R. J. Hollingdale (Harmondsworth: Penguin Books, 1982).

Hofmannsthal, Hugo von, *Selected Prose*, trans. Mary Hottinger and Tania and James Stern (New York: Pantheon Books, 1952).

——, *Gesammelte Werke* (Frankfurt am Main: Fischer Taschenbuch, 1979, 4 vols).

Jameson, Fredric, *The Ideologies of Theory: Essays 1971–1986* (Minneapolis: University of Minnesota Press, 1988, 2 vols).

——, *Signatures of the Visible* (New York; London: Routledge, 1990).

——, *The Geopolitical Aesthetic: Cinema and Space in the World System* (Bloomington: Indiana University Press; London: British Film Institute, 1992).

Lindsay, Vachel, *The Art of the Moving Picture* (New York: Modern Library, 2000).

Mallarmé, Stéphane, *Oeuvres Complètes* (Paris: Gallimard, Bibliothèque de la Pléiade, 1945).

Marx, Leo, *The Machine in the Garden* (New York: Oxford University Press, 1964).

Matthiessen, Francis Otto, *American Renaissance. Art and Expression in the Age of Emerson and Whitman* (New York: Oxford University Press, 1941).

Melville, Hermann, *Moby Dick, or the White Whale* (New York: Oxford University Press, 1947).
——, *Pierre, or the Ambiguities* (New York: New American Library, 1964).
Metz, Christian, 'A propos de l'impression de réalité au cinéma', *Cahiers du cinéma*, 166–167 (1965).
Momigliano, Arnoldo, *Essays in Ancient and Modern Historiography* (Oxford: Blackwell, 1977).
Mulvey, Laura, *Visual and Other Pleasures* (Basingstoke: Macmillan, 1989).
Mumford, Lewis, *The Culture of Cities* (New York: Harcourt, Brace & World, 1938).
——, *The City in History: Its Origins, Its Transformations and Its Prospects* (New York: Harcourt, Brace & World, 1961).
Musil, Robert, *The Man Without Qualities*, trans. Sophie Wilkins (London: Picador, 1995, 2 vols).
Nussbaum, Martha C., *Love's Knowledge: Essays on Philosophy and Literature* (New York: Oxford University Press, 1990).
Poe, Edgar Allan, *The Complete Tales and Poems* (New York: Modern Library, 1938; reprint New York: Vintage, 1975).
——, *Essays and Reviews* (New York: Library of America, 1984).
Poulet, Georges, *Les Métamorphoses du cercle* (Paris: Gallimard, 1979).
Renan, *Qu'est-ce qu'une nation?, Oeuvres complètes*, vol. 1 (Paris: Calmann-Lévy, 1947).
Rodley, Chris, ed., *Lynch on Lynch* (London; Boston: Faber and Faber, 1997).
Rossellini, Roberto, *Fragments d'une autobiographie* (Paris: Ramsay, 1987).
Rossi, Aldo, *A Scientific Autobiography*, trans. Lawrence Venuti (Cambridge, MA: MIT Press, Oppositions Books, 1981).
——, *L'architettura della città* (Padua: Marsilio, 1966). *The Architecture of the City*, trans. Diane Ghirardo and Joan Ockman, intro. by Peter Eisenman (Cambridge, MA: MIT Press, 1982).
——, *Il libro azzurro: il miei progetti 1981* (Zurich: Jamileh Weber Galerie, 1981).
——, *Teatro del mondo* (Venice: Cluva, 1982).
Schmitt, Carl, *The Concept of the Political*, trans. George Schwab (New Brunswick, NJ: Rutgers University Press, 1976).
Schrader, Paul, *Transcendental Style in Film: Ozu, Bresson, Dreyer* (Berkeley: University of California Press, 1972).
Scorsese, Martin, *Interviews*, ed. Peter Brunette (Jackson: University Press of Mississippi, 1999).
—— and Henry Wilson, *A Personal Journey with Martin Scorsese Through American Movies* (New York: Hyperion, 1997).
Shorske, Carl, *Fin-de-siècle Vienna* (New York: Knopf, 1980).
Simmel, Georg, *The Sociology of Georg Simmel*, trans. Kurt H. Wolff (New York: Free Press, 1964).
——, *The Philosophy of Money*, trans. T. Bottomore and D. Frisby (London; Boston: Routledge, 1978).
Slataper, Scipio, *Il mio carso* (Rome: Editori Riuniti, 1982).
Tafuri, Manfredo, 'Per una critica dell'ideologia architettonica', *Contropiano*, 1 (1969).
——, 'Austro-marxismo e città: *das Rote Wien*', *Contropiano*, 2 (1971).
——, *Teorie e storia dell'architettura* (Bari: Laterza, 1970). *Theories and History of Architecture*, trans. Giorgio Verrecchia (New York: Harper & Row, 1980).

——, *Progetto e Utopia* (Bari: Laterza, 1973). *Architecture and Utopia: Design and Capitalist Development*, trans. Barbara Luigia La Penta (Cambridge, MA: MIT University Press, 1976).

——, *La sfera e il labirinto: avanguardie e architettura da Piranesi agli anni '70* (Torino: Einaudi, 1980). *The Sphere and the Labyrinth: Avant-gardes and Architecture from Piranesi to the 1970s*, trans. Pellegrino d'Acierno and Robert Connolly (Cambridge, MA: MIT University Press, 1987).

——, *Venezia e il Rinascimento: religione, scienza, architettura* (Torino: Einaudi, 1985). *Venice and the Renaissance*, trans. Jessica Levine (Cambridge, MA: MIT University Press, 1989).

Tate, Allen, *Essays of Four Decades* (Chicago: Swallow Press, 1968).

Thomson, David and Ian Christie, eds, *Scorsese on Scorsese* (London: Faber and Faber, 1990).

Trakl, Georg, *Selected Poems*, trans. R. Grenier, M. Hamburger, D. Luke and C. Middleton (London: Cape, 1968).

Valéry, Paul, *Oeuvres* (Paris: Gallimard, Bibliothèque de la Pléiade, 1960, 2 vols).

Van Gogh, Vincent, *Lettres à son frère Théo* (Paris: Grasset, 1982).

Virilio, Paul, *Cybermonde, la politique du pire* (Paris: Les Ed. Textuel, 1996).

——, *Esthétique de la disparition* (Paris: Balland, 1980).

——, *La Vitesse de libération* (Paris: Ed. Gallilée, 1995).

Weber, Max, *The City*, trans. D. Martindale and G. Neuwirth (New York: Free Press; London: Macmillan, 1958).

White, Hayden, *Metahistory* (Baltimore: Johns Hopkins University Press, 1973).

Williams, Raymond, *The Long Revolution* (London: Chatto and Windus, 1961).

——, *Culture and Society* (London: Chatto and Windus, 1963).

——, *The Country and the City* (New York: Oxford University Press, 1973).

Index

impressionism, 52, 53, 54, 55, 58
inauguration, 170–1
'Independent Cinema', 208
'intellectual montage', 214
irredentism, 84, 88
Istituto di storia dell'architettura,
    Venice, 110, 118
Italian Communist Party, 108–14,
    116–18, 126
Italian populism, 125–6
Italianamerica (film), 199

James, Henry, 177
Jameson, Fredric, 177, 185;
    'Architecture and the Critique
    of Ideology', 126, 129–30;
    'Existence of Italy', 163–4, 167–71;
    'On Magic Realism in Film', 173;
    Signatures of the Visible, 158, 172,
    174, 175, 176, 178–9
Jules et Jim (film), 207, 208
Jung-Wien group, 50, 53

Kafka, Franz, 55, 56, 57, 124, 136
Kant, Immanuel, 17, 34
Kantian dualism, 175–6, 179
Keitel, Harvey, 210
Keynes, J. M., 110, 117, 120
Kirkegaard, Soren, 119, 120
Kiss Me Deadly (film), 185
Klee, Paul, 142–3, 171, 172
Kleist, Heinrich von, 31
Klimt, Gustav, 50, 51–2, 53, 54–5, 90,
    134
Kokoschka, Oskar, 51, 58, 60
Kracauer, Siegfried, 164
Kraus, Karl, 51, 53, 54, 86, 133, 135,
    138, 141, 144
Kubrick, Stanley, 205

Lacan, Jacques, 122, 160, 173
Lang, Fritz, 163, 186, 188, 189, 206,
    208, 209, 213
language: limits of, 144; multiplicity
    of languages, 136–40, 141, 145–6
Last Waltz, The (film), 215
laterality, 172
Lefebvre, Henri, 129
Leipzig City Advertiser, 151, 155

Lessing, Gotthold Ephraim, 83
Levinas, Emmanuel, 138
lighthouses, 96, 107
Lindsay, Vachel, 188–9
Liotta, Ray, 193
literature: literary Stalinism, 112–13
Livy, 57–8
Lombardy, 98–100, 101
Loos, Adolf, 51, 54, 97, 100, 102, 105,
    114, 115; Cacciari on, 113, 116–17,
    122, 124–5, 127, 133, 135–40, 141;
    Roman architecture, 135–6, 137
Lorca, Federico García, 104
Lost Highway (film), 175, 182–5, 195,
    196, 198, 200
Lowell, James Russell, 14
Lukács, Georg, 63, 64, 117, 121, 122
Lumière brothers, 166
Lynch, David: aesthetic implications
    of *Lost Highway*, 175, 182–5; nature
    in films, 196–7; and Scorsese,
    195–201, 202; soundtracks, 200–1;
    suburban locations, 195–6

M (film), 188
Mach, Ernst, 58
Madonna, 158–9
Majakovskij, Vladimir 112–13
Mallarmé, Stéphane, 12, 48, 81
Manet, Édouard, 48, 66–7
Mann, Thomas, 87, 117
Mantz, Paul, 55–6
Marcuse, Herbert, 129
Marx, Karl, 118
Marx, Leo, 195
Marxist humanism, 129
Matthew, Saint, 5
Matthiessen, F.O., 30
Mean Streets (film), 194, 198, 199, 200,
    205–7, 209, 212
mechanical form, 30, 31–2; distrust of
    Mechanical Age, 69; industrial
    labour, 118–19
media: cultural impact, 150–73, 174,
    183–4; in Scorsese's films, 206–7
Mekas, Jonas, 208
Melville, Hermann, 100, 107; *Bartleby*,
    69; *Moby Dick*, 9, 21, 23; *Pierre, or
    the Ambiguities*, 22, 23, 33, 69